TEN YEARS
THAT SHOOK THE WORLD

TEN YEARS THAT SHOOK THE WORLD

THE GORBACHEV ERA AS WITNESSED BY HIS CHIEF OF STAFF

VALERY BOLDIN

Translated by Evelyn Rossiter

BasicBooks
A Division of HarperCollinsPublishers

Designed by Ellen Levine

Library of Congress Cataloging-in-Publication Data
Boldin, V. I. (Valerii Ivanovich), 1935–
    Ten years that shook the world : the Gorbachev era as witnessed by
his chief of staff / Valery Boldin : translated by Evelyn Rossiter.
      p.   cm.
    Includes index.
    ISBN 0–465–08407–9
    1. Soviet Union—Politics and government—1985–1991. 2. Gor-
bachev, Mikhail Sergeyevich, 1931– . 3. Boldin, V. I. (Valerii Ivanovich),
1935– . I. Title.
DK288.B65   1994
947.085'4—dc20
                                                              93–29231
                                                                 CIP

94 95 96 97 ♦/HC 9 8 7 6 5 4 3 2 1

CONTENTS

PREFACE

The concluding pages of *Ten Years That Shook the World* were written at a time when the Soviet Union was being stripped not only of its Socialist system but of its very statehood. Not for many centuries had our country endured events as dramatic as those of the preceding eighteen months. World wars, revolutions, and the military and economic confrontation between two powerful blocs had been unable to cause the collapse and dismemberment of that great power. The Soviet Union was destroyed by an explosion from within, carried out by a small, influential group of party, state, and opposition leaders who, though originally propounding noble slogans, sought to enhance the power of the country by reforming all spheres of society on the basis of Socialist principles. Power struggles and personal ambitions caused them, however, to sacrifice the interests of the state and the people, and to lead the country to collapse and bloodshed.

I feel it is my moral duty to tell of these events, as I am one of the few people in Mikhail Gorbachev's entourage who are familiar with the distinctive traits of his character, the way his goals were transformed, the driving forces that paved the way for changes in the structure of society and then carried out those changes, as well as many details of events as they unfolded. This book discusses the conditions that fostered the collapse of the Soviet Union: the development of the country, including its economy, from 1981 to 1991; the growing crisis in the party and its leading organs; and the role played by the various state leaders in perestroika and the political power struggle.

Working in the Communist party Central Committee, and also in my capacity as the Soviet president's chief of staff, I witnessed the machinations involved in the process of political decision making, the appointment of members of the most powerful organs of party and state, and the activities of Leonid Brezhnev, Yuri Andropov, Konstantin Chernenko, and the members of the Politburo and their entourage.

While the book describes many events of those ten years, 1981–91, it focuses particularly on the activities of Mikhail Sergeyevich Gorbachev—the conditions under which he emerged among the senior party leaders and the influences that formed his character and propelled him on his ascent to the top. It was his arrival on the political scene that fostered the changes that took place in Soviet society. By the time Gorbachev was elected general secretary of the Soviet Communist party, at a special meeting of the Central Committee plenum on 11 March 1985, he had already made up his mind to carry out certain social reforms, though he lacked a well-ordered scheme for that purpose. Instead, he resorted to cosmetic methods designed to impart a more presentable face to socialism. This, of course, was not the perestroika that later came to be known all over the world for its verbal radicalism and practical impotence.

The reader of this book will learn how the ideas of perestroika came to maturity, who was originally responsible for them, and who proposed the radical reforms of the democratization of society and glasnost. Developments over the final few months of the Soviet Union's existence, and the causes and consequences of the events of August 1991, are also described.

Advocacy of reformist goals caused deep turmoil in the country, fomenting political activity throughout the population. The political leadership's failure to achieve its stated objectives, together with its frequent and abrupt policy switches, led to the dismemberment of the state and prompted the republics of what had once been a great power to flee, in order to preserve their own peoples.

Like any work of this kind, this book cannot present a full account of all events, personalities, and forces involved. Rather, it shows the view from the top of the pyramid of the main characters in this story performing in a series of events still fresh in many people's memories. I hope it makes it possible in due course to analyze more thoroughly and more accurately the reasons for the drama that was played out over one-sixth of the earth's landmass, with its powerful climax and its changing players.

TEN YEARS
THAT SHOOK THE WORLD

INTRODUCTION

ADAM B. ULAM

Few politicians remain heroes to their aides for long. Valery Boldin's closeness to Gorbachev not only failed to inspire him with admiration for or gratitude to his boss but left him with a vivid dislike of the man. But then, few people in Boldin's position would carry their grievances against a superior to the point of active plotting and participation in a conspiracy to remove him from power.

Valery Ivanovich Boldin was a journalist with *Pravda* when, in 1981, he was asked to work for Gorbachev, then a Politburo member and secretary to the Central Committee of the Communist party, in charge mainly of agricultural affairs. Though he professes that he was reluctant to leave the world of journalism for high politics, it is unlikely that this was so. The Politburo was the Olympus of Soviet politics. And Gorbachev, then fifty, was not merely one of the ten to twelve people who collectively exercised absolute power over the vast empire; being also a secretary of the Central Committee, he would be one of the prime candidates for the top position, that of the general secretary, once its incumbent, seventy-five years old and ailing, Leonid Brezhnev, disappeared from the scene. To be sure, there were some party oligarchs ahead of Gorbachev, but they were much older and in poor health. So one could be fairly confident that within a few years the succession to what then appeared the most powerful political job in the world would become open and that Mikhail Sergeyevich, by far (eight years) the youngest of the oligarchs, barring some untoward development, would become the prime candidate for the position once held by Stalin and Khrushchev. In May 1982 Mikhail Suslov, long the power behind the throne of Soviet politics, died. That November, Brezhnev disappeared from the scene. His successors, Yuri Andropov and Konstantin Chernenko, both already gravely ill, were soon also claimed by death, and in March 1985 Mikhail Gorbachev became general secretary. Boldin continued as one of the new leader's closest assistants and gathered appropriate rewards: candidate member of the Central Committee in 1986, full member in 1988. In 1987 he became head of the General Department of the Central Committee, a position of considerable administrative importance, possibly a prelude to his own ascent into the leadership and certainly much more than he could have expected as a journalist.

Alas, as our author advanced, the fortunes of the Communist party rapidly declined. By no means a Communist diehard, he became increasingly appalled at the growing chaos in Soviet politics and at what he came to see as the indecisiveness and incompetence of his chief. By 1990 he realized that the whole Soviet structure was tottering. His conviction, Boldin assures us, that if things were allowed to continue as they had since 1987 the Soviet Union would collapse is what motivated him to join the plot designed to remove the man who had betrayed communism and brought the country to the brink of disaster. As we know, the plot of August 1991 collapsed infamously, thus speeding up what the plotters had tried to prevent: the crumbling of the Union and the utter collapse of the Communist party. Along with the main figures of the conspiracy, Boldin found himself in jail. And it was there, and intermittently in the hospital, that he entered upon this work of self-justification and indictment of his erstwhile boss. He wrote it while still awaiting a trial that Yeltsin's government promised would have taken place in April 1992. Hence, not surprisingly, we are not given much information about the mechanics of the conspiracy to overthrow Gorbachev or of the attempted coup. For reasons that will become apparent, the trial did not take place, nor is it likely to, and Boldin and his fellow conspirators are now free men.

The reader will undoubtedly note how much of the historical catastrophe (as the author views it) that has overtaken his country is ascribed by Boldin to the personal failings of Gorbachev. The picture of Gorbachev given here is quite different from that which was widely accepted in the West during his years of leadership. Instead of a brave reformer, Boldin sees in him a man who never knew what he wanted and who became a prisoner of forces he unwittingly helped release. The writer does not deny his subject a degree of idealism, but in the main his Gorbachev, far from a selfless proponent of democracy, is a power-hungry politician, very susceptible to flattery, very attentive to his personal privileges and material comforts. But for all of the author's prejudices, the book offers us an invaluable insight into the atmosphere attending the last days of what was not only a mighty empire but a vast, unprecedented experiment at remaking history and changing the world.

We cannot understand the historical role of Gorbachev or his personality without reviewing the background of the events that placed him in such a key role at a crucial period of history. Today that background is but dimly perceived, even by the average Russian or Ukrainian, preoccupied as they are by the more recent and burning questions: how to cope with the ever worsening economic crisis; whether and how the democratic experiment can succeed in their countries—the ethnic conflicts within, though for the moment subdued, may still escalate to a level surpassing those in the former Yugoslavia. And for the Western public the USSR, whether as the "evil empire" or as an experiment in socialism, must now appear as distant and unrelated to our current concerns as World War I.

Thus we tend to forget that in 1985, no government of a major state appeared to be as firmly in power, its policies as clearly set in their course, as that of the USSR. Mr. Reagan's and Mrs. Thatcher's mandates were subject to the whims of their electorates, their powers curbed by the legislatures. In the United States and Great Britain an election could—sooner or later was bound to—transform the ideological direction of public policy. In the Soviet Union all threads of power were held by the Communist party or, more precisely, by the handful of men who headed it. They—the members of the Politburo—were selected by cooptation, their "election" by the Central Committee of the party a formality, any restraint on their prerogatives by the legislature or the judiciary a fiction. The rulers, of course, could and did vary their policies, but any dispute or bargaining about them took place within that charmed circle, with even fairly high officials, not to mention the rank and file of the party members, not privy to the discussion nor able to affect the decision. And to all appearances the mass of Soviet citizens, whatever their private feelings, accepted this authoritarian system as a fact of life. Open political dissidence, which appeared in the USSR during the Brezhnev period, was still confined to small groups or individuals, usually from the intelligentsia, and even so it was as a rule ruthlessly suppressed by the regime. Imprisonment or exile awaited the too-vocal critics of any major features of Soviet life.

Nor, before perestroika, could one readily spot those social and economic weaknesses of the system that, within a few years, would contribute to its crash. Agriculture had long been recognized as the Achilles' heel of the economy. The country, once the world's leading exporter of grain, had become largely dependent on imports. Industrial growth, so impressive in the 1950s and 1960s, had slowed down considerably. But the official statistics still presented an impressive picture of the production of such basic commodities as oil, steel and gas. And behind those statistics, only a few experts could perceive that with regard to technology and quality, the Soviet economy was already exhibiting clear symptoms of stagnation. What could not be easily obscured was the fact that the Soviet citizen's standard of living, though it had risen immeasurably since Stalin's time, was still abysmally low compared with that in the West, and was even surpassed by other Communist countries of eastern Europe.

For all the multinational character of the ruling elite and the ample rights "guaranteed" by the constitution, the USSR was very much a Russian-dominated state. The regime was watchful and suspicious of anything appearing to be, even in the cultural sphere, a sign of particularism on the part of non-Russian nationalities. But here again the combination of official repression and of propaganda seemed to have succeeded in keeping the aspirations of Ukrainians, Uzbeks, and the other groups well in check; no one in the early 1980s could have anticipated the intensity and even violence with which those aspirations would erupt within a few years.

One might well object that this balance sheet of strengths and vulnerabilities of the Soviet regime in the years of Mikhail Gorbachev's assumption of power is largely unrealistic, as indeed events were soon to demonstrate. The real weakness of the Soviet system was that it rested mainly on suppression. Once that suppression slackened, there was no way the rulers could contain the people's aspirations to a freer and fuller life, as both citizens and consumers, or the non-Russians' demands for real autonomy or independence. Yet it was the disintegration of the ruling apparatus—the Communist party—rather than a spontaneous revolt of the masses that would bring down the Soviet colossus. And it is the question of whether and how Gorbachev contributed to the fall of communism that touches on Valery Boldin's story.

Whatever its other and numerous failings, communism in Russia succeeded in forging a seemingly indestructible weapon of power: the party. In its seventy-odd years of existence, the Soviet system survived vicissitudes and catastrophes that would have toppled most other regimes. Against overwhelming odds it emerged victorious from the civil war after the Revolution. It survived famines that claimed millions of victims. In Stalin's hands the Communist party became a tool to force the peasants, then 80 percent of the population, into a new form of serfdom masquerading as collective farms. Though it was ruthlessly purged, it was the party, along with the secret police, that subjected the USSR between 1937 and 1940 to a terror unparalleled in history. What other regime could have withstood the catastrophic defeats of the first six months of the war with Germany, when the Soviet armies lost upward of three million soldiers in casualties and war prisoners?

How could one have predicted that in five short years the party's grip on power would grow increasingly tenuous, that even well before the drama of 1991 the organization, nineteen million strong, would become a "helpless giant" (to quote another politician who had suffered a spectacular fall), utterly incapable of controlling the social scene that had been so quiescent and submissive in March 1985? Before that date, not even the boldest Soviet dissident could have dreamed of or demanded an early and complete erasure of communism from the nation's life. For Solzhenitsyn, it was a matter of a fairly distant future. All Sakharov had pleaded for up until his death in 1989 was for the regime to become more liberal and to give life to the hitherto dead letter of the Soviet Constitution. Neither of those two courageous critics of the system could foresee that not only the Communist party but also the Union would be shattered in such short order. The system that had survived catastrophic famines, terror, and crushing military defeats succumbed to what, at least at first, was a modest attempt to reform it.

Was it the case—as one of the proponents of perestroika, the current mayor of St. Petersburg, was to state—that Gorbachev and his followers tried to reform what was unreformable? Could the Soviet system have survived had the new leader been content to follow in the footsteps of his predecessors and confined himself to cosmetic changes? Or, as Boldin argues, although some reforms were badly needed, was it Gorbachev's ineptitude and arrogance that were mainly responsible for the crash of both perestroika and the Soviet Union?

As for the proverbial danger of an authoritarian system trying to reform itself, we must note that the Soviet system had survived one major change in the direction of liberalization: the transition from Stalinism to what at the time (1953–56) was called "collective leadership"— in fact, from the unbridled despotism of one man to rule by an oligarchy, from a society gripped by intermittent waves of terror to one where repression was more in the style of a "normal" police state. Even then there were fears that the change, welcomed as it was by all except diehard Stalinists, might shake the foundations of the Soviet system. As Khrushchev, the main architect of the change, then dubbed the thaw, was to confess, "We were scared—really scared. We were afraid the thaw might unleash a flood, which we wouldn't be able to control and which could drown us. How could it drown us? It could have overflowed the banks of the Soviet riverbed and formed a tidal wave which would have washed away all the barriers and retaining walls of our society. From the viewpoint of the leadership, this would have been an unfavorable development. We wanted to guide the progress of the thaw so that it would stimulate only those creative forces which would contribute to the strengthening of socialism."[*] Well, from 1953 to 1956 the leadership did indeed manage to contain the early version of perestroika. The tidal wave would come thirty-odd years later.

As we know, Khrushchev's struggle, first with Stalin's ghost and then with his fellow oligarchs, was very much on Gorbachev's mind as he planned his own tactics for changing the Soviet Union. On the one hand, it must have convinced him that a major change was possible without undermining the foundations of the Communist edifice. After all, no single pronouncement or proposed reform he advanced could compare with the one that had shocked Soviet society in the wake of Khrushchev's denunciation of Stalin before the Twentieth Congress of the Party in 1956. That supposedly secret speech, and subsequent revelations, shook the foundations of what every Soviet citizen and every foreign Communist had been taught to believe for over thirty years. And yet the thaw did not grow into a flood that would overflow and wash away the barriers and retaining walls of the Soviet system. And presumably that system was quite capable of withstanding other self-administered shocks.

But there was another, less comforting lesson for Gorbachev from

---

[*]*Khrushchev Remembers: The Last Testament,* trans. and ed. Strobe Talbott (Boston: Houghton Mifflin, 1974), p. 79.

Khrushchev's era. His fellow oligarchs grew tired and fearful not only because of his continuing garrulousness about Stalin's sins but also because of his constant innovations in the Soviet economy and administration—his harebrained schemes, as they characterized them. And so they finally managed, through a palace coup, to remove him. Khrushchev fell because he had allowed Soviet politics to continue to be conducted in a conspiratorial way, without letting the people at large know what was going on at the highest level of the party. To avoid a similar fate at the hands of *his* colleagues, Gorbachev had to create an atmosphere that would not allow a few Politburo members to plot in secret behind his back. Hence the need for glasnost, for letting the public know what is going on at the center of Soviet power. It would then not be possible to repeat what had happened in October 1964, when the nation's highest leader became an emeritus overnight, with not so much as a single protest—in fact, no public reaction whatsoever.

This is not to suggest that Gorbachev promoted glasnost for purely selfish reasons. He genuinely wished for a more open society and for less in the way of censorship and control over the media than had been the rule before 1985. And it was only late in the game that he realized that complete freedom of speech and the press was incompatible with party rule, something in which he as a Communist had refused to believe until his overthrow. After 1988 he would have subscribed to Boldin's wistful complaint that "glasnost had gone to people's heads." And, indeed, if one had to isolate one factor that destroyed the reputation and what remained of the morale of the Communist party, and thus prepared the way for the crash of 1991, it was glasnost—a veritable explosion of criticism of the government and eventually of Gorbachev himself.

But how could the general secretary, brought up within the Communist party, solicitous of its reputation and eager to retain it as the ruling organ, fail to anticipate what would happen when the whole sordid past of Communist rule became public knowledge? I think the answer, though the author of this book would disagree, is that there was a considerable element of idealism in Gorbachev's makeup. Just as he wanted to cleanse the Soviet Union from the last excrescences of Stalinism, so he believed that *on balance*, the record of communism in Russia was a constructive and honorable one.

Then, as a politician, he believed that the public's fuller (but perhaps not full) knowledge of the crimes of the Stalin era and of the corruption of Brezhnev's would strengthen his hand as reformer and inhibit his conservative colleagues on the Politburo from trying to trip him.

The Communists never forgot that the Revolution, of which they had become beneficiaries, had been made possible by the czarist autocracy's having lost, long before 1917, its moral authority in the eyes of the educated class. It was the hostile intellectuals, writers, professors, and the like who made imperial power so vulnerable that military reverses in World War I (much, much less severe than those suffered by the Soviets in 1941) plus a few days' rioting in the capital could topple it.

Lenin and his successors never forgot that lesson. From the beginning of the Soviet era, the intellectuals and cultural life in general had been controlled by the regime to an extent that would have been unimaginable during even the most repressive periods before 1917. Relaxed somewhat after Stalin's death, those controls still remained rigorous, and the party's hand lay heavily on writers and the media especially. Technically, there was no censorship. The writers, historians, and journalists knew what to write and, if they somehow erred, then their editors provided the needed corrective. If a novel, film, or historical treatise clashed with the current party orthodoxy, this could only be because just before its appearance, the party line had changed. A previously unknown author's grim description of life in a concentration camp was published only because Khrushchev, then in his anti-Stalinist phase, personally authorized it. After Khrushchev's ouster, Solzhenitsyn's *One Day in the Life of Ivan Denisovich* disappeared from the public libraries and went, so to speak, underground.

The new era of intellectual freedom and Gorbachev's bid for the support of the intelligentsia were signaled by the general secretary's personal telephone call to Andrei Sakharov in December 1986. The highest Communist official told the country's most celebrated dissident (with Solzhenitsyn out of the USSR) that his exile was over: let him come, a free man, back to Moscow and work for the common good. But if Gorbachev thought that this gesture, unprecedented for a Soviet ruler, would earn him the unconditional support of the intelligentsia and disarm the dissidents, Sakharov's first statement after his return must have sounded a warning. Yes, said the great scientist, he supported perestroika, but the government should immediately release all political prisoners and end its military intervention in Afghanistan.

Khrushchev's successors, who had considered his attacks on Stalin unseemly (and dangerous for the party), preferred not to talk about

Stalin at all, but when they did, they restored him to a kind of pedestal: an outstanding party leader who unfortunately committed some errors and abuses. And this, of course, had to be the general approach to that delicate subject, whether in a history book or a novel. But glasnost started what became an open season on Stalin. What the officials themselves said on the subject made Khrushchev's accusation appear pallid—thus Gorbachev on the seventieth anniversary of the Revolution: "Through mass repression and lawlessness, Stalin and his entourage have sinned before the party and the nation. Their guilt is enormous and unforgivable." But as of 1987 the general secretary still found it necessary to qualify his condemnation of what had been not merely one man's and his henchmen's dereliction but a huge chunk of Soviet history. With blatant inconsistency, he still found it necessary to praise Stalin's leadership during the war and his imposing collectivization upon the peasants, lamely concluding: "From the viewpoint of historical truth, it is indisputable that Stalin contributed to the struggle for socialism and to its defense in the ideological struggle. . . . The core of the party headed by Stalin had successfully defended Leninism."[*]

But such "balanced" consideration now sounded preposterous in the light of what newspeople, historians, and even erstwhile servants of the dictator now felt emboldened to tell the nation. How could one find anything positive about the man who, as the mass of material available to the public clearly showed, authorized and directed the mass murder of his own people? The Soviet public could read data from the KGB files attesting how during the years of terror, regional offices of the secret police had been provided with precise quotas of how many "people's enemies" had to be unmasked and liquidated in their districts. They may have suspected it before, but now Soviet newspaper readers were repeatedly and authoritatively told how collectivization had been not a grandiose feat of social engineering but a veritable rape of Russian peasantry, the number of its victims probably surpassing that in Hitler's "final solution." And a number of articles, some by military men, dissipated the legend of Stalin's great services during the war, until then the most enduring of the myths about the tyrant. On the contrary, it was he who, by the massacre of the Soviet officer corps before the war and by leaving the country unprepared for the German invasion, was responsible for the Soviets'

---

[*]*Twenty-seventh Congress of the Communist Treaty of the Soviet Union* (stenographic report) (Moscow 1986), vol. 1, p. 55.

early defeats and the staggering losses of soldiers and civilians.

Against this lurid but overwhelmingly convincing and documented picture, how could one maintain that during that period the Communist party had still somehow maintained its Leninist purity, rather than cravenly surrendering to one man and thus bearing a large share of the responsibility?

In addition, glasnost began to undermine the cult of Lenin. No longer only historians, but the average Soviet citizen would now be made aware of the data that presented the founder of communism as a brutal politician and fanatic not averse himself to authorizing terror on a large scale. What period of Soviet history then remained unsullied by crime and violations of basic human rights, by placing the nation's welfare far behind the interests of the rulers? The ten years of the Khrushchev era remained a gray area. He had tried to mend the system, but had not basically changed it. And his successors, while making life easier for the bureaucracy—no longer periodically massacred, as under Stalin, or bullied, as by Khrushchev—allowed the country to slip into economic stagnation and tolerated widespread corruption.

As Boldin's book unwittingly demonstrates, Gorbachev was too much of a Communist to distance himself from the dreadful legacy of the Soviet past. And he was not enough of a Communist to try resolutely to stop the flood of glasnost when it still could have been stemmed. By 1988 it was too late; both the discipline and the morale of the organization were rapidly eroding. Perhaps the Union and Gorbachev's own leadership might have been saved, but not the monopoly of power of the Communist party. And without that monopoly, the nineteen-million-member party was a helpless giant.

But what was it that perestroika was supposed to achieve? Here we come to the nub of the problem. In some ways the use of the term by the general secretary during the first three years of his leadership was comparable to the exploitation of the slogan "change" by the Democrats in the 1992 U.S. presidential election—an enticing but vague term. What was it that would be restructured and how? Boldin's testimony is again instructive. Then close to Gorbachev and still a believer in perestroika, even he cannot quite spell out what it was all about. Was the structure of the *Union* to be remade so that it would become a *real* federation with real autonomy for its fifteen component republics? Nothing before late 1989 indicates that Gorbachev was aware of the intensity of the nationalist feelings in the Baltic republics, the Ukraine, and, to a lesser extent, elsewhere, or of the fact that unless the USSR was remade in a hurry into a genuine federation, it was likely to fall apart. Would perestroika license other political parties? Again, until 1988 the idea would have appeared inconceivable even to the most reform-minded followers of the general secretary.

Insofar as we can reconstruct Gorbachev's original intentions, they were grounded in the belief that the Soviet system could be rejuvenated spiritually and morally without disturbing its political foundations. As late as 1988 his principal adviser and bête noire of the conservatives, Aleksandr Yakovlev, could write, "The Party took the lead and managed to reveal the reasons for the previous deformation of Socialism. . . . Hence the Party has proved to be a true political vanguard of society." Equally anachronistic was Yakovlev's other evocation of the goal of perestroika: "This presupposes a return to Lenin's ideals of Socialism, to its truly democratic and humanistic image."[*] This definition contained nothing that could not have been said by Khrushchev—a vision of the "masses" being drawn into the task of the Socialist construction, of ending past abuses and finding new ways of developing the creative energies of the people.

To be fair, Gorbachev and his chief lieutenant did have some ideas that, though still not concrete, went beyond the old chestnuts of the post-Stalin Communist rhetoric. The USSR was to be a "state under the law," and most of the police state practices would be discontinued. In the economic sphere, the old "administrative-command" system of running the economy (with all the main decisions being made in Moscow) was to give way to greater autonomy of individual industrial enterprises and managers.

Gorbachev has been much second-guessed for not being more energetic and resourceful with the economic side of perestroika. Yet, while decentralization of the economy was probably the most noncontroversial part of his program, its practical application proved most baffling. Unlike Deng in China, the Soviet leader, though almost thirty years younger, remained much more of a Marxist dogmatist. In agriculture, he would not tamper with the collective farm structure until it was too late. In industry, the notion of privatization remained taboo until the very end.

[*]A. Yakovlev, "The Political Philosophy of Perestroika," in *Perestroika 1989*, ed. Abel Aganbegyan (Elmsford, N.Y.: Pergamon Press, 1988), p. 52.

And so in a move fatal for himself and for Communist power, Gorbachev decided that democratization of the Soviet political structure was the most effective and safe way of putting perestroika into practice. This democratization would stop considerably short of democracy as we mean, for the Communist party would still rule.

The Nineteenth Party Conference of June–July 1988 prescribed new arrangements for the legislative elections in the USSR. Previously those elections, whether at the All-Union or the local district level, had been an empty ritual, with just one party-selected candidate "running" for office. Now there could be, and in many districts would be, more than one candidate. In most cases the party man or woman would still be elected. But to make absolutely sure that the Communists would remain a majority, it was also decided that one-third of the future Congress of the People's Deputies would be selected not regionally but by various "social organizations," such as the Central Committee of the party, the Academy of Sciences, and the like. Those people were sure to be pro-Gorbachev.

Czarist Russia's experience with constitutionalism should have taught Gorbachev that one cannot combine genuine parliamentarianism with semi-autocracy. And, indeed, the election of March 1989 proved a crushing blow to Gorbachev, perestroika, and, eventually, the Soviet system. The pro-Gorbachev wing of the party received a safe majority. But in several cases high party officials were defeated by independent candidates, and some of them running unopposed failed to receive at least 50 percent of the registered vote necessary for election. Boris Yeltsin, publicly humiliated by the general secretary in 1987 and kicked out of the Politburo, scored a smashing victory over the official candidate in Moscow and would now become Gorbachev's nemesis. The long-suppressed but always latent nationalist feelings in the non-Russian republics burst forth, and several independent deputies declared themselves advocates of far-reaching autonomy, if not outright independence of their lands.

And so the Soviet legislative bodies, until now meek servants of the party, became agitated centers of real politics. And Gorbachev, hitherto self-assured master of the political scene, had lost much of the aura of the national leader. From now on he would be increasingly buffeted by the forces of the right and left: to the former, he appeared as the destroyer of Communist law and order; to the latter, increasingly, as the betrayer of the liberal promise of early perestroika. The general secretary, the title once denoting the most powerful politician in the world, was reduced to being just a politician, who, while he would continue to accumulate more and more power on paper, grew increasingly impotent to arrest the drift to political chaos.

It is this latter-day Gorbachev who deserves Boldin's characterization: "His words lacked assurance . . . and it was evident that he feared taking any steps at all." The slogan of perestroika was originally greeted with popular enthusiasm, largely on the assumption that the abandonment of Marxist dogmatism would be effective in raising the standard of living. Freed from the necessity of paying homage to the obsolete platitudes of Marxism-Leninism, most prestigious Soviet economists became overnight enthusiastic believers in the free market. Yet meaningful reforms still encountered staunch resistance from the serried ranks of the Soviet bureaucracy. And the general secretary no longer had the power to impose new laws and changes by simple fiat, as would have been the case before 1988.

Habits and fears bred by decades of collectivism also proved to be a barrier to economic improvement. Peasants finally licensed to leave collective farms were in most cases reluctant to accept new freedom and its responsibilities. The same fear of being on their own without the paternal state guiding them afflicted the industrial managers. A resolute and enterprising leader could have inspired a new spirit throughout the country that would lead to greater self-reliance. But Gorbachev was no longer capable of inspiring the enthusiasm that his launching of perestroika had generated.

Here one cannot quite agree with Boldin when he writes that "during the early days of his administration Gorbachev believed in the people and regarded them as his power base, and later on he came to realize that they were deaf to his new ideas." In fact, Gorbachev was still enough of a Communist to regard some of the "new" ideas—for example, private property—as impermissible departures from socialism.

Similar reluctance afflicted him in the political field. It took a lot of pressure from the legislature to persuade Gorbachev as late as February 1990 to agree to eliminate from the Soviet Constitution Article 6, which proclaimed that "the Communist Party, armed with Marxism-Leninism, determines the general perspectives of the development of society and the course of the home and foreign policy of the USSR."

By then it should have been clear to anyone but a diehard Communist zealot that there could no longer be any hope of preserving the party as the dominant force, and that the question of the hour in the Soviet Union was: Could the Union itself be saved in anything resembling its current form and area? The Communist regimes in eastern Europe were falling like bowling pins. How could the Lithuanians or the Ukrainians remain unaffected by what was happening in Poland, East Germany, and elsewhere, by the sight of their Communist bosses laying down their powers in panic, no longer able to count on Soviet tanks and soldiers to protect them from their peoples?

A realistic politician would have conceded the fifteen republics' right to independence. He might have added that those that were irrevocably committed to claim it (as were the three Baltic ones by 1990) might still preserve close ties to the ones that did not—a relationship analogous to that binding members of NATO and the EEC. Instead, Gorbachev defended the Union in terms that could not but still further irritate the non-Russians. He said in his television speech in February 1991: "History had decreed that a number of big and smaller nations become united around Russia. . . . This process was assisted by the openness of the Russian nation, its readiness to work as equals with people of other nationalities. . . . One can confidently say that our country has achieved a unique type of civilization, the results of joint endeavors of all our nationalities."[*]

With glasnost having vividly demonstrated what kind of "unique civilization" Moscow's imperialism had in fact created, such rhetoric was completely out of tune with the popular sentiment even in the Russian republic. Ironically, in 1990 and 1991 it contributed greatly to pushing the Soviet Union toward its eventual disintegration.

The All-Union elections in 1989 were followed the next year by the elections to the republics' and other constituent units' legislatures. In Russia those elections led to Yeltsin's becoming, first de facto and then in name, president of Russia. And while professing at that time, and probably truthfully, his desire to preserve the USSR, his actions and claims undermined still further the wobbly edifice. Like those in the Southern states before the American Civil War, Yeltsin questioned the superiority of the Union laws over those of the republics and wanted the latter to determine what proportion of general taxation should be turned over to the central government.

By 1991, perestroika had ceased to have any meaning to most Soviet

[*]*Izvestia*, February 7, 1991.

citizens. And those other issues, subject of passionate debate and agitation only a few months before—Stalinism, the role of the party, even democratization—now seemed insubstantial against the reality of ever deepening economic crisis and the catastrophic erosion of the authority and prestige of the central government.

We still don't have a clear picture of Gorbachev's plans and intentions during the hectic months before August. Ostensibly he was promoting a new constitutional arrangement, which, if proposed two years before, might well have enabled the Soviet state to survive, almost undiminished territorially, for quite a while. But, after 1990, it is unlikely that the new federation would have endured, even if the August putsch had not intervened and Gorbachev's Union Treaty had been signed.

Did the president and still general secretary at the same time play with the idea of the use of force to secure what he could not realistically hope to obtain by negotiations with Yeltsin and other republics' leaders—preservation of a viable state? Certainly during those last months Gorbachev had distanced himself from his earlier reform-minded advisers, such as Yakovlev and Shevardnadze, and drawn closer to those who would soon try to overthrow him and turn back the clock. Did he more sensibly than the future *putschists* decide that while the people had lost their illusions about perestroika, they would not passively accept an attempt to return to totalitarianism? Or was it fear of losing his great popularity in the West, by which he set such great store, that kept him from authorizing the recourse to force?

Boldin may have hit upon the explanation of Gorbachev's state of mind in that summer of 1991 when he wrote how prone his countrymen had been to expect a miracle to produce economic and political betterment: "We expected miracles from the revolution and collectivization, perestroika. . . ." At the time it was the phantom of massive Western economic help that held the promise of such a miracle.

It still seems rather strange that Gorbachev could have departed calmly for his August vacation on the Black Sea completely unaware that something was brewing among his closest official collaborators: his vice president, prime minister, minister of war, head of the KGB, and many others. Stranger still was the ineptitude of the plotters. But had they been more efficient, it is still unlikely they could have achieved more than a temporary success. By 19 August 1991, political power in the vast country had become too diffused to be scooped up again or for anyone to be able to restore the pre-perestroika USSR.

The failed coup hastened and made explicit what had been implicit: the disintegration of the Soviet Union and the fall from power of Mikhail Gorbachev. And it was Yeltsin who gave a final push to both. "An indestructible union of free republics was forged forever by Great Russia," proclaims the Soviet national anthem dating from Stalin's time. And now, ironically, when the republics became really free, it was the largest of them, Russia under Yeltsin's leadership, that in effect contributed most to the destruction of the Union.

It is fascinating to observe how the interplay of personalities decisively resolved this great historical drama. Had not Gorbachev chosen to humiliate and punish Yeltsin in 1987, the latter in all likelihood would have remained a follower of the general secretary. And had the choice of the Politburo in 1985 fallen on someone other than Gorbachev, how different would have been the history of the last few years!

Biased though it understandably is, Boldin's portrait of his erstwhile boss provides us with some valuable insight into Gorbachev's personality. This book confirms what has been suggested by other sources: the general secretary's indecisiveness once he had to confront the basic social and economic problems of a rapidly changing society. The man who so cleverly outmaneuvered his conservative colleagues in the intraparty council stood helpless when it came to dealing with the ethnic question or determining the nature and pace of economic reform. Having in effect destroyed the party, Gorbachev badly needed another power base during those two years. The situation cried out for a fresh start—a new party or movement. Yet he preferred to remain nominal head of *the* party, soon a political corpse. Nor did he succeed in gathering around him a body of loyal advisers and lieutenants. Even before Gorbachev's downfall, he, president of the state, had become politically isolated. Today there are still people in Russia who venerate Stalin, but hardly any who are nostalgic about the author of perestroika.

Valery Boldin was a personal assistant to Gorbachev and then, from 1987 to 1991, chief of staff for party affairs. His book provides, for the first time, details about the daily routine of the fallen leader. We are given many examples of his overriding concern for personal power and its material perquisites. To be sure, had the former been Gorbachev's sole aim, he would have never embarked on perestroika—any democratization was bound to reduce the general secretary's authority. Yet, though Boldin exaggerates, the reader emerges with a strong impression of Gorbachev's haughtiness and scant regard for his subordinates' feelings. We cannot reject Boldin's opinion that his adulation by the West went to his boss's head and made him intolerant of criticism and overly hasty in breaking the taboos of Soviet politics. Our author does not take kindly to Gorbachev's altering the hitherto severely masculine tone of Soviet politics and allowing his wife to become a public figure and—worse!—to influence his political decisions and demeanor. In many ways Boldin's views are those of an old-fashioned Soviet bureaucrat; how characteristic of Gorbachev's difficulty in judging people that he allowed a man like that to remain a close associate for ten years.

But let us not be too severe with either Gorbachev or Boldin. How many people could one have found in the Soviet apparatus whose minds had not been flawed by decades of indoctrination and isolation from the outside world? The writer has little to say about one great contribution of his chief: the East-West accord. And, indeed, for all of Gorbachev's sins of omission and commission (mostly the former) in domestic affairs, history will render him his due in having contributed to what might be called the revolution of common sense in international affairs. Boldin's anguish over what happened to the USSR, however, warps his judgment. For him, ending the dangerous rivalry with the West does not compensate for the harm done by Gorbachev in trying to transplant Western ideas and customs to Soviet soil.

And, in a way, there is more than a grain of truth in that complaint. Perhaps one could not inject even a small dose of democracy into the Soviet system without destroying it. In any case, Gorbachev proved unequal to the task. As the author puts it, "He was convinced that by concentrating in his hands the power of both party and state, by securing emergency powers, he would wield unconditional control over a great country. In fact, all he held in his hands was the reins; his teams of horses had bolted long ago"—except for the exaggeration of his boss's predilection for power, a fair description of the political reality during the last two years of perestroika.

This book's message is not merely a nostalgic lament for the past. In addition to recounting the personal drama of a political leader, it shows how no basic reform can be effective unless backed not only by popular approval but also by strong and purposeful political authority. It is on the proper balancing of the claims of freedom and authority that the fate of Russia depends.

1

MOVING INTO
GORBACHEV'S ORBIT

The steel door grates and squeaks on its hinges as I am led into the cell; I then hear the keys rattling as it is locked behind me. In the dim light, I promptly bump into the steel bunk bed. Some minutes pass before I become aware of my surroundings. A washbasin and toilet stand less than two feet away. There is no window, only a steel sheet with holes in it. Glancing around, I can now see that my cell measures about ten feet by six. I sit on the bunk and continue to survey my new abode. Solitary confinement—perhaps just as well. I do not feel like seeing anyone. I am still carrying under my arm the possessions they have left me with. I have no belt, tie, or shoelaces. They have also kept my money and documents. It seems I no longer need a great many things. I lie down on the steel slats of the bunk bed, feeling the chill of the metal against my body.

Some five hours later the door opens, and what passes for dinner is placed directly in the sink. I do not touch my food. An hour later someone is taken upstairs, and I am soon led to a cell where I find two pairs of eyes staring curiously at me. Seeing the condition I am in, the others let me take the lower bunk bed and help me stretch out a mattress made of lumpy padding. I settle in, trying to keep warm, but find myself twisting and turning from discomfort and pain. Worse is yet to come, so I shall have to get used to it.

Earlier that day I had still been lying in a hospital bed; I was awakened just before dawn by the sound of suppressed whispering in the corridor. The door then opened, and the nurse looked in to announce that "the doctors are coming to see you." I could tell from the frightened expression on her face that I was in trouble. They took off their white coats, and one of them handed me an arrest war-

rant signed by Nikolai Turbin, the procurator general of the USSR. The man who showed me the warrant bore an amazing resemblance to Major Tomin from a popular television series called "The Experts Investigate." This particular expert had the same intelligent face and refined manners. I dressed and soon found myself being driven toward Blagoveshchensky Pereulok. The drivers, who obviously did not know their way around Moscow, spent a long time trying to find the right address; moreover, the roads in that part of town had been dug up for building repairs and the laying of sewer and utility lines. Eventually we arrived. The procurator got in, and we drove on to the silence of the Matrosskaya Tishina prison, special isolation unit no. 4.

So here I am, duly frisked and stripped down to the bare essentials. The sequence of events over the previous few days that has brought me—and not only me—to this charming spot keeps going around and around in my head.

"Tomorrow at 2:00 P.M. a plane from the defense ministry will be ready for takeoff at Chkalovskaya airport. You must be there on time." That was the tail end of the conversation at the KGB reception building on 17 August.

"Will you be well enough to fly? Someone has got to tell the president what's really going on in this country. He'll believe you."

For the previous week I had been in the hospital, on an intravenous drip practically every day, feeling really lousy. Yet I was so worried about the situation in the country, which was close to disintegrating, that I simply had to set my personal considerations aside.

There were both military and civilian aircraft at Chkalovskaya when I arrived there on 18 August, which was Air Force Day. The pilots were obviously participating in some special events for the occasion. A number of black Volga sedans drove up to the plane. We exchanged greetings with the crew and climbed the steep, narrow steps to board the TU-154. There was no boarding ramp of the usual kind. The pilots helped us into the cabin. Oleg Baklanov (Central Committee secretary for the defense industry), Oleg Shenin (Central Committee secretary for organizational matters), Valentin Varennikov (deputy minister of defense), and I were seated in the cabin of the defense minister's plane. On one side of the cabin was a couch, on the other several comfortable armchairs and some cushions on the side, with a large table in the middle. We took off our jackets. Some military personnel and others in civilian clothes walked past the wide sliding doors on their way to other cabins. Varennikov gave the order to take off.

The engines started up, and the plane shook and started down the runway. We took off quickly and easily; soon I could see below me the woods, lakes, winding streams, and clusters of dachas of the outlying areas of my hometown, Moscow. After a steep ascent at takeoff, we began a steadier climb. The ground was increasingly hidden by patches of cloud; soon the yellow-green fields, villages, gardens, and lots were visible only from a great altitude. The flight was to last two and a half hours. I began to think about exactly what I was doing. Why was I in that plane? What had made it necessary to speak out about the grave situation in the country?

Since January 1991, there had been regular discussion of the difficulties that loomed ahead. The country was in a political and economic crisis. The president was so concerned that he had instructed several members of the Security Council to prepare proposals for the introduction of a state of emergency. He listened to the proposals but had still made no decision. Several times he had met with Central Committee secretaries Dmitri Yazov, Vladimir Kryuchkov, Nikolai Tizyakov, and Oleg Baklanov, each of whom, from his own particular standpoint, warned that the economy was collapsing and that the state itself could well disintegrate. The new draft federal treaty ignored the desire of the general public, as expressed in the referendum of 17 March 1991, to keep the Soviet Union united. Centrifugal forces were now tugging relentlessly at that Union. Indeed, a "battle of laws" was raging, as the republics adopted decisions proclaiming the primacy of their own laws over those of the Union; legislative chaos was mounting daily. It was increasingly evident that the country's leaders had lost control of the situation.

A crisis was also developing in the army and the defense complex. Without proper control and constant monitoring of nuclear weapons and replacement of their warheads, an irreparable disaster could occur. As a result of neglect, defense industry plants producing nuclear raw materials and building and replacing nuclear warheads had been forced to shut down; qualified personnel were leaving. A group of well-known nuclear scientists warned the president of the impending dangers in the nuclear industry. Personnel cuts had increased the number of officers lacking apartments and other social benefits. The economy continued to decline. Links with suppliers of raw materials and manufactured parts

difficult. It must be said, in all fairness, however, that he studied hard and soon developed a grasp of many ideas. He then began to use them so vigorously that, except for an occasional slip, he managed to conceal his abysmal ignorance and his lack of systematic knowledge of political economy.

Though trained as a lawyer, he never worked as one, spending his whole life in the party organization and agriculture. While working in Stavropol he had acquired a sound knowledge of agriculture, completing a correspondence course at the agricultural institute. After his move to Moscow he continued to think in regional terms, taking a little more time to develop a grasp of the subject on a nationwide scale. When Andropov began to involve Gorbachev actively in the work of the Polit-buro, he turned his attention, with all the vigor of youth, to a wider range of subjects. Here again, however, Gorbachev concentrated on pro-ducing material for publication. He regarded language as his main con-cern and one of the most important ways of getting things done.

Whenever some new issue came up, even something quite difficult, he would say: "We must write an article or a book on this. Sit down and work up a proposal." Even after his return from vacationing in Foros, Gorbachev said at a press conference that, while there, he had written an article dealing with questions posed by a coup d'état.

A sense of hopelessness descended on all those who knew Gorbachev well when they saw him incapable of acting, paralyzed by hesitancy. As the country teetered near the brink of collapse, civil war, and disintegra-tion, there was an urgent need for someone to take action.

In August 1991 preparations for the signing of the new federal treaty were in full swing. Despite my illness I was compelled to go practically every day to check the typesetting of the text. Certain accoutrements were needed: paper, files, cases, ink and pens, flagstaffs, of which there would be more than fifty. On 16 August Gorbachev telephoned me, sounding very agitated, and angrily inquired about the meeting of leaders of the republics in Alma Ata. I was unable to make a sensible reply, as I was unaware of such a meeting; moreover, he could have asked the members of the Security Council or his assistants, who specifically handled such matters. He was annoyed with me for sending too many documents to his vacation home in the south: "Listen, I'm not at work now; I'm on vacation. So cut it out, otherwise I'll send back the ones I haven't read."

That was not an idle threat. Once, while he was staying at the dacha, I sent him some documents that he had kept for two weeks without reading. On that day we discussed, in a calmer manner, a number of other questions pertaining to the country's future.

The plane began its descent. The grayish yellow of harvested fields floated by beneath us, with a few villages, some dusty factories, and a string of cars traveling along a country road; then came the sea, which I had not seen in twelve years. The aircraft shuddered as the undercarriage was lowered on our approach to the airport, where rows of heavy military planes could be seen. The TU-154 touched down, the engines roared as they went into reverse thrust, and we taxied to the main terminal. We had arrived at Belbek military airfield, near Sevastopol. The senior army, navy, and air force officers who were waiting for us on the tarmac nodded curtly in our general direction and then conferred with Varennikov. We walked into the newly constructed terminal, a small, attractive building consisting of a few rooms set to the side and a large reception hall for high-ranking guests arriving on vacation.

"Not long ago a reception was held here for Gorbachev and the republican leaders," said the officer who accompanied us.

It was five o'clock, but we had not had any lunch. A bite to eat would have been most welcome, as I was feeling unwell and increasingly weak. A few minutes later we were invited into the hall, where lunch—borscht, meat, potatoes, and stewed fruit—had been laid out on the edge of a table. We rushed through our meal, hardly tasting the food; then we went outside, where we were met by a number of black and gray Volgas in which we were driven to Sevastopol and then on to Foros.

The last time I had been in either place was 1962–64. I remembered the road and the cliffs with their man-made cavities in which medical units, stores, and command posts had been located during the war. It was a warm day, though the sun could not be seen behind the haze. When the sea eventually came into view, I found it hard to tell at first where the sky ended and the water began.

About thirty-five minutes later I spotted a red rooftop by the sea; it was the summer residence of the president of the USSR. We turned right off the road and entered the property. A number of heavy-set security guards stood by the gate. We drove up to the guest house, a well-designed and solidly built two-story structure with a spacious hall and a broad staircase leading to the second floor, where the clinic was located. As I had to take some medication, I went in; it was empty. Yuri

Plekhanov (chief of personal security for the Gorbachev family) went off to announce our arrival. Either nobody was home, or whoever was there was in no hurry to receive us. It was not until a half hour later that we entered the foyer of the dacha and began to wait. I saw the spacious halls, a large room opening directly out onto the seafront, and then private apartments, a dining room, and a winter garden. The whole place was made of the finest materials, as you might expect in a villa that cost 80 million rubles, according to Plekhanov—not to mention the cost of all the communications hardware. The materials used were the very best, the kind of thing I had never seen before. Rumor had it that the roof was made not of red tile but of a special aluminum with the same color and texture as red tile. The original design was amazing in many other ways, but all that came back to me later.

In about ten or fifteen minutes, Gorbachev came out, looking very agitated. His face was red, perhaps from sunburn but probably from rage. He quickly shook everyone's hand and angrily asked: "Why has the phone been disconnected? What are you doing here?"

"We wanted to talk to you and explain."

"Did you cut off the phone?" he went on, without listening to us. "What does this mean?"

This exchange took place on the way to his office, which was small and uncomfortable. There were two windows, one on either side of the table, and nowhere to sit, Gorbachev himself remained standing. Shenin tentatively began to speak: "We have come to tell you about the situation in the country and to let you know the kind of measures that could correct it."

"Who do you represent? On whose behalf are you speaking?"

Shenin was taken aback. Only the day before, he had been expecting a friendly discussion and a mutually agreed solution, in the spirit of previous conversations. In fact, the trip had been made on condition that there would be a mutual agreement and a decision by the president. And now everything had gone haywire right from the start. Standing near the window as I listened to the discussion, I realized that there was something strikingly different about the president's behavior. Perhaps he had been surprised to see Varennikov among us?

"Who do you represent, and on whose behalf are you speaking?" he repeated.

"Well, we represent a substantial part of the country's leadership," said Shenin, in an attempt to continue stating his case.

"Who, precisely?"

Tension was mounting. On learning that only Baklanov, among those present, had been a member of the group responsible for this initiative, he said: "I want to hear what you have to say; I refuse to talk to the rest of you, since you represent nobody."

Glancing at Plekhanov, he added: "And you have no business being here at all. Get out!" Plekhanov, humiliated by this remark and the tone in which it was uttered, left the room.

Baklanov began speaking, but Gorbachev again interrupted him, to ask: "Who exactly was it who sent you here?" He began to list some names, which the president noted down.

"Well, what did you come here to tell me?"

"I would like to start with the situation in the country. You know that both agriculture and industry are in serious trouble, but that's not what we've come to talk about."

"What do you mean? I know all that already, and know more about it than you."

He would not let Baklanov speak. Varennikov then intervened, referring with characteristic forcefulness to the situation in the country and in the army, describing the great hardship the general public and the officer corps could expect unless emergency measures were taken. He too was cut off.

The president went on the offensive, resorting to those homemade tactics he had been using of late in the Central Committee plenums whenever his performance as general secretary was criticized. He always fought fiercely and uncompromisingly to protect his post.

All this emotional crossfire, which was driven by wholly illogical urges, was pointless. Gorbachev listened distractedly as various options for future action were put to him. Their purpose, as I understood it, was to have the president make emergency provisions for bringing in the harvest and stabilizing the economy, or at least for halting the decline in production; it was intended that he should instruct either the Cabinet of Ministers or anyone else in whom he had confidence to put those measures into effect. These ideas were put forward but, because of the belligerent atmosphere, they made no impact.

"Everything you propose can be done only by democratic means. I shall therefore advise you on the best way to do what you intend."

Then came an abrupt change of tone, which I am still at a loss to understand. In the course of a calm, businesslike discussion, Gorbachev gave matter-of-fact advice on how to resolve the issues raised, explaining the reasons for his policies. "Think it over and let your comrades know," he then said, shaking us each by the hand as we left.

Raisa was sitting in the hall with her children and grandchildren.

"Have you brought good news?" she asked Baklanov.

He told her that we had come with good intentions and that everything would be all right. All we had talked about was our concern over the situation of the people; he added that, as friends, we wished her and her family well.

We went outside feeling quite drained by this unexpectedly distressing conversation. Baklanov, clearly puzzled by what had happened, said: "But he thought that was the only solution. What has changed?"

Plekhanov was again busy in the guest house. But our cars were ready, and we wanted to get out of there as fast as possible. The atmosphere was one of high emotional tension. It seemed we were all acting like robots, not looking at one another or understanding what was happening.

We drove out onto the highway, past the heavy-set security guards at the exit. We passed cars going the other way. I felt somewhat confused and disoriented. The road back seemed much shorter.

In Belbek the plane was ready for our departure. Sitting on a bench next to the terminal, I could see that everyone had already gotten on board and that the military brass had said goodbye and left. Only then did I board. The plane taxied for a long time, paused for a moment at the start of its takeoff run, and then started with a thrust down the runway, quickly became airborne, and after a steep initial climb steadily gained altitude. The ground far beneath us was soon cloaked in the darkness of a southern night, punctuated here and there, on land or sea, by a few dull yellow lights. I settled in for the two-and-a-half-hour trip to Moscow. Someone was saying something, but nobody in particular was listening. Tea and cookies were served, but I could neither eat nor drink.

When we landed in the darkness of Moscow, it was bitter cold. We got into the first cars that came along, not noticing who else was getting in with us or who was already inside. Plekhanov told the driver to hurry. But the cars took different routes. Somewhere near Krasnoselskaya Street we had a flat tire; while the driver, who had pulled alongside the sidewalk, was preparing to put on the spare, another hired car came along and we all got in. Within fifteen or twenty minutes we were in the Kremlin. The corridor on the second floor of the government wing, along which we walked, was full of people, mainly security guards.

In the dim light of the office I could see people seated along a long conference table covered with green cloth. As I sat down at the edge of the room, I at first recognized only Vice President Gennadi Yanayev. The waiters served tea and sandwiches, and I began to listen. This group, which had arrived ahead of us, was being addressed by Shenin, who spoke calmly and thoroughly. In response to a request from Yanayev for further information, Baklanov said a few words, but added nothing of substance. I had nothing to add, either.

The discussion, growing steadily more heated, then turned to what should be done. Opinions were divided, with some arguing that, as the president had refused to agree with them, everything should stay as it was. To which others rejoined: "Did you expect him to agree? That's very naive; that's not the way to go about it." It was impossible, however, either to press ahead or to back down. Several people began talking at the same time; arguments began to break out. People were entering and leaving the room all the time. They were waiting for someone, and trying to contact certain others by phone, to ask advice or to summon them to the Kremlin.

It was now really late and I was feeling terrible. I got up and returned to the hospital, suspecting that my protracted absence must have caused some panic there.

When I fell asleep on the evening of Air Force Day, 18 August, my favorite holiday, I still had no idea what they had decided to do. Nor did I realize at that moment that this would be the last relatively quiet day of my life. There was much more that I did not know at that time: the sheer magnitude of responsibility some people bear for the fate of the nation and its people, as well as the baseness of those who would kick a man when he is down. Until I experienced that, I don't think I really understood life or people.

I could never tolerate flattering, obsequious types who try to ingratiate themselves with the right people. Anyone who possesses such qualities, either manifest or latent, could also betray others or stab them in the back. Could I have avoided flying to Foros? Of course I could have. I had already been in the hospital for about a week, spending hours at a time on an intravenous drip and feeling weak, with a heavy head and frequent pains and dizziness. I could quite easily have declined to take part in any venture whatsoever, but I met with men whom Gorbachev trusted more than himself; indeed, he had instructed me to meet with them whenever the need arose. In such a critical situation, therefore, my contact with them was all the more justified. When I went to Foros I saw no reason to expect anything out of the ordinary, since all aspects of the situation were well known. And it really was essential to change that situation, so as to prevent the collapse of the Union.

On Monday I woke up with a sense of foreboding. As soon as I turned on the television, I realized what had happened. The State Committee for the State of Emergency had been formed, and Vice President Yanayev had assumed control. Slowly and sadly, the announcer read out the documents that had been adopted. Yanayev had taken over the duties of the "sick" president. Surely they could have done better than that, I thought; such a solution did not make sense at all. My first instinct was to go to work and find out exactly what had happened, but it was not that simple. I had to be hooked up to the intravenous line and stay in bed for as long as possible. I arrived at work late. There were armored personnel carriers and tanks in the streets. I was told that Yanayev had been asking for me. There was no answer when I phoned. People were leaving and entering his conference room, which was full; I went in unannounced and sat at the edge of the room. They were discussing further steps to be taken on the economy. Pavlov was not there.

It was my impression that they had been sitting there all night. The discussion was chaotic—and not, as it later turned out, because of lost sleep. Without waiting until the end, I went back to my office. Everyone was busy, so conversation was pointless. I summoned the section heads, many of whom had phoned, to tell them that work should continue as before.

For those three days, from 19 to 21 August, my sole source of information was the hospital TV, which offered little in the way of news but plenty of somber, funereal music. Losing my patience, I decided to go to work, but even there it was hard to find out what was happening. There was no information, and nobody really knew anything. I sorted through some documents, transmitted a decree and several instructions signed by Gorbachev, and perused the manuscript of some articles I had written long ago, which I now found unsatisfactory. I discarded some copies of different versions of the federal treaty and other old papers that had accumulated over the previous few weeks, then returned to the hospital. Something was being broadcast on television, although it was half obscured by crackling sounds and interference. I sensed that the world was about to change. As soon as I felt slightly better I went back to work, only to find myself once again in an information vacuum; so I returned yet again to the hospital. That evening the situation did change, and radically, when I learned that Yazov, Kryuchkov, Ivan Silayev (chairman of the Council of Ministers), Anatoly Lukyanov (first deputy chairman, presidium), and Vladimir Ivashko (a Central Committee secretary), with a few others, had flown to see Gorbachev, that he had consented to see only some of them, and that he was on his way back from Foros. The next morning information was once more in short supply, and the phones had been disconnected. Then I had a feeling of impending doom.

Twenty-four hours, and a long summer night, were yet to pass before I entered the Matrosskaya Tishina prison.

LEAVING *PRAVDA*

Try as I might, I can have no peace, as my restless mind disgorges swarm upon swarm of fresh, sharply etched memories. My head throbs in pain as I watch the whole procession of events, in full color and fine detail, pass before my mind's eye. I can clearly remember the first time I met Gorbachev—that tragic phenomenon of our age. I well remember my hopes and the hopes of millions of others for changes in society. Everyone believed that a better life could be ours, without ethnic strife, bloodshed, cruelty and hatred, without refugees and poverty, the collapse of the state, and the disintegration of the army.

I well remember the day in 1981 when I began my ten years of work with Gorbachev. I mentally replay the scene over and over again. It all started when my phone rang. It was Vasili Popov, assistant to the editor-in-chief of *Pravda*, where I worked, telling me that his boss wanted to see me. As the editorial board meeting had just ended, with nothing said about the work of my section, I was surprised by this request, especially as Yuri Afanasyev, since his appointment, had generally avoided heart-to-heart discussions. Wondering just what he could want, I went down to the fourth floor.

"Gorbachev just called. He wants me to release you so that you can become his assistant. Do you know him?"

My surprise was evident: "No, I've never seen him, and have no idea what he is like."

Genuinely puzzled by my reply, Afanasyev looked at me suspiciously. "Well, it doesn't matter," he said with a frown, throwing back his long gray hair. He continued emphatically: "I told him that I won't let you go. Who am I going to have left here? They've repeatedly raided this place for people. Soon there'll be nobody left working at *Pravda* at all. You see what I mean?"

He began to list the names of journalists who had quit to take higher positions at other newspapers and magazines and in the party.

"Remember, I'm not letting you go; if necessary, I shall complain."

He tried to think of someone to call. Mikhail Zimyanin would not do, as he was only a Central Committee secretary. He could hardly call Brezhnev, who was known to be in poor health. He then suggested two other names—Suslov and Kirilenko—before falling silent.

Staring at Afanasyev in astonishment, I pondered carefully what I had been told. I did not know Gorbachev, but I did know that party secretaries from resort areas, as he was, all had been pampered by fate, and were quite unbearable. Most of them were enmeshed in corruption. They spent all their time hovering around important visitors, seeking to ingratiate themselves. I was fond of *Pravda* and of journalism and so was most reluctant to move to an office job, knowing full well what a grueling proposition it was. Assistants were treated like outcasts, being given the bulk of the work and the harshest abuse; bosses tended to regard them as their personal property and subjected them to the severest criticism.

A few days later I was invited to meet Gorbachev at the Central Committee offices. Without having to wait, I was ushered into the small office of a Central Committee secretary, with a low ceiling and venetian blinds on the windows. The stale air smelled of synthetic materials.

I was greeted by a good-looking man of medium height, with a fine set of teeth and hazel eyes with a kind of inner sparkle. What may once have been a full head of hair had now shrunk to a graying fringe, exposing several purple birthmarks, which extended toward the forehead and eyebrows. Apart from that, all I remember is the smart way he dressed: a brownish suit, made by a high-class tailor, a foreign-made and doubtless expensive cream-colored shirt, matched by a brown tie and shoes. It seemed as though his clothes had been made only the day before and had not yet been worn enough to develop wrinkles. He came over to me, holding out his soft, limp hand like a trophy.

"Haven't we . . . ," he began, but I disposed of his doubts, saying: "No, we have never met." We both sat down and spent a few minutes talking generally about agriculture. Then, as if the issue had already been resolved, Gorbachev explained what he expected from me and which questions I would have to deal with. Uncertain whether Afanasyev had conceded defeat and agreed to my departure or whether Gorbachev had no intention of asking either his or my permission, I said nothing. In any case I needed to know exactly what he wanted. I told him that besides my regular job, I taught a higher economics course for the state planning agency, Gosplan, and was anxious to continue doing so; moreover, a book of mine was being prepared for publication, and I was also working on a number of articles.

"That's fine," he agreed. "All to the good, in fact."

I could not then have known that, once in his employ, I would never again be allowed to write or, in particular, to hold a teaching job. Holding more than one position was strictly forbidden in the Central Committee, where it was felt that all of one's energies should be devoted to one cause, one passion.

Dispirited, and without giving my consent to work for him, I left. That evening a rather diffident Afanasyev said that he had been under pressure; the next morning he made an indignant speech claiming that *Pravda* was being torn to shreds and that he was not going to stand for it. He did not, however, say to whom he was going to appeal. The experienced Zimyanin, whose advice he apparently sought, recommended that he refrain from further protest and remember that the poaching of personnel was not a one-way process, as members of the Central Committee staff had at various times been sent to *Pravda*.

That was how my career at *Pravda* ended. I always regretted leaving, and hoped that one day I would be able to return to journalism, in any capacity, because the spirit of freedom and creativity prevailing at *Pravda* even in those days could not be supplanted by any other temptations. Apart from anything else, a transfer to the Central Committee meant an immediate 50 percent cut in salary. That, however, was the least of my concerns, as a generally difficult and uncertain future lay ahead.

Yet I did not realize, then or later, that I would find it quite so difficult to live in that stuffy atmosphere with its rigid, antiquated, and sacrosanct rules. All that I could definitely anticipate was a tempestuous life of frantic struggle, reflecting the gathering storm of deep dissatisfaction that pervaded the atmosphere of society as a whole. I wondered whether I would be able to survive and perform any useful work at all in the midst of that torrent of passions.

THE ECONOMY ON THE
VERGE OF COLLAPSE

Another day passes, another midnight comes. It is precisely at night, which is known to be conducive to both miracles and crimes, that my mind begins to be filled with some extremely fanciful visions. I think that it has all been a dream, and that I shall soon awake in my own bed at home, horrified by the nightmare I have witnessed. I even try to touch the wall and the iron post of the bunk bed. But there is no miracle, just as there has been no crime. I lie with my eyes open, yet not seeing, while the succession of events plays itself back before me, as in a film.

In May 1981 I started going to my new place of work by 9:00 A.M., often earlier. I went up to the eighth floor and into the small, seedy room, which was papered from floor to ceiling with a plastic wallcovering. The air conditioner was pumping stale, sour air, as if hundreds of others had already breathed it and the residue was coming through to me. I opened a small window, contrary to recommendations, and set about my paperwork. My job was to delve into the details of agricultural production, including technology—something I had largely forgotten about, given my interest in economics and politics.

I sat staring at tables showing the structure of areas under cultivation for various crops, the animal feed balances, and much more. It would have made more sense for this kind of material to be dealt with in the Ministry of Agriculture or, better still, in its local branch offices. But the Agricultural Department of the Central Committee comprised an enormous apparatus, including dozens of agronomists, zootechnicians, agrochemists, experts on fruit and vegetables, economists, engineers, and other specialists who, having done their own share of reaping and sowing on the farm, were determined to advise others on harvesting techniques, on what buckwheat gruel was like and how it should be eaten.

The department head was V. A. Karlov, a mature and tough individual who had once been "exiled" to Uzbekistan as second secretary of its Central Committee. Now, as head of the dynamic agriculture department of the party's Central Committee, he, to a large extent, decided farm policy. The apparatus under his control dictated all the twists and turns in the development of agriculture and appointed members of all the central and local agrarian organs, as well as the directors of agricultural departments in the republics, regions, and districts.

I found myself imperceptibly drawn into the work of this vast, unwieldy organization, espousing its interests and following the course laid down over decades by its structures and officials. Like a grain of sand I moved along with a huge landslide, trying at the same time to save my individuality from being overwhelmed.

The severe consequences of the 1981 drought had lasted many years, inflicting heavy economic damage on farming areas and on the entire country and emptying the coffers of the state.

Tension was high in the Politburo, the Central Committee Secretariat, and the Council of Ministers, as resources were being sought for the purchase of grain. Dutifully, but without much conviction, I prepared memorandums and documents. I had so far not been in contact or reached a mutual understanding with Gorbachev. The apparatus of the agricultural department had drawn him, like many others, into consideration of the fine points of agricultural production: crop cultivation, new methods for plowing, feeding livestock, preparing animal feed, and certain other details that I felt were of minor importance. Here again there was a lack of mutual understanding. In my opinion we viewed each other with silent contempt: I thought it was entirely inappropriate for him to be delving into matters such as the diet of hogs and hens, which would have been a waste of time even for me, but especially for a member of the Politburo. He was aware of my attitude and resented it. I also saw other reasons for failures in farming, including the abysmal ignorance of the true state of affairs on the part of many senior officials. After consulting my colleagues, who shared my opinion, I decided to organize a series of publications emphasizing that poor relations between producers and consumers and our antiquated notions of economics had driven the farming regions to a desperate condition. These frank, hard-hitting articles received a great deal of attention.

The economic situation was further aggravated by a loss of faith in the political leadership. The country's finances were in appalling condition, with many industrial and construction organizations operating at a loss. Labor discipline was extremely poor: every day hundreds of thousands of people failed to show up at work. At the same time the quality of goods produced deteriorated, thus destroying the value of a huge volume of resources, both human and material. Agricultural machinery arrived on the farm in such abominable condition that it could not be used without an additional input of labor. This in turn meant that one-third of the food harvest was lost.

Public awareness of the prevailing disorder and economic ineptitude did nothing to increase people's enthusiasm for work. Shortages of goods, coupled with the inflationary process, meant that workers, both blue- and white-collar, spent more time hunting for goods in short supply than actually producing anything. A situation fraught with the gravest consequences was developing in the country. There was a need for decisive and carefully elaborated measures to cure the country's economic ills.

The current leadership, however, was incapable of acting. It was clear to all that Brezhnev and his entourage were increasingly helpless. An atmosphere of alcoholic indulgence was pervasive. As I came to realize during my trips around the country, guests were always welcome, no matter who they were: dinner parties were laid on for them, while the hosts, ignoring their visitors, simply drank and engaged in rounds of gift giving. One could never be sure that after a visit to a collective farm, for example, the trunk of one's car would not be found to contain some expression of goodwill, as a souvenir of the visit. Gorbachev often said how difficult it was to receive the large numbers of guests coming to his region on vacation, to indulge their whims and to provide them with gifts.

It was hard to fight illegal activities. We once received among our documents an internal Central Committee memorandum from the Central Committee secretary P. Medunov, complaining that the office of the procurator was biased against the inhabitants of the Kuban region. This matter was discussed in the Central Committee, and I, realizing that many of the secretaries were inclined to support Medunov, naively went to Gorbachev and told him all that I knew about the underhanded dealings of the leadership of that resort area. He listened to me but said nothing. He must certainly have known all about this affair, but he preferred not to stick his neck out. I later learned that Viktor Naidenov, the deputy procurator general in charge of the investigation, was not merely criticized in the Central Committee Secretariat but morally destroyed and soon dismissed from his post.

This story left a grievous legacy, especially as it was soon confirmed. Such practices, which were occurring in many regions and republics, later became one of the reasons for the public's loss of faith in the party. Some way out of this situation had to be found. Industry and agriculture needed an injection of new principles and attitudes.

Late one evening toward the end of 1981, I had a frank discussion with Gorbachev. Rummaging through his papers, he talked of the difficulties facing agriculture and the economy in general. For me it was an opportunity to talk about everything that had been tormenting me for several years. When I broached the need for new ideas and new approaches to the development of society, he frankly stated his own views and suggested that some thought should be given to the choice of people who could elaborate some new concepts for the development of the economy. A list of economists, many of whom I knew personally, was drawn up; I also knew industrial managers who espoused bold ideas. I warned him, admittedly, that meetings of the sort he envisaged could hardly pass undetected and that such an initiative would certainly run into opposition, as economic issues generally were the province of other members of the Politburo, who jealously watched for encroachments on their special fields. And that is what eventually happened. Yet meetings with experts began and continued for quite a long time. Either directly, or through me, Gorbachev invited economists from Gosplan, the Ministry of Finance, the Committee on Labor and Salaries and many other organs. Gatherings of this sort, sponsored by Gorbachev, soon became habitual, almost a ritual. Most of the directors of economic research institutes, academicians, and noted university scholars attended them. In a sense they served as training for Gorbachev, introducing him to the problems at hand and teaching him how to speak the language of political economy.

Meanwhile, the state of the agro-industrial complex was going from bad to worse. Gorbachev, deeply worried by these trends, was anxious to find some way of achieving results at least equal to those of the Central Committee plenum held in March 1965. The idea of a food program and preparations for a Central Committee plenum to consider all aspects of agrarian policy date from this time.

Many experts from the Ministry of Agriculture, Gosplan, and scientists from VASKhNIL, the Lenin All-Union Academy of Agricultural Sciences, began to compile a draft food program. Gorbachev then instructed the academicians[*] V. A. Tikhonov, A. A. Nikonov, and I. I. Lukinov to compress the results of their labor into a document of usable size. A vast amount of time and effort went into what I felt was an essentially pointless operation, in which high-sounding language created the illusion of substance.

---

[*]An academician is a member of an academy, usually the Academy of Sciences.

What was really needed was a new injection of resources into the farm economy, the cancellation of debts, and an increase in the prices paid to farmers for their produce. Here Gorbachev fought hard to persuade the Council of Ministers and particularly Vasily Garbuzov, the finance minister, that instead of canceling the debts of collective and state farms each year, it would make more sense to pay the same amount in the form of price supplements, thereby at least promoting a rise in the quantities produced. The lack of understanding on this question, however, was absolute; indeed, the plenum would have reached no conclusion at all had it not been for Brezhnev, who, on hearing of the outcome of this quarrel, told Kosygin, then chairman of the Council of Ministers, that he would not go to the rostrum in a Central Committee plenum empty-handed.

That did change the situation; though, as later events showed, it was a bit like applying a poultice to a dead body.

Funds were sought, not for the first time, to buy grain in the United States, Canada, and Australia. In 1981, a year of drought, so much grain was bought that the world market reeled from the impact. A wave of indignation spread across the globe: Russia's appetite was effectively denying grain to those who really needed it. However, the deed was done: the grain was bought, even though the price was exceptionally high. Such operations had traditionally brought those involved an abundance of high awards, including the title Hero of Socialist Labor—and that at a time when foreign and Soviet freighters stood idle for months, waiting to be unloaded. In some cases the grain rotted, leaving nothing to be unloaded at all.

Little thought was given to money in those days, while the awards so liberally dispensed obliged their recipients to remain silent about failures. The special services regularly reported on this situation to the leadership, but those who spoke out ran the risk of criminal charges. Those responsible for the crimes committed were immune from prosecution.

In the fall of 1982 it became evident that another grain shortage loomed. Gorbachev was frantically trying to bring in the harvest, arrange for purchases of foreign grain, and find hard currency with which to pay for them. At the same time he sought to attract attention to himself and the problems he was dealing with. He was always eager to make speeches or write articles. For that reason, when I was ordered to write a book showing that we had reached or were approaching the levels of food consumption in countries like Great Britain, France, and

Spain, that we were actually surpassing them in calorie intake, and that hunger had in the past been an integral part of Russian life, I immediately became suspicious.

It was true that the history of hunger in Russia reached back many centuries and had also occurred in this century: the landowners and large grain merchants sold grain to Europe while Russians were dying of hunger. That fact could not be denied. Yet claiming that the situation had been rectified and that the food program would lead to new heights of prosperity was at the least wishful thinking. As for comparisons between nutrition levels in Great Britain and the Soviet Union, the less said about that, the better.

When I told Gorbachev all these things, he still insisted that I proceed with the book. I began to collect material and to study the literature. Gorbachev began to give me an increasing volume of work, including the preparation of documents for meetings.

The more I worked with him, the more I was impressed by his capacity for hard work and his memory: he could remember dozens, even hundreds, of items of statistical data. He manipulated with consummate ease everything he heard from expert advisers. His growth during those years was quite rapid. He also made progress on his most vulnerable front: culture. Both Gorbachevs had clearly made a point of familiarizing themselves with the arts, particularly music and theater. Twice or three times a month they would attend the theater or visit the ancient historic sites of the Zolotoi Kolets, surrounding Moscow. Yet Gorbachev rarely said anything about these visits. Nor did he offer his opinions about plays he had seen or the performances of individual actors. His domestic life was a closely guarded and private preserve. Work, ambition, and the desire for acclaim dominated his life.

He continued to take particular care with his appearance, changing suits almost daily and meticulously choosing shirts, fashionable ties, and elegant shoes. I was often astonished by how concerned he was with external considerations. I wondered, for example, how such an immensely busy man could find time to focus every day on his large tie collection, always remembering exactly what it contained and carefully matching each day's tie with his suit and shirt. While traveling with him, and on various other occasions, I saw for myself that he knotted each tie when putting it on, rather than simply slipping it, already assembled, over his head, the way many other men did. Perhaps this reflected a

desire to make up for lost time, dating from his poor youth. Even as a young man, despite his straitened circumstances, he always strove to be fashionable.

Early in November 1982 the situation in the Central Committee was extremely tense. Alarming developments were taking place in the country. Despite its best efforts, the Politburo's decisions were not being carried out. People had lost faith and looked forward to substantial changes.

It had become increasingly apparent that Brezhnev was no longer capable of running the party or the country. At meetings of the Politburo, whose duration tended to shrink steadily, he would sit with a vacant stare, seemingly quite unaware of his surroundings, the identity of those present, and the business they had come to discuss. More often than not he would read out a note prepared for him by his assistants, printed in very large characters on a special typewriter. He often got so confused that he read the same sentences over and over again, and then looked around pathetically, as if acknowledging his helplessness. In order to cut short the tortuous business of reaching conclusions and agreeing on proposals, Chernenko would help him bring the meeting to a close; everyone would promptly concur, and then, in an atmosphere of general consternation, file out of the room.

With all his flaws, Brezhnev was much more congenial than Gorbachev in his dealings with his subordinates; he often engaged them in friendly conversation and seemed to take a genuine interest in their domestic lives. Some of Gorbachev's speechwriters who had just finished a report for him once hinted to me that he might perhaps wish to hold a reception to thank them for their efforts; when I passed on the suggestion, however, he declined. When I asked him to sign a few copies of the report and give them to all those who had put their minds, hearts, and souls into this very demanding task, he reluctantly took four copies of the book and scribbled, "To Comrade X, respectfully, M. Gorbachev."

A less respectful gesture would have been hard to imagine. When I handed them out, feeling deeply embarrassed, several people joked sourly about it, noting the curt, halfhearted manner in which he had voiced his respect for them. Deeply hurt, they wondered whether he had found the report unsatisfactory. Anticipating further tactlessness on his part, his aides never again asked the general secretary to sign any published material they had prepared for him.

THE DAWNING OF
PERESTROIKA

Outwardly at least, it appeared that, after the appointment of Andropov as general secretary in 1983, Gorbachev's position remained unchanged: he was still in charge of matters pertaining to the agro-industrial complex. Yet his real influence on decision making underwent considerable changes. A careful observer would have noticed how he slowly but ever more confidently became the most influential member of the Politburo, at the expense of the second-ranking man in the party, Konstantin Chernenko, who controlled the party secretariat. The frequency and character of Gorbachev's phone conversations with Andropov, his long absences during which he met personally with the general secretary, and the fact that he was now being given assignments in fields other than agriculture all suggested to me that his fortunes were improving. He was increasingly involved in decisions on a wide range of economic problems, as well as on the organization of the party and personnel matters. Gorbachev's ascendancy caused tension between him and Chernenko. Andropov did not like Chernenko, though he was always mindful of the need to placate his power base.

Organizational and personnel questions were perhaps the field in which Andropov felt least competent. Gorbachev was not particularly well equipped to deal with them, either, as he did not personally know many industrialists or economists and found himself increasingly obliged to seek advice from a variety of people, some of them as poorly informed as himself. However, as solutions needed to be found for a host of problems and as the situation demanded many new appointments, Andropov tended to trust and rely on Gorbachev to do the job.

Early in the spring of 1983 he asked me whether I knew Yegor Ligachev, the first secretary of the Tomsk *obkom*.* I told him that I did not know the man personally, though I had seen him in the early 1960s and had heard a lot about him.

For a while he had worked in the Central Committee apparatus, where he dealt with organizational and ideological questions within the Russian

---

Oblastnoi komitet, the party committee in charge of an *oblast*, a territorial and administrative unit subordinate to its union republic.

Federation. In those days members of *agitprop** regarded him as a resolute and incisive person. After Ligachev's election to the post of first secretary of the Tomsk *obkom*, friends of mine from the area told me of major changes that had been brought about largely as a result of his energy. In addition to economic problems, he also focused on the development of culture, education, and science. I reported all these facts to Gorbachev.

"I've known him for a long time," he replied. "We worked together in Czechoslovakia in 1968."

About that time he often mentioned the names of individual party workers, economists, and industrial or farm managers, asking my view of people on the spur of the moment, perhaps in an attempt to gauge the accuracy of his own assessment or to find out something new. At first I paid little attention, but his purpose later became evident to me. In April 1983 the Politburo appointed Ligachev head of the party's Organizational Department. This was a crucial sector of the Central Committee's work as a whole, as it encompassed all cadres, as well as appointments not only in the party but in many other organizations as well.

Gorbachev and Ligachev jointly set about injecting fresh vitality into the party structures, recommending to Andropov new candidates to fill various posts. They had ample opportunity to appoint necessary and reliable specialists to key posts in the party apparatus, although Gorbachev often remarked that there was no one to choose from. Little attention had been paid to appointments in the middle echelons of the party apparatus, with the result that those occupying second-ranking positions were less competent and even older than the first secretaries of the party's *obkoms*, *gorkoms*, and *raikoms*.[†]

"In Stavropol the district committee secretaries are more powerful than many of the people now in charge of the *kraikoms*[§] and *obkoms*," he

---

*The Agitation and Propaganda Department, founded by the Central Committee in 1920 and part of the Ideological Department since 1988. Its purpose is to use the media to advance the party's policies.

[†]*Gorkom*, from *gorodskoi komitet*, is the party committee in charge of a town. *Raikom*, from *raionny komitet*, is the party committee in charge of a district, a small territorial and administrative unit similar to a county in rural areas or a borough in towns.

[§]*Kraievoy komitet*, the party committee in charge of a *krai*, a large, thinly populated territorial and administrative unit. A *krai* is comparable to an *oblast*, being distinguished only by the presence within its boundaries of small non-Russian ethnic groups living in autonomous regions. Stavropol is one of six *krais*.

was fond of saying, doubtless having in mind those *raikom* and *raiis-polkom* (district executive committee) officials he himself had selected.

And he did make many personnel changes; he once boasted that he had replaced all the Communist party *raikom* secretaries in a mere year and a half. As a Central Committee secretary himself, he naturally relied on people from Stavropol. On the whole, those I met were energetic and well educated.

When I started work with Gorbachev in the Central Committee, I resumed and consolidated my relationship with Aleksandr Yaklovlev, which had lapsed when he was sent to Canada as ambassador in 1973. We had known each other since the early 1960s, when we often worked together on various issues while he was an agitprop instructor for the Central Committee and I was on the staff of the Central Committee secretary Leonid Ilichev. Ilichev, an academician whom I had known while working at *Pravda*, held Yakovlev in high esteem and made a point of entrusting him with the most delicate assignments.

I met Yakovlev while he was on leave from Canada. We discussed the numerous changes occurring in society, as well as in the development of agriculture. Feeling that Canadian agriculture was highly efficient and that its methods lent themselves to use in the Soviet Union—a view with which I concurred—he asked me to persuade Gorbachev to go there and see for himself. After the two men had met, it was agreed that Yakovlev would send a telegram from Ottawa inviting Gorbachev, on behalf of the government, to visit Canada. The telegram was duly sent; and Andropov, under pressure from Gorbachev, though not without some doubts of his own, agreed to let him travel for a short while to Canada.

The trip to Canada had a decisive impact in that it enabled the future author of *Perestroika* and *The New Thinking* to understand in much greater depth the processes occurring in the Western world, and to familiarize himself with a variety of options for the future development of the Soviet Union and with questions of democratization, freedom, and glasnost. As Gorbachev later told me, during this trip Yakovlev expounded his vision of development in the Soviet Union and the world as a whole, suggesting ways of improving our society.

The Canadian trip also played a crucial role in Yakovlev's career at a time when the authorities back home seemed in no hurry to have him return from his diplomatic assignment. Eventually, after Yakovlev successfully sought help from Gorbachev, Chernenko, and K. M. Bogolyubov, then head of the Communist party General Department, his return to

Moscow was formally approved. He was given a new job. The Academy of Sciences, acknowledging his merits as well as his position as director of the World Economy and International Affairs Institute, soon elected him as a corresponding member. Yakovlev embarked on a more exalted, but also more turbulent, phase in his life.

This was how the prime movers in both the theory and the practice of perestroika came to join forces.

Yakovlev became an ever more frequent visitor to my office on the fourth floor of the Central Committee building. Together we worked on the speeches and articles we had been instructed to prepare for Gorbachev and discussed many other matters, pertaining mainly to international policy. We worked hard for long hours, in an effort to keep up with the fast pace of developments. I tended to get back home around midnight, for a few hours' rest from the myriad demands on my attention. The mounting tension in the party and the Central Committee was matched by a steady increase in our work load. Although few people realized it, Andropov was critically ill. He spent more and more time in the hospital, grew tired very easily, and found it increasingly difficult to speak.

INFIGHTING

After Brezhnev's death in 1982, the Politburo decided to retain his assistants in the Central Committee apparatus, creating for this purpose a special advisory group attached to the Central Committee Secretariat. They had nothing particular to do, and nobody consulted them or sought their advice; yet their independent status, coupled with their knowledge of the secret motives for the appointment and promotion of many individuals, made Brezhnev's advisers a distinct nuisance.

I remember witnessing the first signs of the collapse of this advisory group. Gorbachev phoned Chernenko to tell him that, at the time of Brezhnev's death and burial, one of the advisers had been enjoying himself with friends at a hunting lodge just outside Moscow.

Chernenko suggested that the adviser be severely punished: "That's outrageous! You draw up the papers and have him fired; what do you think?" he asked Gorbachev.

"You're quite right," he replied. "Such dissolute behavior has got to stop."

It must have seemed illogical to dredge up events from two and a half years earlier and to punish someone for them, but nobody challenged the decisions of the general secretary. In this way a man who had helped Chernenko rise to power was dismissed, as were several others in due course. The advisory group was disbanded, leaving no witnesses to the ascent of the general secretary and several other leaders to the highest positions in the Central Committee apparatus.

The election of Chernenko to the post of general secretary, in March 1984, left Gorbachev depressed and alarmed. He must have hoped to secure the top post for himself, thus breaking free from all constraints. He was young, sufficiently well educated, and ambitious. Yet he now found himself, once again, forced to stand in line, pulling other people's chestnuts out of the fire.

At the same time the prospect of Gorbachev's appointment as second secretary of the Central Committee seemed uncertain. Chernenko had apparently announced in the Politburo that Gorbachev would be the new head of its Secretariat, thus making him the second-ranking member of the party. However, as the Politburo had made no decision on the subject, he continued to occupy the same seat at the table in the Politburo conference room. To his profound distress, he was not invited to move to the right of the general secretary, facing Tikhonov, the chairman of the Council of Ministers. The fact that his status as second-ranking member had been only half acknowledged, and the duplicity with which he had been treated, left Gorbachev deeply embittered and upset. Occasionally, in the company of close associates, he was unable to contain his anger and lashed out at Chernenko and all the other old men. He often held long conversations with Marshal Dmitri Ustinov, the Minister of Defense, during which he unleashed his pent-up frustration. Ustinov supported and encouraged him, urging him to keep on working calmly and promising to raise the matter with Chernenko.

Even so, Chernenko's attitude toward Gorbachev remained ambivalent. Tikhonov and certain other members of the Politburo, viewing Gorbachev as the main threat to their comfortable existence, were fiercely opposed to his appointment and did their utmost to humiliate him, sometimes in petty ways. They could never forgive him for rising so far under Andropov. The standoff continued until Ustinov lost his patience and announced at a meeting of the Politburo that Gorbachev should occupy his new seat, whereupon Chernenko, as if suddenly coming to his senses, ratified this move. At this point a disjointed chorus of approval was heard, as many other members, realizing that the question of the No. 2 post had in any case been decided, added their own endorsement. The only one who did not alter his position was Tikhonov, who, throughout the rest of his tenure as chairman of the Council of Ministers and member of the Politburo, remained firmly opposed to Gorbachev. It was not until eighteen months later, when he was already retired, that he sent Gorbachev a letter of apology, though he later came to regret it.

Gorbachev disclosed the contents of that letter to the party leadership; coming from a man who had very nearly ruined his career, it was most gratifying to him.

The issue that had troubled Gorbachev for so long was now resolved in his favor. He looked happier and more authoritative; more important, he began to work with great vigor.

Having worked hard to demonstrate his influence, Gorbachev sensed an increasing alienation between him and the general secretary. He was only rarely invited to become involved in making important decisions, and experienced none of the mutual trust to which he had grown accustomed while working with Andropov. Gorbachev was worried. Despite his attempts to improve relations with the general secretary, the chill between the two men persisted. Mutual understanding with the Council of Ministers also eluded him. He often spoke of his isolation, and assured anyone in whom he confided of his dedication to Chernenko.

Ligachev, as I soon learned, had talked to the general secretary at Gorbachev's request, trying to convince him of his personal loyalty. As a result, or perhaps for other reasons, Chernenko did warm to him slightly. Gorbachev began to meet and talk with the general secretary more often. Notwithstanding many restrictions, he began to implement Chernenko's plans. He once confessed to me that he had met Chernenko the day before and told him that, regardless of any malicious gossip he might hear, he would do his utmost to support the general secretary, help him in his work, and do whatever was required. For my benefit, he then added: "You've got to avoid squabbling in the party and feeding the rumor mill. I'm just going to work with the general secretary, the way I'm supposed to."

Gorbachev felt that this statement would assuage those who regarded him as an ambitious upstart. One cannot be sure how sincere his words actually were; but he certainly did not, and could not, give his full support to Chernenko. This was a collision not merely between two personalities but between two philosophies. Lamely acceding to Chernenko's wishes would have been disastrous for Gorbachev, as it would have equated his understanding of the problems at hand with that of the general secretary.

When I mentioned this point to Gorbachev, he maintained his customary silence. His ability to ignore the remarks of others and leave questions unanswered was, and still is, a characteristic trait. Even a no from him often signified consent. I sometimes observed that, despite his silence, ideas that had been put to him by others did not fall on barren soil; instead, they tended to blossom forth some time later in his actions, masquerading as the fruit of his own reflection. Some ideas took several years to achieve recognition and reappear as his own. Gorbachev had developed sleight of hand to the level of virtuosity. Nobody seemed particularly offended, however, as everyone just assumed that such procedures were an inherent part of the exercise of political power.

Gorbachev's duties now involved him in many new subjects. In addition to agriculture, he also dealt with the chemical industry, light industry, and trade, and he conducted meetings of the Central Committee Secretariat. This meant that he took a considerable part in the deployment of party cadres and managers from industry and agriculture. I realized how anxious he was to keep control over all new appointments when in a fit of temper he once voiced his resentment over Ligachev's habit of taking personnel issues directly to Chernenko. "He doesn't consult; he immediately goes right to *him*," he said bitterly. "I didn't expect that from Yegor."

He restrained his emotions nonetheless, and initially tried to mend his relations with Ligachev. At the same time he filed everything away in his memory; then, given the first opportunity, he barred Ligachev from decisions on many personnel issues. Such matters were thereafter entrusted to Georgi Razumovski, who had been chairman of the Krasnodar *kraiispolkom.** But that was later. From mid-1984 on, Gorbachev played an extremely active role in the Central Committee apparatus, working hard himself and forcing others to do likewise. He did his best to make an ever increasing number of questions his own exclusive province. As for his methods and his choice of words, they were often dictated by his vigorous and assertive style.

Kraevoi ispolnitelny komitet, or regional executive committee.

ON THE EVE OF
BIG CHANGES

Gorbachev's status remained uncertain and unstable. The members of Chernenko's entourage were frightened by his rise through the hierarchy and did their utmost to belittle his role in the party. During the general secretary's illness Gorbachev was again denied a chance to conduct meetings of the Politburo, although, according to a long-standing tradition in the party, the official in charge of the Secretariat could also serve as chairman of the Politburo. Now, however, Politburo meetings were regularly postponed; only when the gap between them grew too long did Chernenko summon Gorbachev, at the last minute, and invite him to convene a meeting. Gorbachev would be furious. Not ready to conduct a Politburo meeting and not having mastered the subjects on the agenda, he sincerely believed that such ploys were intended to embarrass him by making him look incompetent. He was probably right. Yet he controlled his impulses, and eventually was gratified to have been able to preside over these meetings and to sit in the chairman's seat.

The list of agenda items was drawn up mainly by Chernenko's assistants and Bogolyubov, head of the General Department. On account of the general secretary's failing health, the agendas for the Politburo were kept brief, and serious issues were either raised and then not discussed or simply kept off the agenda altogether. As had been the case in Brezhnev's time, meetings lasted thirty to forty minutes, ending with the adoption of prepared resolutions. During his term as chairman, Gorbachev did not change this practice, though he was already placing emphasis on the gravity of the problems posed and the difficulty of resolving them.

It was said that as his condition worsened, Chernenko had to be practically carried into the room, placed behind the chairman's table, and handed all the necessary documents, before the other members were allowed to enter. Panting and turning red in the face, he would say a few words and incoherently read out whatever his assistants had prepared for him. Meetings became shorter and shorter. I had never seen the Politburo members and the Central Committee secretaries in such a panic-stricken state. Sensing the inevitable outcome of his illness and realizing that they were responsible for recommending his candidacy to the Central Committee plenum, they discussed the situation frankly. To many of them the future seemed grim indeed.

Meanwhile, Gorbachev was hard at work. As second secretary of the Central Committee, he wanted to address an ideological conference that had been decided on at the Central Committee plenum of September 1983, while Andropov was still alive. Such a speech would enable him to consolidate his position as No. 2 man in the party and as a leader who formulated party policy. It had previously been decided that Chernenko would deliver a report at the conference, but his poor health and his new status as general secretary now precluded such an option. Gorbachev promptly took advantage of that fact, in the belief that party ideology should be in the hands of the second-ranking leader. That had been the custom under Mikhail Suslov, whose example was imitated by his successors.

When a final decision had been made to proceed with preparation of the report, Gorbachev summoned his aides and told them to assemble a group of experts on ideology and to start work on the report. The members of the group were N. Bikkenin, Yakovlev, V. Medvedev, G. Smirnov, S. Sitorian, together with several members of the Ideological Department. In the fall of 1984, at dacha No. 19 in Serebriany Bor, they went to work.

With the benefit of hindsight the resulting text can be said to include the philosophical basis for the restructuring, or perestroika, of all spheres of our society that would be elaborated at the Twenty-seventh Party Congress in February 1986. It had always seemed to me that our difficulties derived to a large extent from the shortcomings inherent in the principles of economic development we had been following all along. The planning methodology devised in the 1930s for a poorly developed country with widespread shortages was simply copied and remained in use even under changed circumstances. It ignored, and even actively rejected, scientific and technical progress. The mistake of the late 1950s, which was built into the party's twenty-year program, led us to continue, with a persistence worthy of a better cause, to build up the sheer volume of output of steel, cement, coal, oil, and mineral fertilizers. By 1980 we had neither met nor come close to meeting our targets under these indicators.

If the United States and the other Western countries had been focusing on those same economic indicators, the Soviet Union would have equaled or surpassed them. However, time and the progress of science and technology played a fatal joke on us. By 1980 our objective was to reach a certain point, where we assumed we would find ourselves in the company of the United States; and we had moved quite close to that point. The trouble was that the United States and a number of other capitalist countries had moved in a completely different direction. Instead of striving to fulfill quantitative indicators, they had relied on the international division of labor, by buying many industrial goods such as coal, oil, and metals from foreign suppliers, while even reducing their own domestic production. On the other hand, they strongly boosted their electronic and chemical industries, developed the aerospace sector, and made numerous other technological gains. In this way they canceled out all our efforts, while cutting their own costs, enhancing their economic efficiency, and using resource-saving principles of production.

The Soviet Union engaged in a global assault along the entire front of economic growth, but the United States surged ahead by means of thrusts spearheaded by scientific advances. Not only did we end up in an economic crisis, with monstrously bloated industrial sectors demanding constant infusions of cash, but our economy came to be cut off from scientific and technical progress. From the standpoint of economic efficiency, our model of development was a dead end. The Communist party Central Committee, the Council of Ministers, our planning bodies, and our economists thus committed a fateful blunder with strategic implications.

Thence came the idea of restructuring the economy, changing planning methods, and shifting to reliance on scientific and technological advances. There was an urgent need to resolve these problems, while at the same time accelerating socioeconomic development and raising living standards.

That was one of the ideas put forward in the report, along with various possible ways of rectifying the current situation. It is interesting to note that the more active use of market mechanisms was already being proposed then, although when the matter was discussed among the speechwriters there were differences of opinion. Gorbachev had often been told, in convincing detail, that monetary and commercial relations also existed under socialism and that such methods could not be ignored at a time of economic crisis. Yet he took a rather cautious view of the subject. A great many dogmas had become so deeply rooted that it was hard to renounce them.

Gorbachev's caution was no doubt due to his memories of all the upheavals that had attended the issue of market mechanisms in the mid-1960s, as well as the eventual results of the use of ingenious methods. His reaction was perfectly understandable, when one considers that while preparing for his new post, he was anxious not to frighten those who could not even utter the word *market* without the foulest curses. On the other hand, it is quite possible that he may truly have failed to understand the problem and sincerely believed that "developed socialism" needed no markets at all. As I cannot be sure what his exact thinking on the subject was at the time, I hesitate to ascribe particular views to him, though it may be assumed that he was juggling in his mind many different considerations, including his own future.

Though the contents of the report are now public knowledge, few people are aware of the difficulties that preceded the speech itself. Before the document was circulated, in keeping with standard practice among the Central Committee secretaries, Gorbachev held talks with Chernenko. The general secretary was reluctant even to contemplate holding such a conference, arguing that a Central Committee plenum had already dealt with the issues, which therefore needed no further discussion. Gorbachev, however, had anticipated this turn of events, as he was familiar with all the arguments used by Chernenko's entourage, and the general secretary himself, to oppose the holding of the conference and his plan to address it. His response was that he was fulfilling the decisions of the Central Committee plenum and for that reason wanted the general secretary to make an introductory statement at the conference. Gorbachev was very persuasive, especially when dealing with people like Chernenko. Even when much younger, the general secretary had never been particularly firm or confident, and disliked rejecting proposals that were put to him directly.

On this occasion he also gave in quickly, especially with regard to his speech. But Gorbachev's troubles were not yet over. Chernenko obviously could not deliver a speech himself, but he was even reluctant to send his greetings. Moreover, after studying the report, on which his assistants had commented, he frankly voiced his dissatisfaction. It did not contain even a reference to his own speech at the Central Committee plenum of September 1983. Here again, Gorbachev was ready, arguing that Chernenko should really be quoted not as the former leader of the party's ideological front but as the current general secretary. Further clarifications were needed on various other issues. When Gorbachev really needed something, his behavior could be insistent and aggressive, even at times uncouth. And it worked. It was obvious that the conference would go ahead and that Gorbachev would deliver his address. Before doing so he looked over Chernenko's comments, and asked us to include some that did not involve matters of principle.

Having repeatedly analyzed the outcome of the conference, including both its substantive aspects and its external impact, I am increasingly inclined to believe that it played a pivotal role in Gorbachev's advancement to leadership in the party.

The man who strode to the rostrum was young, vigorous, and, in his own way, engaging. Although his delivery left something to be desired, the speech itself was full of new ideas and seemed to cover a vast amount of ground.

Those present, mainly writers and other intellectuals who had grown tired of Brezhnev, Andropov, and Chernenko, suddenly realized that the party leadership now included certain new young members who could carry on its work and change the situation in the country. Gorbachev's speech also contained some significant new thinking and in particular some new economic notions, which were adopted in varying degrees later on.

On the whole the audience was favorably impressed, although certain factions did their best, during the subsequent debate as well as in the press, to distort and belittle the report's significance. Gorbachev duly registered all these things, and years later he would still list the names of individuals and newspapers that had been disinclined to support the stand he had taken at the conference. In fact, many of those working in the ideological sphere later found that their fate hinged on their reaction at the time; despite their best efforts, some of them were later unable to rectify their mistakes. Now, of course, these things are of little importance.

The death of an important protector, Dmitri Ustinov, shortly before the conference seriously upset Gorbachev's plans and left him suddenly feeling vulnerable. He was genuinely worried about what the future held in store for him. However, Chernenko's grave illness and his own successful performance at the ideological conference meant that he was now a force to be reckoned with.

A few days after the conference Gorbachev flew with Yakovlev to London, where he held his first meeting with Margaret Thatcher. Even at this early stage, she had discerned in him a promising leader and supported him to the utmost. She was, of course, not only perspicacious but well informed.

Soon I was once again in the hospital, this time recovering from a heart attack brought on by overwork and the harsh demands made on my services, as well as by my own dedication. Although I did not feel well, I was still required to draft a report for publication and to prepare other texts. After a month in the hospital I went to a sanatorium to convalesce, slowly emerging from the crisis. At this point, Gorbachev was particularly insistent, calling frequently to find out when I would be returning to work and issuing various instructions. The doctors, on the other hand, were in no hurry to discharge me; in any case I was so weak that it hardly seemed likely that Gorbachev would find me very helpful.

As elections to the Supreme Soviets of the whole country and the Russian Federation drew nearer, the political scene was becoming increasingly active. The campaign consumed a great deal of my time, as I found myself once more busy writing speeches. Whereas Gorbachev had agreed to run in Stavropol for a seat in the Supreme Soviet of the Union, his position in the elections for the Supreme Soviet of the Russian Federation had taken a new turn. In his capacity as second-ranking member of the leadership, he should have been a candidate in Moscow—a prospect that both he and his entourage found worrisome. His meeting with the people of Moscow was crucial, as it meant that this "promising outsider" was to be inspected by the inhabitants of the capital. His trip to Stavropol, of course, was also crucially important.

The rule was that *Pravda* would allot over half a page to the coverage of his speech, in the light of his status as No. 2 man in the party, thus enabling him to put forward numerous ideas that were certain to be well received by the public. The speech he was to deliver at his meeting with the voters was soon ready, and a date was set for his departure for Stavropol.

About this time, however, the intensity of "palace intrigue" and infighting rose to new heights. The increasingly sick Chernenko now spent much of his time in the hospital. As his strength ebbed away, he sensed the looming presence of the young agrarian expert, who struck him and many others as a mysterious, alien, and even hostile figure. All the factions still supporting Chernenko now made a last-ditch effort to prevent Gorbachev from assuming the post of the ailing general secretary. While Gorbachev had succeeded, with help from Ustinov, in taking his rightful place at the Politburo table, he had still been unable to move into the office of the second-ranking member of the party. Gorbachev's opponents had succeeded in keeping him in his old office on the fourth floor. Those familiar with the pecking order in the party organization viewed this whole affair as a humiliating snub for the second secretary of the Central Committee. That was certainly how Gorbachev perceived it.

The official excuse for the delay in Gorbachev's move to his new office was that Chernenko had not yet completed the removal of his own possessions. Now, it was argued, he was too sick to decide which things to leave and which to take. It was not until the day before Gorbachev's departure for Stavropol that permission was granted, quite unexpectedly, for Gorbachev to move into his new office on the fifth floor. Gorbachev issued orders for the move to take place immediately and then flew to Stavropol.

However, he had to endure further acts of petty harassment and humiliating decisions in matters such as the press coverage of his campaign speech. While we were staying at the two-story official guest house in the downtown area, Gorbachev decided to take yet another look at the text of his speech. He nervously began to insert various passages, while deleting others, leading me to fear that the text would be gravely impaired, perhaps even ruined. I always felt that last-minute, improvised insertions never did any good, and often led to mistakes and misunderstandings.

At that very moment, just as we were rushing to finish the job, the representative of TASS came in to announce that Gorbachev's speech would be allotted the same amount of space in the newspapers as those of the other members of the Politburo. That was a bad sign, suggesting that Gorbachev's opponents now had the upper hand. Acting on his instructions, I phoned his secretary in Moscow to find out what was going on and whether someone had halted his move into the new office; but I was told that his things were still being moved and that there was nothing wrong.

When I told Gorbachev he listened nervously, constantly butting in as I spoke. He habitually vented his frustrations on those present, often deliberately hurting people's feelings in the process. From my own observations over the years I knew that he tended, in a moment of irritation or when someone was making a particularly sensible remark, to insult whomever he was talking to. Gorbachev did not like advisers. Being convinced of his own importance as a perpetual leader, he could neither listen to others nor accept their ideas readily. On hearing a new proposal he would sometimes react by saying that he had already explored the idea himself and that he had intended all along to do what it entailed; or he might enlarge upon the idea, explaining the reasoning behind it, and thereby demonstrating his understanding of the problem. Many other people also told me that Gorbachev's attitude made it very difficult to offer him any kind of advice or to work effectively with him.

At the meetings of the Federation Council at Novo-Ogaryovo, in 1991, this trait was particularly evident. Gorbachev's grasp of the problem at hand was often so poor that he was unable to arrive at any meaningful conclusions; he would therefore interrupt a speaker and endorse his ideas, passing them off as his own. On one occasion Yeltsin objected publicly and in quite strong language, telling Gorbachev to allow him to finish speaking and not to interfere. By then, of course, Gorbachev no longer regarded these barbs as an affront. He would fall silent for a minute, looking at the protestor apologetically with his big moist brown eyes. This man, who only a short while before had commanded wide respect, now made a pathetic spectacle as he continued to lose face and ingratiatingly sought to assert himself by means of feeble, unconvincing arguments.

Back in the spring of 1984, harassed and unsure of himself, he had criticized his speechwriters for their work, even though the text had already been approved. On the other hand, Gorbachev did not always bear grudges: his mood could change quickly, erasing from his memory the impolite and occasionally offensive remarks he had made. Despite all the difficulties, I did my best in those days to convey my thoughts to him and offer advice. During preparations for his trip to the Stavropol region *krai*, he and I differed sharply over the choice of itinerary. He was inclined to visit the most remote, isolated villages, to see small farms where he had never been before, whereas I believed that since he was already fairly well known among farm workers, he should focus instead on large enterprises, spend some time among the workers at big industrial facilities, and perhaps visit some institute or other. The first secretary of the regional party committee, Vsevolod Murakhovski, was inclined to agree; but Gorbachev stubbornly pressed ahead with his plan. Only after two days on the road, during which he met forty or fifty livestock farmers and shepherds, brought in specially from dozens of miles away, did he realize his mistake. Its consequences were varied: few people showed up to meet him, and press coverage was delayed by the remoteness of the places he visited. As a result his visit became less and less newsworthy. Then he changed his itinerary, and things went better.

The presence of the cameras of the central TV station, and the realization that his words were being broadcast nationwide, made Gorbachev nervous as he delivered his campaign speech; once it was over we were able to relax at a farewell supper. We then boarded the plane, looking forward to some rest and pleasant company. I sat with the security officers and the doctor in one of the cabins, drinking tea. Neither before or after did I ever feel the slightest urge to sit with Gorbachev and Raisa and have supper with them. I cannot say that either of them was lacking in hospitality: Raisa always tried to treat guests well, yet it was difficult to feel relaxed in her company. I often heard similar reports from others, who also found relations between the Gorbachevs and their guests to be strained and artificial, as if the couple were shielded behind an invisible veil of animosity and alienation.

Suddenly the Gorbachevs summoned me into their cabin, invited me to take a seat, and offered me a cup of tea. The ensuing conversation left a permanently nasty impression in my memory, though I managed to hide my emotions at the time. They told me that, as I had lived up to their expectations, they had decided to keep me on as their assistant. They asked a few questions about myself, expressed a few preferences, and offered some advice. I was only vaguely aware of what they were saying, however, as my rage boiled within me. As soon as the opportunity presented itself, I got up and left.

"What was all that about?" I wondered. I had thought all along that we were all working together for a common cause, but it turned out that they had merely, as it were, renewed my lease. When I had gone to work for Gorbachev, advancement through the ranks was not what motivated me, as I knew that a poor performance would cost me my job, while a good one would cost me my freedom. All I wanted was to help this vigorous man improve the state of the country, strengthen its economy, and raise the living standards of the people. The land of my ancestors, family, friends, and acquaintances had always been a source of great pride for me. I was proud that in that great country I had many friends, not only in Moscow but also in the republics—Georgians, Armenians, Uzbeks, Tajiks, Ukrainians, Belorussians, Moldovans, and Kazakhs. I sincerely loved and respected the ethnic groups that had stood shoulder to shoulder, during the harsh war years, with Russians, Belorussians, and Ukrainians, defending our great Fatherland from fascism at the cost of immense losses. The Uzbeks, Kazakhs, and others who, during the war, had shared their bread, offered shelter to women and children from many western regions of the country, and given orphans a home and an upbringing had all earned my undying friendship. Having been an evacuee myself, I know that nothing could ever erase the memory of the valiant selflessness of the brotherhood of all the peoples of the Soviet Union.

Well aware of the arduous nature of the task I had set myself, I had gone to work for one of the leaders of the party in order to make sure that the country's moral prowess would henceforth be matched by economic might. Both my character and my convictions prevented me, however, from becoming anyone's personal property; nor could I accept having my fate decided in a family setting. It was a grave mistake to construe my diligence at work as submissiveness. This attempt to impose on me a three-year period of probation, followed by the magnanimous announcement to the effect that I would be allowed to continue working sixteen hours a day, seemed utterly ludicrous. I seriously began to consider whether I could work with a man who had so badly misread my cooperation with him and who viewed his subordinates as servants. In an effort to account for such behavior, I was increasingly inclined to the view that Gorbachev's rapid rise from a modest rural background to the very pinnacle of power had outstripped his command of the social graces and his culture. His lordly manner and contempt for his subordinates had already become evident to me in the past. What I had heard from inhabitants of the Stavropol region who had studied the man carefully now seemed fully justified.

Yet our common cause, which I then understood to be the strengthening of our Fatherland, compelled me to transcend personal affronts and to dismiss much of his behavior as a mere awkwardness in the expression of his wishes. Yet the scars remained in my heart.

Chernenko died on 10 March 1985, at 7:20 P.M., at the age of seventy-four. Having already been notified of the impending crisis by Yevgeny Chazov, the Minister of Health, Gorbachev knew what was to happen in the near future. As soon as news of the general secretary's death spread, the members and candidate members of the Politburo, and the Central Committee secretaries, assembled at the Kremlin. In a walnut-paneled room just before the conference room used only by members of the Politburo, Gorbachev briefed everybody on Chernenko's illness and the causes of his death. Many of those present then learned for the first time of the severity and range of the ailments that had afflicted the general secretary. Forthcoming arrangements were discussed, but without much concrete detail. Gorbachev then suggested that the gathering should move into the Politburo conference room, where other senior party and government officials had assembled.

That evening Gorbachev again became aware of latent but powerful opposition to his advancement. With the outcome still unclear, he hastened to convene a plenum of the Central Committee. It was agreed that the plenum would be held the next day. Though many issues remained unresolved, the Politburo meeting then adjourned. The fate of the new leader was now in the hands of those closest to the party's channels of communication and organizational structures, those who were able to contact members of the Central Committee and who controlled the Central Committee apparatus. That night a telegram was sent to all republics, *krais*, and *oblasts* throughout the country announcing a plenum the next day at 5:00 P.M. Other documents, including proposals to honor his memory, were prepared in connection with the death of the general secretary. The staff of the Central Committee apparatus set about their work, which was to have a crucial impact on the outcome of the extraordinary plenum of the Central Committee.

The next morning Gorbachev called me: "There's going to be a Central Committee plenum at five this afternoon; we're going to need a brief but substantial speech. Get to work on it, and call Yakovlev."

As soon as Yakovlev and I sat down to draft the speech, we agreed that it should not cover the great merits and achievements of the deceased general secretary, but should look ahead, outlining certain new courses of action. In its final form it did just that.

On that memorable evening when word came about Chernenko's death, the higher echelons of the party promptly found themselves embroiled in high-stakes political maneuvering, compromises, and game playing. It is doubtful that the appointment of any other general secretary was ever scrutinized or debated so thoroughly or enjoyed such powerful organizational backing. Few people could have realized, at the time, that all that preparation was the prelude to the onset of a new era in the life of the Soviet Union—an era of exploding myths, collapsing statehood, and disintegration of the army, an era of discord among the national groups of a once great country.

2

THE MAKING OF
A GENERAL SECRETARY

Once again Red Square was filled with vast throngs of people, though this time nobody seemed anxious to appear mournful. The stands were again filled with dignitaries from the various republics, *krais*, and *oblasts*, as well as foreign diplomats. Once again Margaret Thatcher, unaccustomed to the Russian cold, tapped her fashionably clad feet together in an attempt to keep warm. With the same purpose in mind, a small group of guests inside the mausoleum sipped from glasses of hot toddy.

Funerals had by now become something of a tradition, and the teams assigned to perform the various rituals knew exactly what to do. This funeral gathering was different, however, in just one respect: the still unfamiliar figure who walked up to the podium on the mausoleum, Mikhail Sergeyevich Gorbachev, was to be the youngest general secretary in many decades. The brief valedictory speech he carried in his pocket was no eulogy; nor did it deal only with the sorrow felt by people around the world, and by the world Communist movement, at the untimely passing of a leader. But it did set forth a vision of the future, pointing to ways out of the country's crisis. I had pressed hard for the inclusion of these ideas, so that the need for reform and improvements could be emphasized from the outset. Perceptive listeners realized that some serious work lay ahead, with a view to bolstering the economy and raising living standards.

After the memorial rally was over, I left Red Square and went to the Central Committee building. At last, after a veritable avalanche of events over the previous three days, I had a few moments in which to mull over what had happened. Ludicrous though it may seem, the first member of the Politburo to mention the possibility that Gorbachev might be elected general secretary was Viktor Grishin, who raised the idea late in the evening of 10 March in the Walnut Room. Could he have been resorting to an artful ploy of his own, on the assumption that some member of the Politburo would duly reject Gorbachev's candidature and nominate someone else?

Gorbachev later recalled his reaction to Grishin's remarks: "At the time, I said there was no need to hurry. Let's think about this carefully overnight, and take account of all the facts. Let's make a decision tomorrow."

It was a flexible reply, and in a sense the only thing he could have said. Grishin's proposal got no support; in fact, even the question of the chairmanship of the funeral commission was left pending, and nobody was in any hurry to appoint Gorbachev. Sensing the uncertainty in the air and mindful of the need for thorough groundwork before his next move, Gorbachev suspended the discussion. The final decision was to be made at the Politburo meeting the next day. In the meantime there was a frenzy of backstage intrigue. Everything depended on the opinion of Andrei Gromyko, chairman of the presidium, and the republican, *kraikom*, and *obkom* first secretaries. The astute Vladimir Shcherbitsky (Central Committee member) had chosen not to fly back from the United States for Chernenko's funeral, thus arguably helping Gorbachev's cause. Given his popularity and reputation for seriousness, Gromyko's voice would clearly be crucial, though his age doubtless excluded him as a contender. On the other hand, he could not stay on much longer as foreign minister. Perhaps he could be offered the post of chairman of the presidium of the Supreme Soviet of the USSR, where his international experience could stand him in good stead? Gorbachev had no intention of taking that second-ranking post, so he would need someone with international experience and good contacts with foreign leaders, especially as he, a young agrarian specialist, had yet to develop a grasp of international affairs. Once Gromyko had been informed of this proposal, matters took a new and more hopeful turn. In addition to Ligachev and Nikolai Ryzhkov, the elder statesman of Soviet foreign policy now began to intervene in Gorbachev's behalf.

The majority of the secretaries of the party Central Committee, *kraikoms*, and *obkoms* tended to side with Gorbachev, though there was a kind of trade-off at work, with some of them wanting to stay in their jobs and others to move to Moscow. Pledges flowed freely, as the need arose. But there were also some doubters, who were aware of the attitudes of Tikhonov and several other Politburo members opposed to the election of Gorbachev.

Both the morning and the afternoon of 11 March 1985 were extremely busy. The Central Committee was preparing for the plenum; Ligachev and Ryzhkov were busy greeting members of the Central Committee, the secretaries of the party *kraikoms*, and *obkoms*, and the directors of industrial and agricultural enterprises. The imminent election of Gorbachev to the post of general secretary was now being discussed openly. The views of the participants of the plenum had to be ascertained no later than 3:00, when the Politburo meeting was scheduled to begin in the Kremlin, and support for the young candidate had to be assured. The Politburo had only one item on its agenda: the election of the general secretary of the Soviet Communist party. Although everything had been arranged behind the scenes, last-minute surprises had to be avoided. When the meeting began, Gromyko, the oldest member of the Politburo and the most authoritative figure in the party and the nation, asked for the floor. Gorbachev knew he could count on him, as he had agreed to give his support after private consultations. As good as his word, Gromyko nominated Gorbachev as the party's new leader and asked to be allowed to speak first at the Central Committee plenum. As he enjoyed practically universal support, his words marked a watershed in the mood of Politburo members. Having made their decision, the Politburo members got ready to move into the plenum.

Just then the members of the Central Committee, many of whom had arrived long before the start of the meeting, were filing into the plenum conference room. They were milling around in the elegant marble lobby, forming occasional clusters or rushing to the buffet tables. All of them anxiously inquired about the course of events in the Politburo. The day before, many *obkom* secretaries had met with their counterparts in the Central Committee. The prevailing view among the members of the Central Committee was that aged leaders, incapable of working and likely to die before long, should no longer be elected; if they were, members of the party organizations would want to know why. What the country needed was tough, resolute leadership.

Many people were mentioning Gorbachev's name, though there were doubters like the hard-nosed *obkom* secretaries who, while acknowledging his abilities, nonetheless felt that the man from Stavropol lacked the required experience, had only a superficial knowledge of the economy, and knew nothing about production and the industrial work force.

The plenum hall gradually filled up; bells rang to announce the start of the meeting. The Central Committee members took their seats, while I sat close to the door in case I needed to leave suddenly. A hush descended on the hall, as a door on the left of the stage opened; Gorbachev emerged, eyes downcast, followed by other members of the leadership in order of seniority in the Politburo, party, and state. Gorbachev walked to the center of the presidium table, stood there silently for a few minutes, and then said that the Politburo had asked him to declare open the extraordinary plenum of the Central Committee.

Reading from his text, he said: "We have all heard the sad news." It seemed to me that this phrase had already become somewhat hackneyed: the party had been hearing plenty of "sad news" of that same sort in recent years, as if it consisted entirely of people who believed in the immortality of sick, aged leaders.

"Yesterday at 7:20 P.M. the general secretary of the Central Committee of our party, the chairman of the presidium of the Supreme Soviet of the USSR, our friend and comrade Konstantin Ustinovich Chernenko, breathed his last," he went on, in a blurred voice. His face bore the imprint of the grief and profound pain caused by an irreparable loss. He described Chernenko's career and his valuable contributions to the building of socialism.

"The loss of a comrade, friend, and leader," Gorbachev continued, "compels us to close ranks ever more tightly, and to continue with ever greater energy our common task, in pursuance of the noble purposes of the Communist party, the well-being and happiness of the Soviet people and stable peace on earth."

The members then stood to observe a minute's silence in Chernenko's honor.

"There is one question on the agenda of this plenum," said Gorbachev, now speaking in a louder voice; "it is the election of the general secretary of the Soviet Communist party. I call on Mr. Gromyko to speak on behalf of the Politburo."

The hall became strangely quiet, the only audible sound being the members' breathing. They were perplexed: Why had the foreign minister been given the floor? Did this mean there had been a power shift, and that Gromyko now aspired to be general secretary? Andrei Andreyevich Gromyko strode to the podium and, head on high, gazing straight at his listeners, said in a rasping voice: "It has befallen me to propose to the Central Committee plenum a nomination for the post of general secretary of the Soviet Communist party. The Politburo has unanimously agreed to recommend that Mikhail Sergeyevich Gorbachev be elected general secretary of the Central Committee."

Even before the last words were out of his mouth, applause broke out in the hall, effectively relieving the tension many had felt over the previous twenty-four hours. All eyes turned to the presidium, and Gorbachev, who sat for a while with head bowed, looked up and tried to halt the applause. His gesture, however, had the opposite effect.

When calm was restored, Gromyko began to talk about the substantive discussion of the matter in the Politburo and described the atmosphere that had prevailed there. It was, for him, a most unusual speech, full of figures of speech, surprising adjectives, unorthodox arguments, and convoluted logic. He stated that Gorbachev was a worthy candidate for the post, with immense experience of party work and the priceless attributes of a leader: principles, convictions, the forthright manner of a Lenin, and considerable analytical ability. Gromyko listed a number of other merits and accomplishments, both current and previous. Everyone listened with rapt attention, as if he had been listing the twelve labors of Hercules, although in the minds of most of those present he had performed only one such labor—the ninth.*

Other members of the Politburo and the Central Committee also endorsed the nomination, pointing out that Gorbachev could be counted on to assure the continuity of party policy and to work for the Leninist cause. At the climax of the meeting, Gorbachev was unanimously elected. After the applause had died down, the new general secretary addressed the meeting. He pledged to follow unswervingly the strategies adopted by the Twenty-sixth Party Congress in October 1980. This meant that he undertook to accelerate socioeconomic development; to make far-reaching changes throughout society, including the material and technological foundations of social relations, on the basis of a planned economy; to develop democracy and enhance the role of the councils of government known as *soviets*; to remain faithful to a policy of preserving the peace, cooperating with Communist and workers' parties,

---

*The ninth labor of Hercules was to obtain the girdle of the queen of the Amazons.

and actively promoting all revolutionary forces. He thanked everyone for their trust in him and swore to be a loyal servant of the party, the people, and the great Leninist cause.

With that speech Gorbachev brought to a close both that landmark plenum of the Central Committee and the mourning phase of developed socialism. Having risen to the pinnacle of party and state power, he could now say what was on his mind and reshape the country according to his understanding of its problems.

The participants in the meeting then dispersed, though all of them thought it their duty to seek out the new general secretary and offer him their personal congratulations. Gorbachev basked in the warm glow of triumph and adulation. When I looked into the reception area of his office, I could hear the secretaries of *obkoms* and *kraikoms* emphatically endorsing the new appointment, talking of new plans and new ventures, and calling for the expulsion of hangers-on from Brezhnev's time. Each of them was evidently anxious to shake the new leader's hand one more time, to assure him of their support, and to ask for his advice.

Sensing that my services were not in demand, I soon went back home. I now saw all that had happened in a new light. It was as if I had been taking part in some incredible, hypocritical farce, in which all the players acted out roles they had studiously rehearsed: even those who privately hated the young upstart from Stavropol and were deeply upset by his ascendancy nonetheless lavished praise on him, while laughing along with all the others. The assumption of the post of general secretary by a new young leader was, of course, a cause for optimism. At the very least it would put an end to the joke that had been making the rounds in Moscow, to the effect that each member of the Politburo was determined to die as general secretary. The main issue was Gorbachev's ability to fulfill his responsibilities. Though aware of his many positive attributes, I also knew he was lacking in some important areas. His blurred articulation and provincial accent (a mixture of Ukrainian and Russian) could certainly be rectified; but if it were not, no harm would be done. People quickly get used to the speech habits of their rulers, and even unconsciously adopt them. Virtually the entire nation and even radio and TV announcers had imitated Khrushchev's palatal pronunciation of the *z* in *kommunizm*. So there was no reason why people should not adopt Gorbachev's innovations, too—pronouncing Azerbaijan as *Azerbarzhan*, and putting tonic stresses in the most peculiar places. There was nothing particularly disastrous in all this; after all, not all high officials were well educated, especially when one considers that most of them came from the first generation to get any kind of real education. A more serious matter was whether Gorbachev had the right character traits and whether he was sufficiently tough and resolute. There were doubts about him even then, though I tended to dismiss them. Nonetheless, I was still not sure; I began to wonder whether the events of 11 March 1985 had not been a historical and political conjuring trick.

At the time, if anyone had told me that the man taking over as general secretary had less strength of character than all his predecessors and that he would steer the ship of state on a tortuous and stormy course, I would have refused to believe it.

On Staraya Ploshchad the first person I met was Yakovlev. We went up to his office, ordered some tea, and sat there for a long time in silence.

"Now comes the hard part," he said finally. "It's going to be a real grind; I don't envy you."

"What can I do? I got into this job myself because I could see we were heading downhill," I replied. "I'll do anything I can to improve the economy. The trouble is, I don't know what I will be allowed to do and what I can decide myself. There's a long hard road ahead, but I'll just do my level best."

Yakovlev thought aloud: "What we need now is some really good ideas. And a firm policy—without that, we're in real trouble. The old way of doing things is going to get us nowhere."

Thus ended the mourning phase of developed socialism. The country now entered uncharted waters. Everyone talked about better days to come, but wasn't the road to hell paved with good intentions?

GETTING DOWN TO WORK

Gorbachev wasted no time moving into the office of the general secretary, known as No. 6, located on the fifth floor of the main Central Committee building. His new premises had long attracted him, just as throne, orb, and scepter once attracted the great rulers of the Russian Empire. Practically overnight the domestic staff had everything in order, replacing the carpet runners, polishing the floors, and sprucing up the walnut paneling. A little more work needed to be done in the lounge, but Gorbachev was not deterred and began receiving visitors in his new quarters.

It was a big office. Size, in fact, was one of the distinguishing features of all the offices on the fifth floor of the Central Committee building: they were all big and all located along one side of the corridor. To the right of the entrance there were wide windows looking out onto the passage leading to the end of the building occupied by the party's Moscow City *gorkom*. The windows had cambric french shutters that were always closed. Near the door opposite the entrance, closer to the windows, there was a massive writing table with a large top and a leather swivel armchair—the general secretary's chair. A portrait of Lenin hung over the table. In keeping with Central Committee custom at the time, only high-ranking party officials could actually sit beneath a portrait of Lenin; in other offices lower down the chain of command the portrait was hung slightly to one side.

To the left of the armchair was a communications panel, consisting of a huge walnut case crammed with electronic gear and wiring. Its upper section contained the apparatus for intercity secret and top-secret communications, the keys of a special telephone that was used to keep in touch with the leadership. It was connected to all the offices of members and candidate members of the Politburo, Central Committee secretaries, vice chairmen of the Council of Ministers, senior members of the Supreme Soviet of the Union, as well as a number of ministers in important sectors for which the general secretary was responsible. These included the KGB; defense, foreign, and domestic affairs; the chiefs of staff; the Military Industrial Commission; the editor of *Pravda*; and Gorbachev's advisers and assistants. Members of the Politburo, assistants, and a number of other individuals had two-way communications. All of them could at any time contact the general secretary, who almost always answered.

Gorbachev clearly enjoyed his new accommodation and the communications panel, which enabled him to call any foreign leader—indeed, to make calls not only throughout the Soviet Union but anywhere in the world. Later he would hold frequent conversations with the presidents of France and the United States and the leaders of the Socialist countries, to wish them happy birthday or to send greetings on some national holiday.

Not everything in the office was to his liking, however. He felt somewhat caged in; I attended meetings at which the need to enlarge the general secretary's accommodation was discussed. He suggested converting the entire fifth floor into his own personal apartments, with his own TV studio. The head of the party's Department of Administrative Affairs, Nikolai Kruchina, often dropped in to talk to me, looking extremely worried. He could not figure out where to put the conference room of the Central Committee Secretariat or how to supply a replacement for Ligachev's fifth-floor office. It was soon decided, however, that a cinema in an adjacent building would be converted into a Secretariat conference room, and Ligachev would be moved to the third floor into an office built especially for him. Plans for the reconstruction were completed by the time Gorbachev was elected chairman of the presidium of the Supreme Soviet of the Union and then president of the USSR. He then spent most of his time in the Kremlin. However, that move was still years away; in the spring of 1985 everyone looked forward to positive changes and was prepared for hard work.

After completing the necessary formalities related to his election as general secretary and disposing of several urgent matters, Gorbachev considered what his next political move should be, in order to bring about change and demonstrate his seriousness of purpose. Before his election there had been much discussion of the impending changes, but, when they inevitably collided head-on with stark reality, they turned out to be so much wishful thinking. Gorbachev's associates naturally knew more or less what needed to be done, but none of them had any idea of how or where to start. The mere accession of a new leader did not necessarily mean that his reforms made any sense or that he had worked out a thorough system for the implementation of changes in all spheres of society. The fact that he, as general secretary, was destined to operate by means of trial and error while bearing responsibility for the fate of the entire country distressed Gorbachev. Behind-the-scenes maneuvering and palace intrigue were now of little use. People expected real change. And the conditions for it were unusually favorable.

Shortly after being elected general secretary, Gorbachev called in a number of Central Committee secretaries, assistants, and other trusted associates to discuss action to be taken by the new leadership. As I recall, the discussion focused on three points. First, the need to accelerate the appointment of new people, replacing those senior officials who, having been closely associated with previous general secretaries, were incapable of supervising areas in which urgent improvements were needed. All kinds of personnel changes were thus justified. Second, Gorbachev's policy was to continue the acceleration of scientific and technological progress, with special emphasis on machine building, as the basis for all changes in production. Having been convinced for some time that all our woes derived from the poor performance of the machine-building sector, he vigorously set about modernizing industrial plants, introducing double and triple shiftwork for machine tools and using rotor complexes. Third, attention turned to the question of travel by the general secretary throughout the country and visits to industrial and agricultural enterprises. Problems related to agriculture and construction naturally arose during the discussion, but were deferred for further study and proposals.

Gorbachev decided that his first visit should be to an industrial enterprise in the capital. He asked me to make the necessary arrangements, but to keep it entirely confidential. The general secretary wanted to go to the Likhachev car factory, a local hospital, a school and a store. I prepared his itinerary, but it was not a surprise visit, as he had disclosed his intentions to Grishin, who was at the time secretary of the Moscow party *gorkom*. Everything, of course, was ready for the general secretary's visit. While it may be difficult to make substantial changes in factories in a matter of days, hospitals were another matter: the one Gorbachev visited had changed so radically that I barely recognized it. The sidewalks, paths, and drive to the main entrance got a fresh coat of asphalt, from which steam and the smell of hot tar were still rising. On the floor we inspected, patients were not allowed out into the corridors, in case something they said might grate on the ears of the distinguished guests. As I later found out from members of Gorbachev's security detail, in the two or three wards Gorbachev was supposed to enter, the beds were occupied by healthy, well-fed security officers with closely cropped hair, who warmly commended the medical staff and the hospital food, while finding it difficult to be precise about their ailments. The doctors, sensing their confusion, seemed very nervous about the possible outcome of the visit.

We got the same "Potemkin village" treatment in a few other places, too. For example, we were invited, supposedly at random, into the new apartment of an "ordinary worker," who happened to have on hand some excellent hors d'oeuvres, candies, preserves, and other delicacies. On closer inspection it became evident that these goodies had been obtained from the specialized suppliers of foodstuffs to the security men. That being so, one could not rule out the possibility that even the carpets on the walls and other furnishings had also been borrowed for the occasion. Gorbachev talked cordially with the worker, inquiring about his occupational and family affairs, shook his hand warmly, and wished him the best at home and at work.

The interesting thing about the visit was not the petty tricks used to impress us, but the fact that Gorbachev, doubtless aware of the large-scale fraud being perpetrated, nonetheless played along, allowing the correspondents to take pictures of it. Not long afterwards, flying back from one of Gorbachev's trips around the country, I mentioned the incident; with Gorbachev listening, I told Raisa about the ill-conceived visit in Moscow, assuming that the truth about what happened would have a sobering effect. I personally felt that one should have nothing to do with deceitful practices of this sort and that anyone who tried to fool the general secretary should be held strictly accountable. Raisa's reaction, however, came as a complete surprise: "Well, what did you expect? When you invite people to your house, don't you tidy up and lay on the best spread you can manage?"

It was hard to rebut her argument. If I expected guests I certainly did tidy up. But my guests were not members of a high-level delegation; and an apartment is not the same as a hospital or some other state-run concern. It had been a political visit, not a casual get-together of old chums. I felt like pointing out that the general secretary was not a guest, but rather the master or leader of the country; but I said nothing for fear of being misunderstood. It was now evident, at least, that such performances were acceptable and could be expected to occur repeatedly. Yet I hardly thought that the whole of our life would soon turn into a stage for a single actor.

While preparing for the trip to the Moscow car factory, I made it clear that if the new leader of both party and country wanted to learn about the working and living conditions of the workers, then he ought to make his way to the factory just as they do—by bus, subway, or tram—so as to see from the outset how hard things were for ordinary people. I proposed that he travel by bus from the factory to the local hospital, and from there to the new housing development where many of the factory workers lived; after all, the leader of the workers' party had no reason to fear unscheduled encounters with the workers. But Gorbachev, no doubt viewing my proposals as eccentric nonsense, rejected them all. I realized that he would find it quieter in an armor-plated limousine, but what can you see from behind bullet-proof windows? During that trip the general secretary did manage to see whatever he was shown, and the local bosses were able to show him whatever they pleased. Their purpose was clearly to prove that Moscow was a model city whose elders worried day and night about how best to ensure the well-being of the capital and its inhabitants. Everything is relative, of course, and what had once been intolerable would now have been received with widespread gratitude. In any case it is doubtful that the general secretary was actually trying to learn anything new on his trip: media coverage of him visiting with workers in the capital was all that was needed.

A number of other urgent economic and political measures, later implemented in some form or other, were proposed. Given their extemporaneous nature, however, they did not address the full magnitude of the reforms society was demanding. People wanted change. Countless families yearned for a higher standard of living, with better housing and greater freedom. In those days nobody could predict the effect that the experiment begun in the spring of 1985 would eventually have on the Soviet Union and its many national groups. At the time, however, most of the proponents and supporters of perestroika were sincere in their desire for rapid improvements.

Once he acceded to his new post, Gorbachev started work in earnest. One of the first assignments he gave to Ryzhkov, and about which he also consulted me, was to draw up a list of priority issues on which the public was expecting action. Ryzhkov was a congenial, no-nonsense democrat, with whom I had excellent working relations. We quickly identified the most pressing issues, proposing nothing particularly new, especially by today's standards. Our main emphasis was on a matter that had been uppermost in my mind at *Pravda:* the need to give people land, to ensure that all city dwellers had a plot of land. With my agrarian background and my contacts with the Moscow city bosses, I had succeeded in getting a plot set aside as a fruit and vegetable cooperative to be run by the editorial staff. It took some doing, but the land was apportioned from the holdings of the Fiftieth Anniversary of October state farm. The cooperative is still going strong today, and many members of the *Pravda* staff spend time there, for their own and their family's benefit.

I also advocated using the paper itself as a vehicle for providing all those interested with plots of land; I also proposed that the staff at various enterprises be allowed to take over vacant plots and decaying rural communities. Things moved ahead until Andropov came to power; the entire process was then reversed as people were taken to court on charges of wasting land and breaking laws governing the construction of dachas. Eventually the distribution of land was completely halted. Ryzhkov and I now sought to resurrect this sensible idea. We also proposed ways of improving housing, medical assistance, and the like. These ideas later began to be couched in the form of concrete decisions. Much of what we proposed was actually carried out, particularly with regard to the distribution of land. In addition to measures intended to meet the current and urgent needs of the public, the Politburo and government drew up and adopted a number of decisions designed to accelerate socioeconomic development. These applied to areas such as the intensification of production, enhanced efficiency, improved technology for the top-priority sectors of machine building and power, the reconstruction of the iron and steel industry, better planning, capital investment, and the introduction of high technology and computers. Work also began on the better management of closely related sectors and the more efficient use of labor, in response to a Politburo decision.

A careful analysis of the titles and substance of the decisions adopted about that time reveals that they contained little that was new. They were essentially stopgap measures, designed to plug holes in a sinking ship. Each successive trip Gorbachev made around the country inevitably led to the adoption of an increasing number of decisions on the economic development of the regions he had visited. Resources were thereby dissipated and the efficiency of investments reduced.

Although the word *perestroika* was already being bandied about in various parts of the country, there was still no overall concept of the kind of changes that society needed. The first few impulsive measures of economic reform quickly foundered on obstacles and restrictions. Priorities for economic development had been chosen in a haphazard manner. Gorbachev had been told repeatedly that unless there was a unified concept of development and unless general issues were addressed first, it would be impossible to move ahead on specific details. Now that the proper conditions—both subjective and objective—existed, there was a pressing need for a serious theoretical basis for change, as well as logical and consistent action to back it up.

Over the previous few years dissatisfaction had been steadily building in society, to the point where it could explode at any minute. This was widely understood, particularly among the country's intellectual elite, traditionally the source and conduit for progressive ideas: scientists, experts from various economic sectors, managers, several top military commanders, and the intelligentsia as a whole. By the mid-1980s the members of that elite had generated plenty of suggestions for the democratization of the USSR and the improvement of social relations, and had done the groundwork for faster scientific and technological progress.

A large store of reform ideas that had accumulated over the years, however, had never been brought out into the open. Since people no longer feared for their lives after the Khrushchev thaw, many of our sociologists felt free to make proposals for social reform. The Central Committee and the government then received a vast amount of mail containing proposals for change. Together with the younger intellectuals, these were the sources of many of the economic reforms attempted by Kosygin in the mid-1960s. Indeed, their ideas, to a considerable extent, formed the basis of the transformations that began in the 1980s.

I frequently had occasion to meet with prominent scientists and scholars from many fields, as well as educators, cultural figures, and writers. These were highly progressive people who knew what was wrong with our system and our method of government. Economics and politics were not the only subjects being frankly discussed in those days: it was perfectly obvious that rigid, backward leadership was stifling many promising ideas. The sheer age of those in control of the party and state structure prevented them from looking ahead or giving any thought to the prospects for the development of their country.

Since the Twenty-sixth Party Congress, it had become obvious that most members of the Politburo stood little chance of surviving till the next Congress. Our history had entered its mourning phase. All of this was well understood by those intellectuals who had long been alarmed by the balance of forces in the leadership and were familiar with the capabilities of each Politburo member.

For this reason Gorbachev's emergence on the political scene attracted the attention of certain intellectual circles. Initially, of course, he was viewed with disfavor, as it was generally felt that agrarian experts like him had failed to remedy the nation's food problems. Certain promising traits of his were gradually discerned, however: he belonged to a relatively new generation, was well educated, and could, when he liked, be charming; he had something of a gift for uniting the reform-minded people who had long been looking for an energetic leader. They backed Gorbachev and helped him gain popularity and move through the labyrinths of power, although they did not all support him from the beginning or without hesitation.

The thinking of progressive intellectuals was greatly stimulated by the advent of a new general secretary. Scientists, scholars, experts, and managers laid their proposals before Mikhail Sergeyevich Gorbachev, driven by the general pent-up desire for change. For months on end they sat in closed government and party dachas, refining new ideas for economic reform, the democratization of society, the improvement of the political system, and international relations.

Ryzhkov's team worked hard on a set of proposals for the restructuring of economic relations. There was a surfeit of constructive ideas, some of which Gorbachev took with him when he went to the podium. But an integrated conceptual framework was still lacking. Gorbachev, feeling that logic could only hinder perestroika, did his best to prevent such a framework from emerging. Many people, including speakers at the congress and the party conference, wanted to know where we were headed; but their requests fell on deaf ears. It has since become evident, as we shall see, that he had another, genuine reason for opposing it.

Gorbachev enjoyed wide support until 1988, when he began to lose confidence and to shift his ground constantly. The flow of fresh ideas then started to dry up, as many members of the academic and scientific communities turned away from him. He made frequent changes in the ranks of the assistants and consultants whose job it was to prepare his reports, speeches, and interviews, while compelled to rely increasingly on exhortation to get things done.

The theoretical side of perestroika and the selection of personnel were greatly influenced by Yakovlev, whose outstanding experience in similar matters dated back to the days of Khrushchev and Brezhnev. I understood that while serving as ambassador in Canada, he had worked out a whole program of changes applicable to key sectors in the Soviet Union. As head of the Gorbachev brain trust, Yakovlev brought in many experts; then, on the basis of a synthesis of their findings, he designed both a conceptual system for the restructuring of society and a set of practical measures for real change. Besides being constantly in charge of the teams of speechwriters, he also generated the basic language of the general secretary's reports and speeches. The Gorbachev brain trust also included some eminent economists and sociologists, such as V. A. Medvedev, Leonid Abalkin, Abel Aganbegyan, S. A. Anchishkin, S. A. Sitaryan, N. B. Bikkenin, Stanislav Shatalin, N. Y. Petrakov, and V. P. Mozhin. Numerous experts were called in from research institutes on economics and international affairs, the Soviet Foreign Ministry, the Central Committee, the Council of Ministers, and other ministries and departments. This was the team that spawned the basic ideas of perestroika, drawing on the valuable contributions of many intellectuals. In the final stages of work on his reports and speeches, Gorbachev and a few hand-picked assistants would become involved themselves, withdrawing either to his office or the state dachas at Novo-Ogaryovo or Volynskoye.

The large and highly motivated team of well-qualified experts could certainly have drafted a coherent theoretical framework for change, but was never asked to do so. My attempts to produce such a framework met with blank incomprehension. The only result of the team's efforts was an analysis of the situation in the party and the country in the mid-1980s. Meanwhile time was slipping by. Much of the work tended to be intuitive and haphazard, with little regard for the consequences. People carried out the general secretary's instructions in the naive belief that he knew what was most urgently necessary.

One global problem that Gorbachev tackled head-on as soon as he took office was the need to accelerate progress through the development of high technology. He had heard a great deal about earlier preparations for a plenum on science and technology, and he decided to take up the matter again, on the basis of strong personal conviction. He believed that since all the woes of the Soviet Union were due to the inadequate development of machine building, this one link could be used to set the whole economic chain in motion. An important Central Committee meeting on the matter was scheduled for June 1985, requiring the preparation of a report. So a team of experts, industrialists and ideologues left for the Volynskoye-2 dacha, where they toiled for two months.

The meeting took place in the plenum room of the Central Committee, a fairly recent structure adjoining the existing building of the Supreme Soviet of the USSR. Though inconvenient, it was considered to be an architectural masterpiece harmoniously blending with the rest of the Kremlin, and earned a Lenin Prize for those involved in its design and construction. Floors and walls were of Italian marble; the cornices were adorned with marble sculptures of workers, peasants, and soldiers. The decor and furnishings were imported from all over the world. Like the tables, the chairs were made of Karelian birch; they were comfortable and equipped with amplifiers. In fact, they were so comfortable that one often heard the sounds of snoring from those in them, especially while routine reports were being read out.

This was where academics, industrial bosses, ministers, and Central Committee members all gathered for the meeting. Gorbachev delivered his report, which had been thoroughly prepared for him, to an attentive audience. Then, with the television cameras rolling, a lively debate took place. It was a sensation. All over the Soviet Union viewers could see a frank debate, much of it unscripted, about problems of great concern to all. The new general secretary made a good impression; he was certainly unlike his predecessors, who stood stiffly at the podium, their eyes riveted to the text from which they were reading, though in this latter regard Gorbachev was still somewhat hesitant.

Party members and the general public felt increasingly confident in this businesslike new leader and his ability to break away from the shackles of the past. That fact was extremely important at the time, because words later lost much of their value.

I wish to emphasize that Gorbachev's policy statements from 1985 to 1987 were based on a firm understanding that socialism in the USSR was a great triumph of the people and that it should continue to be developed. Socialist principles, which were sacrosanct, would lead to the attainment of the ultimate objective: the building of a Communist society. These assumptions at first underlay all of Gorbachev's thinking, to the exclusion, in my opinion, of all else. This attitude to the heritage of the past certainly accorded with the feelings of the majority. The entire population wanted radical change in economic and foreign policy and a radical democratization of society. They expected a new system of incentives and greater freedom for the party committees and organizations, in addition to the social guarantees to which they had grown accustomed. The party had long supported Gorbachev, especially as he claimed that the accomplishments and values of socialism would be preserved.

It was not long, however, before something quite different began to happen. Actual events during the first year had already shown that quick results were out of the question. Gorbachev had argued that as soon as agriculture was freed of its shackles and all those wishing to do so were allowed to use different types of leasing arrangements, there would be plenty of food for all within a year or two. This one statement alone demonstrated how far removed he was from real life.

When he decided to insert this argument in the report, I objected that it was unrealistic. He was furious: "Don't you know anything about the way peasants think? Just look how fast things moved in China, and we're no worse than them." In his text, though, he did delay the onset of abundance, making it "within two or three years."

This kind of simpleminded view of perestroika's potential led to the adoption of hasty decisions and the use of unorthodox incentives, methods of management, and organization in the economic sphere. Worst of all, personnel at all levels of government, even in Gorbachev's immediate entourage, began to be replaced rapidly. Without carrying out the proposals of one expert group, he would latch on to the ideas of others. The kaleidoscopic whirl of ideas and individuals seemed to express the general secretary's own state of panic. New ways of accelerating economic growth were forever being suggested; yet with each successive change, one was left with the impression that a fundamental shift to capitalist methods of development was in the offing. Those methods, moreover, belonged to the primitive and immature stage of capitalism. Although we still heard talk of "building socialism with a human face" and of the "Communist perspective," these were mere words, a kind of ideological fig leaf masking the naked fact of deviation from policies approved by the plenum meetings and congresses of the party.

Such theoretical waffling was also a consequence of Gorbachev's character. Ever since his early years, from school and institute to the Komsomol (the Communist Youth League) and his work in the party, he had grown accustomed to following a course devised at what we call the center, and had come to expect success, approval, and applause as his due. At the age of sixteen he won a government award, graduating with distinction from high school, where he had been head of the Komsomol organization; he was admitted without examinations to Moscow State University, where he again headed the Komsomol, and eventually graduated with honors. Throughout all those years Gorbachev had known nothing but encouragement, approval, and often enthusiastic praise for his abilities. The same trend continued after his graduation from the university. Instead of taking some tedious job as a procurator, in which one cannot make one's mark without a great deal of hard work, Gorbachev found himself at first working for the Komsomol and eventually in charge of party organs, where he continued his ascent to the summit in a similar manner. Working for the kind of organizations in which he spent much of his career gave him valuable public exposure. At no time, however, was he held responsible for his performance, or punished for failure: he never graduated from the practical or industrial school of life. The fact that he spent virtually his entire career in the party apparatus was not his fault but his misfortune: it made his backbone soft and pliable, rather than firm and persistent. Consequently, when his reforms ran into practical difficulties, he would quickly lose interest and switch to something else. It is perhaps not surprising, therefore, that his sphere of activity was reduced to making speeches to be reported in the press or shown on TV, as well as trips to the West, where, as representative of the Soviet Union, he was welcome and honored.

At the time, however, he had just assumed the burden of responsibility not only for the fate of the party but also for the well-being of millions of people throughout the country who expected their new leader to produce more than rhetoric, of which they had heard plenty over the years. Now they wanted to feel they were following a well-charted course toward a specific destination; they wanted things to get better, or at least not to get worse. I could tell that Gorbachev was finding the situation increasingly oppressive. His abilities and talents were of no avail: when far-reaching experiments were started in 1988, the economic situation promptly deteriorated in real terms. The Politburo, the party, the public, seeing that words were not being followed by deeds, began to lose confidence in him. A profoundly distressed Gorbachev was aware of this, too. He then cast about for miraculous remedies, proposing one new idea after another. About this time he began to receive suggestions that had apparently been endorsed in several other countries. First he proposed to follow the Hungarian model and then those of Sweden and Austria.

There was nothing wrong with this approach. Capitalism had successfully borrowed a great deal from socialism. But it would be difficult for us to use foreign methods of management without making profound changes in the system as a whole. Soviet industrial managers were not happy with such piecemeal imitation, seeing in it a destabilizing influence on the economy.

Sensing that the party and the Central Committee were now suspicious of him, Gorbachev became nervous and depressed. Since change could no longer wait, his former methods were of little use; yet he also shied away from a gradual transition to a market economy. Between

1988 and 1991 hesitation became an essential feature of his policies. He did not dare move either forward or backward, thereby alienating many radical factions while failing to unite the hardline traditionalists behind his policies. Party leaders at all levels, as well as democratically minded segments of the public, feeling that Gorbachev's penchant for vagueness and inconstancy was leading nowhere, lost confidence in him. It was a tragedy for Gorbachev, the party, and the entire nation. He eventually stood alone, despised by his own party, and mocked by the democratic faction of society.

But four years would elapse before this came to pass. At the time, approaches to the structuring of the whole of society were still being formulated. The wind of change was blowing across the Soviet Union. The people acclaimed Gorbachev as their protector and their hope. They yearned for greater freedom, more glasnost, and a chance to speak their minds about the hard questions. The qualms Gorbachev had aroused in party, industrial, and governmental organs were swept away in the general euphoria. Letters addressed to Gorbachev started to pour in from all over the country and from abroad. People started writing poems exalting the new general secretary and likening him to a messiah.

I reviewed those letters before briefing Gorbachev on their content. He was so fond of them that he would sit for hours rereading passages that he liked and quoting excerpts from foreign individuals.

"Listen to this," he would say, before reading out a confidential report from TASS. "The constructive changes in Russia, started by its leader Gorbachev, are eliciting a growing response in the countries of eastern Europe. It is unlikely that their leaders will be able to cope with the mounting wave of change demanded by their peoples."

I cannot tell for sure who first noticed Gorbachev's fondness for reading flattering reports about himself—the Western intelligence agencies or our own ambassadors. But the general secretary's egotism was used to the full. Information praising the new leader poured in from all sides. So every Soviet representative abroad felt duty-bound to send along some clipping from a Western newspaper or magazine extolling the mighty deeds of Mikhail Sergeyevich Gorbachev, and took whatever opportunities he could to tell Gorbachev how popular he was with both leaders and "ordinary people" in the West.

The mail from abroad certainly swelled to many times its normal size. Many people sent Gorbachev keepsakes, family heirlooms, money, and valuables. In many foreign countries medallions and coins of gold, silver, and platinum were minted in his honor. In this way he collected large amounts of valuables in the sincere belief that they had been sent to him as a reward for his achievements. He still believed this even when people began to turn away from him, realizing that he was concerned not with the country or the people but with his own renown.

PERSONAL INFLUENCES

Another day passes, and another night. Then everything repeats itself. I am scarcely aware of my cellmates, having failed to notice for some time that one of them has been taken somewhere else. Seeing the state I am in, the second young man, Dima, an intelligent, pleasant fellow who has been protesting his innocence for two and a half years, does what he can to help and to defend my rights.

"It's no use fighting here, you won't get anywhere," he would say. "That whole business of the presumption of innocence is a lot of baloney. They all know you're a criminal and treat you like a murderer, a rapist, or an enemy of the people. So don't let it upset you. There's no one to defend you. If you want to make it, keep your wits about you; otherwise you're finished."

Even I understand that, though there's no fight left in me. I find more and more that I tend to stay in bed and my thoughts drift back in time.

Having worked with Gorbachev for ten years, I feel entitled to draw certain conclusions about his character, moral standards, abilities, and working methods, all the more so as he himself identified certain influences as having helped form his character and his capacity for leadership. First, the genetic makeup he inherited from two ancestral lines: the Gopkalo family of Chernigov through his mother and the Gorbachevs of Voronezh through his father. He attached much importance to his genetic side. One can only guess at the lives of his more distant ancestors, but his grandfathers' lives were hard, at times tragic. They witnessed the birth of the collective farm movement and ran afoul of the Soviet authorities. All of this undoubtedly affected Mikhail's character. He combined the diffidence, gentleness, and kindness of his father and the toughness and, in many respects, the harshness of his mother. These traits were not, however, evenly distributed, as could be seen from the example of his brother Aleksandr, a nice colonel with big, sparkling eyes and the forthright manner of a child. This latter trait frequently got him into tricky situations, from which he had occasionally to be extricated.

What I liked about Aleksandr was his candor, unpretentiousness, and lack of guile. I remember pointing this out to Gorbachev, who replied that his brother was a good man who had inherited much of his character from their father.

Gorbachev grew up a bright, able, and hard-working member of a peasant family, endowed with a powerful memory and a fair amount of guile. Over the years this latter trait was honed to perfection, though those who knew him well found the devious schemes he had invented to be obvious and predictable, even those of the homemade variety, which he had stored up in vast quantities for use in all circumstances. His most striking attribute was the ability not only to outwit his opponents but to manufacture no-lose situations for himself regardless of the course of events. Newcomers were baffled by his game plan. He knew how to compel his opponents to let him steer the conversation as he wished and to end up espousing his views, thus putting them on the defensive.

As early as their summit meeting in Geneva in November 1985, Reagan's aides spotted this trait and advised him not to allow Gorbachev to dictate the run of play or the agenda, or to stray from the agreed topics during negotiations, or to keep changing the subject. Though Gorbachev's mastery of this technique reached its peak while he was general secretary, its roots undoubtedly went back very far, to the period of his political coming of age in Stavropol.

Even as a child and an adolescent Gorbachev seemed destined for leadership. At school as previously mentioned, he headed the Komsomol Pioneer organization, was always at the forefront of student activities, took part in amateur theatricals, and performed on stage himself. Gorbachev once recalled the day he halted all classes in order to lead the students out to witness the arrival of the water that had started gushing along the canals into the parched, sunbaked steppe. The idea of suspending classes came naturally to him, because in such an arid area water was cause for celebration. His political judgment, even at that early age, was clearly superior to that of his teachers, since it never occurred to them to observe an event that, while obviously of great value to the farm economy, also had political overtones. People were ready to forgive Gorbachev many things because he had an excellent academic record, was engaged in socially useful work, and, in later years, was a good helpmate for his father at the machinery and tractor station, responsible for all mechanized operations on the collective farm.

Like many others in the region, Gorbachev started work in the fields at an early age. The rural work force was greatly reduced, and agriculture seriously impaired, during the difficult wartime years. The war also left a deep imprint on the character of the young Mikhail Sergeyevich Gorbachev; in later years he would reminisce about the time he was whipped by a Kalmyk in the service of the Germans and about how he hid in remote farmhouses to avoid being shot or sent to fascist Germany. He did not, however, witness the kind of atrocities the Germans committed in Belorussia and many of the western regions of Russia. Nonetheless, they left their mark on the character of young Mikhail, who respected strength and authority. After the war he won recognition not only from his contemporaries. At the age of sixteen he received a government award, the Order of the Red Banner of Labor, for the work he had done helping his father on the combine harvester. During the harsh wartime years, while his father was still away in the army, he was reponsible for ensuring that his family did not lack the basic necessities of life. He therefore certainly proved his mettle as a hard worker by managing to survive hunger and devastation.

The rest of his life was the product of those sound inherited traits, toughened by the hardship of wartime. Moscow University merely broadened his knowledge and his capacity to work independently; it can hardly be said to have enriched him greatly from the professional standpoint, especially when one considers that he spent only a few days working in his specialized field. He was at first assigned to the office of the procurator general, and was in fact waiting for an opening there. At the time, however, people in that office who had compromised themselves during Stalin's time, when the rule of law was nonexistent, were being weeded out. Moreover, the process of the rehabilitation of wrongfully convicted persons was also under way. As Gorbachev himself said, vacancies were being offered only to candidates with legal experience. Nonetheless, the fact that he was not offered a job must have hurt him deeply, and he would harp on this point relentlessly. In my opinion it was an insignificant episode. He later said that he had been given to understand that there was some chance he might be offered the post of procurator general, but that he had said that, as a young secretary of a party *kraikom*, he could not accept it. He had in any case forgotten much of his former knowledge of the law, as became evident when the time came to implement measures of democratization and political reform: he frequently found himself at a loss and constantly had to turn for help to Lukyanov.

In the mid-1970s, as Gorbachev himself acknowledged, he refused to head the Central Committee Agitprop Department on the grounds that it was too late in his career for him to consider such a post. Being well connected in the Politburo, Gorbachev had a fairly good idea of his own worth; unlike most party members, he was unwilling to go wherever the party sent him, and waited for something more suitable. He was right.

Moscow University gave Gorbachev something more than a knowledge of the law: it enabled him to try out his strength as a political militant in the youth movement. The chance to lead thousands of students, of course, was attractive; it satisfied the vanity and ambition so common among young people. The university was where he met many able people whose ideas were later to gain wide acceptance. In fact, it was where he met Zdenek Mlynarzh, who used to stay with him in Stavropol. Theirs was a close friendship that Gorbachev always referred to with real pleasure. Mlynarzh referred often to Stalin's death, which shook the Soviet Union as well as the fraternal Socialist countries and much of the rest of the world and, Mlynarzh feared, meant that the Soviet Union was "finished."

Their paths and their views of socialism diverged thereafter. A chill descended on their relationship during the Prague Spring, when they found themselves on opposite sides of the barricades. Gorbachev remained loyal to the Communist choice, while Mlynarzh left Czechoslovakia; but there was no open rift between them.

After Gorbachev had risen to general secretary, Mlynarzh published an article about the new Communist party leader in an Italian newspaper. Gorbachev kept the article. Once he took it out and began to talk about Mlynarzh, hinting that they had been friends; he perused it again, and said there was nothing wrong with it. Soon their friendship revived. Mlynarzh was a fairly frequent visitor, offering Gorbachev advice about how to proceed and warning against the dangers of a hasty dismantling of existing structures. He certainly influenced Gorbachev over the years their acquaintance lasted, though it is hard to say to what extent.

Extracurricular work at Moscow State University gave Gorbachev a chance to expand his social circle and become involved in the activities of the elite segment of the student body; this in turn helped his career by exposing him to the mechanisms by which one could rise to positions of power in the capital city—even if it concerned only the Komsomol.

Gorbachev graduated with high honors from Moscow University Law School and then married Raisa Titorenko. He then had to return to

Stavropol, where obscurity and uncertain living arrangements awaited him, together with the numerous other difficulties that normally beset young graduates. He and Raisa endured hardship, renting a small room, unheated throughout the bitter cold of winter; but they were young, healthy, and determined to improve their lot as soon as possible. Gorbachev returned to his native region as a theoretically well-trained young Communist eager to work hard and rise in the world.

RAISA

It is hard to say how his life would have developed had he not married Raisa. His wife's attitude and character played a decisive role in Gorbachev's fate and, I believe, to a significant extent in that of the party and the entire country.

With her tough, harsh, and domineering character, she knew how to bend others to her will, how to get her way one way or another. She became the First Lady of the Soviet Union quickly, or at least in less time than it took Gorbachev to feel that he had truly established himself as leader of the party and the state. She had no qualms about issuing orders over the phone to the general secretary's aides and to several members of the government, especially those she knew personally. Raisa left no doubt about who was in charge, by assuming the role of leader and organizer of the constellation of wives of top officials. She occupied a senior position in the All-Union Fund for Culture and was, in effect, its leader. On instructions from her, government phones were installed in the offices of many cultural organs and of many radio, television, and press organs. Communications equipment similar to that provided for the general secretary was also installed in her car and those of her KGB escorts.

Raisa soon made contact with the wives of the diplomatic corps by giving a reception for them on 8 March, International Women's Day, 1986. I got a call from Gorbachev around midnight one night while I was still at work. He often phoned at a very late hour to issue instructions on unexpected matters that had occurred to him after his evening walk with Raisa. This time it had to do with this reception. It had been decided that the event would be organized by the Foreign Ministry and the Central Committee's International Department. That decision, however, had been issued by the Central Committee Secretariat, whereas he was asking me to have it converted into a decision of the Politburo so that arrangements would proceed more smoothly. Soon the Politburo decision was issued, whereupon it became more binding than any law.

The reception took place at one of the official government villas in the Lenin Hills. It was attended by the wives of the leaders, of ambassadors, and of a number of senior officials of the party and state, as well as by well-known actresses and women from the arts and academia. Many of the participants came away profoundly impressed by the splendor of this ceremonial event. The women waited in a long line for a chance to shake the hand of the general secretary's wife and to greet her on the occasion of International Women's Day. The First Lady herself looked rather prim, as she scrutinized, with a practiced eye, the clothes and jewelry worn by the guests. The women then proceeded to take their seats at tables laden with every conceivable delicacy, where they patiently listened to the welcoming speech. In those days receptions tended to be quite lavish, with performances by famous artists. The entire operation cost the state coffers a pretty penny, but nobody seemed to care how much was spent. It was customary for women attending receptions to be given gifts of flowers and various kinds of souvenirs.

I know for a fact that many of those attending such functions found them rather tedious, but went anyway to avoid offending the First Lady, who, as they soon realized, had an excellent memory; moreover, the identity of any who chose to show disrespect toward the general secretary's wife by declining to attend could easily be checked by a glance at the lists of those present. The main reason why I also found them tedious was that several months before the reception Raisa would ask me to write her a speech. She had an aide of her own, although he was technically on the general secretary's staff; but for some reason she was not happy with his style. She was a fussy and whimsical person to work for, quick to hand out rebukes for what she deemed to be omissions and to make caustic remarks. With each passing year writing such material became more difficult, as I sought to avoid repeating myself. Anxious to avoid her barbs and humiliating lectures on work that I was not even supposed to be doing, I soon hit on the idea of sending three or four versions of the speech for her to choose from, often drawing on the services of people with fresh views and no idea of what had been said at the previous year's reception. Though her criticism continued even then, she made her speech from the prepared texts anyway. It was only later that I realized that the purpose of the criticism was to show the need for revisions. This is what later happened to G. Pryakhin, one of Gorbachev's consultants, who was commissioned to write a book for Raisa. Both Gorbachev and his wife severely criticized him for being such a poor writer, complaining that the whole thing would have to be revised because of his failings. Yet as far as I recall, the book was published as written by Pryakhin, although the Gorbachev family probably made certain amendments.

By virtue of her education and experience as a university lecturer on Marxist-Leninist philosophy, Raisa's views were those of a dedicated Communist; in fact, she frequently upheld her convictions in private and in public. She taught hundreds of students in the same spirit, instilling in them a sense of loyalty to Marxism-Leninism. As Gorbachev used to say about his family, in which everyone except the very young grandchildren were committed members of the Soviet Communist party, Raisa was the head of "our family party cell." She was not only its head, but also its very soul and standard-bearer. She laid down policy not only in the family cell. When making policy decisions, she strove to ensure that her husband, as a member of the domestic cell, applied the agreed line involved throughout the Soviet Communist party itself. I assure you that this is only a slight exaggeration.

I personally saw how Raisa day after day kept hammering away relentlessly at some idea with which she was obsessed, and how she would eventually get her way with her husband. With his rather mild character and his inability to stand his ground, Gorbachev often found himself under the influence of his wife's decisions. Sometimes I could actually see ideas germinating in Raisa's mind; in fact, she often tried them out on me to assess their chances of survival.

There was a certain sequence of events. I knew that on certain issues Gorbachev had prepared decisions in response to the demands of a given real-life situation and with the support of advisers or members of the Politburo. But some time would pass and his viewpoint would change. All of a sudden I would hear him uphold some new approach, with which I was already familiar from talking with Raisa. This was how the general secretary and president formed his opinions, not only about statements in the press or the positions taken by newspapers, magazines, radio, or television but also about individuals and their abilities and potential.

I do not wish to name certain public figures and politicians, including several ministers who, in some instances without realizing it, owed their very jobs to Raisa. But all of them passed a tough test of their personal loyalty and diligence.

Raisa not only pursued policies of her own but also, when traveling with her husband, insisted on getting appropriate attention focused on herself and on having the necessary events arranged for her benefit. While we were in Kuibyshev, she said to me: "Let me tell you what the wife of the first secretary of the party *obkom* said to me: she was supposed to escort me on a trip around town, but she told me she couldn't make it because she had no one to leave her dog with. Have you any idea what that means?"

We laughed at this strange excuse, while wondering whether it meant that people were unhappy about the visits made by the general secretary's wife to enterprises and organizations, that the woman was really fond of her pet, or that she may have simply failed to understand who exactly had deigned to visit the *oblast*. In any case many people who knew of the incident did not envy Yevgeny Muravyov, then first secretary of the *obkom*—a man not unduly burdened with ideas, who was at the time under the strain of a huge work load as well as the barrage of criticism then being leveled at senior provincial officials in general.

If, as we did, you also feel a twinge of apprehension about Muravyov's fate, you are quite right: he was passed over, in favor of V. Afonin, former secretary of the Stavropol *kraikom*, who was later transferred to the Central Committee and after Gorbachev's visit to Kuibyshev would be a strong candidate for promotion to first secretary of the *obkom*.

Yakovlev, who thoroughly understood the complex relations between Gorbachev and his wife, was particularly afraid of incurring her wrath. Even so, he got himself into trouble that led to severe disagreements with the general secretary over various ideological issues. The Gorbachevs took the problems of Marxist-Leninist ideology very seriously indeed, and their opinion had to be taken into account. Many people in public life—politicians, writers, and the like—sensed Raisa's growing influence on cultural policy and would write letters to her, pressing their own agenda, complaining of their lot, and asking her to help museums, schools, or libraries and to intercede on their behalf so as to get their works published or enable them to move into a better apartment. Amazingly, most of these questions were resolved favorably and quickly. In cases where Raisa's wishes and her phone calls did not get results, the general secretary himself would issue a resolution, which was carried out promptly.

It became increasingly obvious that the general secretary's wife was not merely his adviser or a kind of shadow cabinet. She was a political figure in her own right, who asserted herself not only on trips abroad but also back home, taking a strong stand on the issues and sidelining many politicians in both party and government.

Eventually the Gorbachevs, while on their numerous trips, would jointly lay wreaths and flowers at various monuments, even if protocol provided otherwise. Their travels required extensive media coverage, and people grasped the significance of that fact. On their TV screens they saw not only the wife of the general secretary but a political figure of increasingly independent stature. She was constantly accompanied by guides and escorts from the security service and the Foreign Ministry, whom she ordered around unceremoniously. The point was not lost on foreign dignitaries, who found her arrogant behavior amazing.

When describing her meetings with Raisa, Nancy Reagan drew attention to her habit of moralizing and the lordly way she treated her entourage. In a matter of minutes, Nancy sized her up, finding her to be like one who has descended from on high to reveal to the world certain facts of momentous importance:

> If I was nervous about my first meeting with Raisa Gorbachev—and I was—she was probably even more nervous about meeting me. I didn't know what I would talk about with her, but I soon discovered that I needn't have worried. From the moment we met, she talked, talked and *talked*—so much that I could barely get a word in, edgewise or otherwise. Perhaps it was insecurity on her part, but during about a dozen encounters in three different countries, my fundamental impression of Raisa Gorbachev was that she never stopped talking.
>
> Or lecturing, to be more accurate. Sometimes the subject was the Soviet Union and the glories of the communist system, sometimes it was Soviet art. More often than not, it was Marxism and Leninism. Once or twice, she even lectured me on the failings of the American political system.
>
> I wasn't prepared for this, and I didn't like it. I had assumed we would talk about personal matters: our husbands, our children, being in the limelight, or perhaps our hopes for the future. I was prepared to tell Raisa about our drug program, because the first ladies of many other countries had found it relevant to their own societies. But when I brought it up, she promptly dismissed the subject, by assuring me that there was no problem in the Soviet Union. Oh, really?
>
> When she came to tea in Geneva that first day, she struck me as a

woman who expected to be deferred to. When she didn't like the chair she was seated in, she snapped her fingers to summon her KGB guards, who promptly moved her to another chair. . . .

I couldn't believe it. I had met first ladies, princesses and queens, but I had never seen anybody act this way.[*]

Nancy Reagan thereby summed up the very essence of Raisa's personality. These are bitter words about the character and temperament of the former First Lady of the former USSR. They could easily cause hurt feelings. Yet the Gorbachevs were not the kind of people who were unable to suppress such feelings: Raisa swallowed Nancy's reproach, and during the trip to the United States in May 1992 she affectionately held Nancy Reagan's hand, just as two children might while crossing the road on the way to school.

The greater part of the Soviet population also resented Raisa's influence. Intuitively sensing who was truly in charge of affairs of state, people wrote increasing numbers of letters expressing their feelings. At first individuals voiced astonishment at the First Lady's inexplicable behavior, but soon letters started arriving from the secretaries of party committees at various levels, as well as from the party organizations of industrial plants and occasionally of entire regions.

Was Gorbachev aware of this mail, and did he realize that it was doing serious, in fact irreparable, harm to his authority? I do not doubt that he knew of its existence, but I can only guess whether he realized the effect it was having.

Lukyanov, head of the party's General Department, also began to brief Gorbachev on the matter. He joked about it, saying: "You know, I decided to show him everything. I've got nothing to lose but my spare parts."

Lukyanov did not know at the time that plenty more could be lost, including one's freedom. I did not know that, either, and I reported to the general secretary on mail of this sort. He was once so upset and even frightened by what he heard that he phoned Gromyko, in my presence, and said: "Andrei Andreyevich, I need your advice. I have to travel a lot, and I need someone I can trust along with me, for help and support. I am now used to traveling with Raisa, but I see that this has set off a flood

---

[*]Nancy Reagan with William Novak, *My Turn: The Memoirs of Nancy Reagan* (New York: Random House, 1989), pp. 338–39.

of negative mail, some of it from party officials. What should I do?"

I could imagine Gromyko on the other end of the line, biting his lip for a moment, thinking carefully, and then beginning by pointing out that this was how it was done in international practice. Gorbachev, however, was not interested in international practice. He wanted an answer.

Gromyko went on, slowly, to point out that inside the USSR, of course, it was a delicate matter; then, sensing that Gorbachev wanted to hear something else, he added that if Gorbachev really deemed it necessary for the performance of his duties, he should do whatever was expedient.

"So you think there's nothing wrong with it?" said Gorbachev hopefully.

In response, Gromyko probably said, without much conviction, that he supposed the established practice could continue.

Gorbachev sighed with relief and handed me back the letters. I had no idea what to do with them next, and for that reason I diligently forwarded them to the general secretary with his mail; though I was afraid they might somehow—God forbid—end up at the dacha.

The Gorbachevs continued their travels together, on an ever grander and more majestic scale. Raisa soon said she wanted a special map of the world on which the countries she had visited would be marked. Having no idea of where to get such a map, I phoned some cartographers. Yashchenko, the chief of the department, promised to help, and eventually produced a map accurately depicting their itineraries inside and outside the USSR, with red lines radiating from Moscow to foreign capitals and to the republics, *krais*, and *oblasts* of the USSR. Moscow came to look more and more like a sun whose rays extended in all directions.

A special KGB security detail was needed for the general secretary's wife on her many trips abroad, in the Soviet Union as well as around Moscow. Various options were put to her, but she liked none of them. The agents who had been protecting the family before Gorbachev became general secretary were dismissed as unsuitable in a single day. Perhaps they knew too much or were deficient in some other respect, but Gorbachev told me: "They got to be really lazy; they could hardly keep up with me when we went walking, and apart from anything else they were used to the old way of doing things. I told Plekhanov to replace the lot of them. And the doctor, too."

Confusion reigned as a matter of course when one general secretary replaced another. The head of the Ninth Department of the KGB was directly subordinate to the general secretary, diligently carrying out his instructions, all of which emanated from the general secretary; occasionally he would report on these matters to the director of the KGB. When Gorbachev arrived, however, the confusion was quite marked; for his personal bodyguards he needed new people, who had to be young and extremely fit. Suitable candidates were quickly selected. But Raisa's security arrangements hit a snag: in addition to a general security detail, she needed an adjutant who would be with her all the time. She was not happy with what was proposed. A hunt started throughout all branches of the entire KGB to find the right man. Eventually a congenial officer with a higher education was found in Sochi. Yet he lasted only a few months, before being summarily dismissed as unsuitable for the First Lady. That came as no surprise, as she had also deemed unsuitable a whole host of cooks, cleaning ladies, and chambermaids; indeed, the turnover among such household staff at the Gorbachev dacha was very high even before her husband became general secretary. As they were all in uniform, they were then assigned to the dachas of various other Politburo members, where they promptly divulged the truth about the lifestyle of the Gorbachev family. When such rumors reached officials of the Central Committee and the Council of Ministers, and thereafter were picked up by the finely tuned ears of the Moscow populace, I decided the time had come to act. Disregarding my own rules, I took the first opportunity to tell Gorbachev that a rapid turnover of staff was bad for his authority and that something should be done to rectify the situation. He understood exactly what I was saying, but remained silent. I do not think that my exhortations had any effect on his wife's conduct, but when Gorbachev became general secretary the party was over for the house serfs in his service. Escape was impossible, and even dangerous. In any case salaries had been set at the same level as those of university lecturers, academicians. Just one difficulty remained. Doubtless for good reasons of her own, the candidates Raisa tended to choose for her staff were not the nicest and youngest women she could find. This kind of personnel policy placed the head of security in a predicament. Sounding desperate, he would often come to complain to me: "Where on earth am I going to find those kind of people? They're all going to have to be trained from scratch, and each given a title: it'll take *ages!*"

Gorbachev certainly knew of his wife's whims, but he lacked willpower and could not withstand her overwhelming energy.

As I noted earlier, Raisa eventually became a constant participant in the preparation of documents for party congresses and conferences. I take it for granted that she also scrutinized other documents, letting her observations and wishes be known. Gorbachev was sometimes placed in a manifestly awkward position when drafting prepared by two Politburo members, Yakovlev and Medvedev, was rejected because of his wife's corrections; he was then obliged to smooth things over. Yakovlev was furious, and glanced at me from time to time while muttering to himself. Medvedev looked around fishing for sympathy and did his best to defend his wording. They were wasting their time, however; Raisa had the last word, especially if the draft involved questions of ideology and culture.

Besides ruling her household, Raisa also unfailingly took part, wherever possible, in policy making and also in the deployment of personnel. Above all else, she formed the character of the general secretary and president, helping him steer through a hazardous sea roiled by many political undercurrents. Her actions may be judged in various ways: as civic-minded or as interference in the president's sphere of competence. He may have willed that interference, but it did limit his freedom of action and his authority.

STAVROPOL

Gorbachev once said, while reflecting on the formative influences that enabled him to become leader of the party and the country, that the sociopolitical environment in which he began work in Stavropol played a major role. With its harsh natural setting and climate, the region certainly gave many local people a chance to develop their abilities and strength. Some prominent industrialists and directors of collective and state farms, who were well known throughout the USSR and even abroad, worked in the Stavropol area. The large number of highly educated people who had for many years gathered in the spa towns of the nearby foothills had left a perceptible mark on the local cultural and academic environment. Gorbachev was certainly not the first political leader to have emerged from this background. Andropov was born in Mozdok, and both Suslov and Fyodor Kulakov (head of the Agricultural Department) worked in the area. Aleksander Solzhenitsyn and other world-famous writers came from these parts, as did a number of other prominent public figures.

The hard-working, energetic people who grew up in the Stavropol region, which was inhabited by dozens of different ethnic groups, formed a favorable environment for the development and growth of talented and enterprising people. Gorbachev often talked about the naturally gifted but uneducated peasants who became successful managers, demonstrating the enormous potential of hard work. He was grateful to these people, who taught him a great deal of worldly wisdom.

The rapid growth of Stavropol over the previous two decades and its great potential offered an environment in which leadership could be manifested in a variety of ways. There was a substantial agricultural sector spread over several climatic zones: from the Caucasus foothills to the arid steppes of the Pridon, virtually from the Caspian to the Black seas. Practically all crops, except tropical ones, were grown there, and conditions were favorable for livestock, particularly sheep. Canals had been built to supply water to the arid land, and irrigation permitted the intensive and guaranteed cultivation of vegetables, melons, animal feed, and other crops.

Industry was also on the rise. There had been a substantial growth in the electronic, farm machinery, and machine-building sectors in recent years. Substantial development had also taken place in the traditional spas, medicine, and the network of sanatoriums and vacation homes. The educational level of the population had naturally risen in the Stavropol region, which was an interesting and productive place to work.

The party and Komsomol organizations, whose ranks included thousands of competent people, had long been strong in the Stavropol *krai*. With the dynamism and capacity for hard work characteristic of the area, many local people had risen to prominence in the party, government or economy, especially in agriculture. It was not, however, unique in this regard: many other regions could match or in some instances far surpass its record.

Lastly, Gorbachev would never have become general secretary and president had he not worked in a resort region and earned the support of highly placed officials who relied on him and gradually helped him up the hierarchical ladder.

People tend to be more talkative as they get older. They tend increasingly to look back, recalling memorable events of which they can be proud. This foible, which may well be universal, was certainly to be found in Gorbachev. In conversations among friends after he had been elected general secretary of the Communist party, he was fond of talking about meetings and conversations with former Politburo members such as Brezhnev, Kosygin, Andropov, Suslov, Kulakov, Mikhail Solomentsev, and V. I. Vorotnikov. The meetings he referred to had taken place not in anyone's office but usually while the party and government leaders were on vacation with their families at Mineralniye Vody.

As did many party secretaries from resort areas, Gorbachev used to meet, entertain, and escort members of the Politburo and government. Such occasions were informal, often taking place in the countryside, in the mountains and foothills of the Caucasus, or in the scenic ravines and valleys of mountain rivers, where the Minister of Health Yevgeny Chazov and the Central Committee administrators had built a number of handsome villas with excellent hunting facilities. Guests would spread a tablecloth over the fragrant grass, lay out an abundance of hors d'oeuvres, and then relax, in a cordial, frank, and grateful mood, to recover from the exhausting pressures of high office. It was in this kind of setting that Gorbachev forged many links with the leadership of the country.

I remember seeing photographs showing the Gorbachevs receiving some Politburo member or other in a casual atmosphere of trust and candor. Such visits could, however, involve delicate situations. In something of a ritual, it had become customary for visitors to receive souvenirs to commemorate their stay in the Caucasus. Recalling that period, Raisa once said: "Some of them were quite blunt about it, and the wives of the senior officials themselves stated which souvenir they would like to get." She then named some wives who had aspired to receive this or that souvenir—Caucasian coins, original pieces made of fine porcelain, or other expensive items.

"It set us back a pretty penny," Raisa went on, "and we had to find some way to wriggle out of it."

But wriggling out proved impossible, so it was just as well that Gorbachev was soon transferred to the Central Committee, and the nervewracking business of receiving guests, while wriggling out of acquiescing to their demands, came to an end.

His informal links with the leaders of party and government doubtless helped Gorbachev's career, as they sponsored and supported him, grooming him for later responsibilities. For his part Gorbachev spoke fondly of Andropov, Brezhnev, Suslov, and several other Politburo members. In all the years I have known him, I do not remember him making derogatory personal remarks about Brezhnev, and when among Politburo members he always referred to him respectfully. These contacts were fondly remembered in later years, and Gorbachev may well have been grateful for what Brezhnev did for him.

One January evening in 1982 he started reminiscing, and spoke warmly and sincerely of Suslov: "What a remarkable and intelligent man he was. Now he has such a lot of work in the Secretariat and Politburo. I'm amazed how he copes with it all."

At first the transition from young *kraikom* secretary to member of the Politburo guaranteed Gorbachev only a huge amount of work but not a chance to rise to higher levels. For that purpose he would still have to graduate from the school of the party apparatus, learning how to make his way in the Moscow bureaucracy. Here again he found it helpful to have been an official in the Caucasus foothills, where many ministers took their vacations, thereby often meeting the right people in an informal setting at the various spas. He did not do this with all visiting officials, however. For example, he was not particularly kind to his colleagues, the other *obkom* secretaries, some of whom occasionally took the initiative by calling him themselves and inviting him to meet them. In the mid-1970s I remember hearing from certain secretaries comments such as the following: "It's gone to his head, having all those important people paying attention to him like that; they ought to send him along to us in the Trans-Ural region or Lake Baikal, in Siberia. That would bring him to his senses, and maybe he wouldn't be so arrogant."

I hardly think a man should be condemned in this way for happening to be in charge of an area where guests came pouring in, all demanding attention. Gorbachev knew exactly which of those guests he should get to know and treat cordially. When he moved to Moscow those contacts helped immensely in his relatively fast ascent through the bureaucracy.

A knowledge of the balance of power in the Central Committee, the Council of Ministers, the Supreme Soviet, the ministries and government departments, and among the various organizations is a *sine qua non* for anyone seeking to get to the top. The art of human contact, of winning the support of those who count, is also vitally necessary. It took Gorbachev several years to acquire the minimum levels of these skills. He was thoroughly scrutinized and tested by various methods before any judgment was passed on his merits.

He soon mastered the art of maneuver, compromise, and pleasing everybody, however—skills he may have acquired back in Stavropol. He grasped with relative success the rudiments of Moscow class intrigue as practiced at the various levels of power, including the ability to say one thing while meaning another, to bluff, and to charm everyone with a broad smile.

At first his ability to attract the attention of the intelligentsia, especially writers, was very important to him. He often went to the theater—in fact, he was noted for it—and he spoke to journalists in cordial, heartfelt terms, even ingratiatingly, though he could roar at them when something was, in his opinion, amiss.

When Gorbachev began the final stage of his ascent he was still a fairly raw politician, with poor oratorical skills. When addressing large audiences he would read from his prepared texts nervously, though he progressed rapidly. He worked very hard to ensure that he was perceived as an imposing, polished figure; had he not possessed certain innate gifts, however, all that effort would have been to no avail.

MARXISM-LENINISM

I would be remiss if I were to omit a reference to the role played in his growth and ascent by his sound knowledge of Marxism-Leninism and the body of theory bequeathed by Lenin. The fact that he was well versed in the history of the Communist party and the writings of Lenin, and often put this intellectual baggage to use, made him unusual among the members of the party and representatives of the local economy in Stavropol and, indeed, in Moscow as well. Many Politburo members, particularly Brezhnev, could remember little of Lenin's works—not surprisingly, perhaps, as the day-to-day business of politics, including the running of the economy, had occupied the bulk of their time over the years. Apart from the first volume of *Das Kapital*, many of them had not read Marx at all and merely quoted suitable passages from Lenin as the occasion required. Even Gorbachev had not read the works of Marx, Engels, or their predecessors. The Central Committee secretaries naturally had well-educated aides with a good theoretical background, though this was no substitute for a knowledge of the sources of the teaching on which the party leaders based their efforts to form a classless society.

Gorbachev was free of many such shortcomings. During the second and third years of perestroika, he suddenly took an unusual interest in the writings of Lenin, discovering some passages that he found particularly edifying. When I went into his office I would always see on his huge table several volumes by the founder of the Socialist state. He would often pick one of them up in my presence and read aloud, comparing it to the current situation and extolling the author's perspicacity.

When that was not enough, he would show how well read he was by asking me to take a certain volume from the bookcase and find a particular quotation for him. Whenever I hesitated he would indignantly remark on my poor knowledge of the founders of Marxism-Leninism. As a matter of fact, I did not think that quotations had to be learned by heart, but even when taken out of context they could usefully illustrate some aspect of society.

In 1986 and 1987, when Gorbachev was strongly under the influence of Lenin's writings, it was my impression that he was anxious to propose some concept that might continue Lenin's thinking and perhaps shake the world as powerfully as anything the founding father of the Soviet Union had done.

When his speeches and articles were being drafted and prepared for publication, Gorbachev did his best to supply a theoretical foundation for the proposals they contained, so as to show the unbroken link between them and the teachings of the founders of Marxism-Leninism. In most cases these attempts at theorizing are clearly discernible. And Gorbachev, as we have seen, loved to get into print. With him it was a veritable passion. In a short time he had had so many works written on his behalf that they filled an imposing row of blue volumes.

While still a student, and especially while engaged in Komsomol and party work in Stavropol, Gorbachev had developed a fondness for communicating with the masses through newspaper and magazine articles. He once asked me to collect everything written by him in Stavropol. The result was an album so heavy that one person could hardly pick it up, let alone carry it. Its physical weight was not matched, however, by the substantive weight of its contents. Everything he wrote in Stavropol makes it clear beyond a doubt that in his mind the inviolable basis for the development of Soviet society was the practical implementation of Marxist-Leninist ideas, the decisions of party congresses, and the thinking and conclusions that Brezhnev presented to society at the time. Those were the ideas that he unswervingly carried out, first as secretary of the *kraikom*, then as a secretary of the Central Committee, and finally as general secretary.

When speaking at the solemn meeting in Moscow devoted to the 113th anniversary of Lenin's birth, he began by describing Lenin as a man "whose name has become a symbol of the revolutionary renewal of the world, and whose teachings have captivated the minds of progressive people everywhere and been embodied in the practical affairs of society on a historic and worldwide scale."

In 1987, on the seventieth anniversary of the October Revolution, he again faithfully espoused Lenin's ideas and his testament: "Seven decades is but a moment in the many centuries during which civilization has grown, but no other period in history can possibly match the accomplishments of our country since the victory of the great October Revolution. There is no higher honor than that of following the path of the pioneers and committing all one's strength, energy, knowledge, and abilities to the triumph of the ideas and purposes of October!"

It may be said that I am quoting selectively here. However, there is still no logical explanation for the later metamorphosis in his thinking, for the political and ideological about-face, whose causes—and particularly whose timing—remain a mystery.

It could be that when devising perestroika he did not burn all bridges to the past because, as he himself said, the process had still not been set in motion; or he may have failed to understand the nature of the changes proposed by his advisers and consultants. In any case, when addressing the Twenty-seventh Party Congress in February 1986, he again declared that the economic, social, and cultural achievements of the Soviet Union were clear proof of the continued vitality of Marxist-Leninist teaching.

Historians will eventually figure out when and why Gorbachev's policies underwent such a radical change. What could account for his transition from advocacy of socialism and the Communist outlook to praise for the capitalist path of development?

Sooner or later Gorbachev will be compelled to explain to the world that sharp change of philosophy and principles. He surely will not want to be thought of as a weathervane, turning whichever way the wind is blowing. For my part I am inclined to agree with those who suggest that it was not his choice. The general secretary found himself bound hand and foot by those forces within the USSR and abroad that had laid out snares to entrap him, and he was compelled to lead his party followers to the slaughterhouse from which he alone emerged unscathed and enriched. Perhaps he intended to start all over again.

3

ON THE ROAD
TO PERESTROIKA

As far back as the spring of 1985, while preparing for his visit to enterprises in Moscow, Gorbachev described his plans for future travel within the Soviet Union. "Of course, I have to visit the maximum number of industrial centers and major agricultural regions," he said. "I must get to know the country and the problems that people are worrying about. But I think it's best to start with the biggest economic and political centers. I've already been to several such places in Moscow; now it's time to go to Leningrad, the cradle of the revolution. Then Kiev, and after that we can decide where else to go, as the need arises."

His later schedule followed that pattern. In the summer of 1985 he made a quick visit to Leningrad, then to Kiev and Dnepropetrovsk, where he addressed party members and workers at industrial plants. For many people it was a memorable occasion. For the first time, party officials, industrial bosses, and workers saw a general secretary who was very much alive and kicking. He did not have to be propped up by aides, and he could answer questions cogently. He also departed now and then from his prepared text, showing a detailed grasp of matters of concern to the people working at the industrial or social facilities he had been visiting.

He liked his Leningrad speech so much that he ordered it shown from beginning to end on television. That was when he became confident of his ability to speak without excessive reliance on a text. It was not a felicitous move, as his extemporaneous remarks took more time and were so diffuse that he occasionally missed key points. Nonetheless, it was an unusual practice—a throwback to the days when gifted revolutionaries, with no written texts at all, inspired the crowds to do great things. That time, however, has gone. In 1985 it was not rhetorical but organizational skills that were needed.

Early in the fall of 1985, prompted by declining oil production and the consequent heavy losses of hard-currency earnings, Gorbachev made a trip to Tyumen, in western Siberia, and Kazakhstan. His advance team, consisting of Central Committee secretaries, deputy chairmen of the Council of Ministers, members of the government, and other senior officials, made very thorough preparations for the trip.

Gorbachev flew to Tyumen with Raisa. In those days such joint travel may well have been the only source of public displeasure with the couple's conduct.

Raisa took great care with her appearance. Wearing fashionable clothes made to measure or bought ready-made outside the Soviet Union, as well as highly original jewelry, she certainly made a striking impression. However, the workers of Tyumen, especially the women, just could not understand. The contrast between the sumptuous attire of the general secretary's wife and the harsh living conditions of the wives and children of the oil and gas workers, many of whom lived in cramped, barrack-style communal dwellings, with few amenities, and who all wore the plainest of clothes, provoked a sullen, resentful silence.

To make matters worse, Raisa in those days still had no special "lady's schedule" of events arranged for her. Accordingly she accompanied her husband practically everywhere he went, from oil wells to meetings with local party officials. Even so, the public gave Gorbachev a triumphant reception on this visit. Huge crowds turned out to greet him, forming a solid wall of people around his motorcade at his first stop. Being unused to the sight of such illustrious visitors, people flocked to set eyes on the Gorbachevs. In Surgut and Yamburg vast crowds gave the general secretary a joyous and noisy welcome. In fact, provincial officials, not expecting such a tumultuous reception, became quite nervous as they surveyed the scene, fervently hoping that everything would go smoothly and that the distinguished couple's visit to the oil region would be a success.

This was one of Gorbachev's more outstanding trips, and one whose impact on the country was made all the greater by television. Pleased with the outcome of his trip and the welcome he had received from the workers, he expressed a thought that I had heard from him previously: "We have to rely on the people; they will help us get ahead on any issue."

So during the early years of his administration, Gorbachev believed in the people and regarded them as his power base. Only later on did he come to realize that they were deaf to his new ideas, backward in their development, and incapable of understanding the changes he proposed.

Solutions were then being sought for a number of problems pertaining to the extraction of oil and gas in Tyumen. At the meeting reports were heard from suppliers of hardware, pipelines, and various materials. Social issues were also being tackled, with plans for the accelerated construction of housing and the supply of more consumer goods, especially warm clothes. The one issue on which Gorbachev emphatically disagreed with his northern hosts was their request for expanded cooperative construction in more southerly regions, in the center of the country.

"This is where you should live, right here," he proclaimed confidently to the vast throng surrounding him. "This is where you should raise your children and where you should stay after you reach retirement."

He obviously could not have thought very carefully before making this pronouncement. His remarks were met not only with silence but with vigorous and even at times vehement opposition, as people argued that the far north was nothing like Stavropol, in the Crimea, or even the Perm region, in the Ural mountains. They told him that in the freezing polar winter, with few hours of sunshine and breathing air low in oxygen, their children got sick more often and old people found it extremely difficult to survive. But the general secretary was unmoved, arguing that it was essential to develop the far north and live there year-round because the conditions were so good and the housing was of such high quality. He hammered away at his theme with such fervent conviction that I found myself wondering whether we would ever get back to Moscow, and whether we, too, ought not to settle in the far north, since life was evidently so pleasant there.

From the area north of the Arctic Circle, however, we quickly and quietly flew to Tyumen, where Gorbachev was to deliver a major speech. As he wanted to make amendments to the text, he compelled Yakovlev and me to revise it at night. When I woke up the next morning the text was gone. Gorbachev had apparently gotten up earlier, come looking for the speech, and begun working on it himself.

His speech dealt with the problems involved in boosting oil and gas production. It severely criticized certain wasteful methods of oil extraction, the failure to apply intensive production methods in the oilfields, the low levels of technology then in use, and the poor quality of the equipment. Socioeconomic issues, relevant not only to Tyumen but also to the whole of Siberia and the Far East, were also given thorough consideration. In addition, however, the speech dealt with one particularly sensitive question: the anti-alcohol program recently adopted by the Central Committee, the Politburo, and the Council of Ministers.

THE ANTI-ALCOHOL PROGRAM AND OTHER POLICIES

As I have noted, the leadership of the country was now in the hands of a group of relatively new people, some of whom, at least, had some extravagantly bold ideas. Unfortunately theirs was the boldness and fearlessness of children who are simply incapable of recognizing danger when they see it. As the Central Committee and the government had, in recent years, received many letters from doctors and scientists, women and writers, denouncing the drunkenness that had swept the country, afflicting all segments of the population, Gorbachev ordered the elaboration of a set of measures to eliminate this scourge.

About that time some rather drastic measures were planned, including the reduction in the output of the sweet, fortified, nongrape wines known collectively as *bormotukha*, which, being cheap and plentiful, were deemed particularly harmful; vodka production was to be reduced gradually. Brandies, dry wines, and champagne were not affected. However, when the draft of the decree was submitted to the Politburo for discussion, its members, driven by a noble desire to wipe out evil without further delay and rendered even more zealous by their own fiery oratory, decided that the proposed measures were inadequate and that more needed to be done. When Ligachev and Solomentsev were put in charge of monitoring the program, it seemed to me that people would stop not only drinking liquor but even sniffing it.

Unfortunately, my sense of impending disaster was again confirmed by actual events. Officials of Gosplan, the Ministry of Trade, the processing industry, and farmers defended the cause of alcohol as best they could, arguing that the proposed measures would cost the state budget billions of rubles, ruin the grape growers, and close down much of the capacity of the wine-making industry. But trying to reason with people who are convinced they are working for the good of the people is futile. Such an abundance of arguments were put forward and so much authoritative advice was offered that further discussion became pointless. Those who advocated a gradual reduction of liquor production were branded as reactionaries determined to perpetuate alcoholism among the Soviet people. It was not an easy battle, but the Politburo eventually got its way.

After such a victory and several pep talks at the party Control Committee with Solomentsev, the plan was put into effect, with results even more drastic than those originally intended. Cuts were made in the production not only of vodka and *bormotukha* but also in that of brandies, dry wine, and champagne. Purchases of foreign liquor dropped sharply, driving the wine-making sector of the Socialist countries close to bankruptcy. As has often happened, in our zealous commitment to the noble cause of the fight against evil, we forgot to warn our own friends of our plan to curtail purchases of their liquor, confronting them with a virtual fait accompli due to a sudden fading of the Soviet people's interest in alcohol.

These decisions, and the attendant collapse of the processing industry and of wine making, dealt a severe blow to the state budget. It was not long before the financial organs felt their effects. Gosplan, the state planning agency, and the Ministries of Finance and Agriculture did their best to slow down the pace of the changes, and at least to limit them to the levels contained in the decision itself; unfortunately, however, the Party Control Committee intervened constantly. Solomentsev, who in his seventy-two years had consumed his fair share of liquor—and, in the view of some, considerably more—was unyielding. While actually attending Politburo meetings, its members were united in their vigorous demands for the eradication of the evil of liquor; yet when I discussed the subject with them individually, I found that many of them were inclined to dismiss these decisions and the pace of the cutbacks in liquor production as sheer nonsense, while remaining steadfast, as far as I could tell, in their own personal drinking habits. Needless to say, our example was not widely followed at the time in other countries.

For others the decree was still valid. At Tyumen, Gorbachev declared: "We shall uphold the norms of sobriety unswervingly. We are going to do a thorough job, and stand by our principles."

This rash decree had a grave impact on the country's economy and the authority of its leadership. The general public did not understand or accept these hastily conceived and ill-considered measures.

At the next reception, in November 1985, the number of guests had sharply declined. They gazed sadly at hors d'oeuvres that were not intended for consumption with mineral water and juices, while foreigners, surveying with a well-trained eye the first fruits of perestroika, shook hands cordially with the leaders, congratulating them and wishing them further successes on their chosen path, before quickly withdrawing. The message was clear: at all subsequent receptions, in violation of their own decisions, the senior members of the government always laid out wines and in some cases brandy as well.

Later on, it was widely felt that the anti-alcohol decree had been the only one in the entire perestroika program actually to have been carried out. Even that, however, was untrue, as its implementation was patchy. The Central Committee was inundated with thousands of indignant letters, as those same women who had demanded action to fight alcoholism in order to save collapsing families and protect their husbands and children from this scourge now called for increased sales of vodka, as their husbands had switched to drinking cologne, tooth powder, and even shoe polish. Unused to the taste of these products, the men cursed and grumbled. The entire populace began to wage a secret war against the government and the law enforcement agencies. The first casualty was the state monopoly on liquor, which later proved impossible to restore. Homemade liquor production, based primarily on sugar, began on a massive scale. From that point on, sugar remained a scarce commodity.

The government panicked. At Politburo meetings many members glared at the decision's sponsors with palpable hatred and showed unmistakable hostility toward Gorbachev, Ligachev, and Solomentsev. But the initiators of the anti-alcohol program, who were fond of reminding everybody that they had saved vast numbers of people from disaster, stood their ground for several more years, like good Bolsheviks, refusing to deviate from their chosen course. Moreover, in the early days, both crime and the incidence of injuries declined, as did the number of drunks. Admittedly, boilers exploded at nuclear power stations, ships sank, and trains collided. But that could have been due to protracted abstinence.

Around the time of Gorbachev's visit to Tyumen, the alcohol issue was only beginning to receive serious consideration. The local women were making speeches praising Gorbachev for saving the public from degeneracy and helping families stay together. Their menfolk maintained a sullen silence, convinced that northerners would never allow such innovations to pass, as supplies of liquor had already been delivered for the winter and they would certainly not allow anyone to take them away.

Such were the conflicting impressions left by Gorbachev's trip to the oil and gas producers.

This was followed by a flight to Tselinograd, in western Kazakhstan, for another meeting that, like many others of its kind, failed to make the slightest impact on the performance of the rural sector. The speech Gorbachev intended to make dealt with the question of raising retail prices for bakery products, among other issues. Action on this matter was certainly long overdue. Yet I very much feared that hasty decisions, made without detailed discussion, could lead to a host of unforeseeable consequences.

There was another worrisome aspect. No one had calculated the impact of this measure on the price of other products. As my colleague from *Pravda* put it, "when the price of gold goes up, ordinary people do not take much notice, since they do not buy precious metals; yet whenever the price of gold goes up, the price of a bunch of radishes at the market changes too." That principle was beyond question. Seeing that all the details of a price increase for bakery products had not been thoroughly analyzed, I was compelled to tell Gorbachev of my objections and to make as good a case as I could for my views. He listened in silence and made no reply. Yet the problem of prices was clearly in urgent need of attention.

In those days I did not favor keeping prices at their previous levels. For many years prices had failed to reflect the real state of affairs in the economy. It was precisely about this time, while the government still enjoyed the trust of the public, while the volume of goods in circulation was quite large, and the backing of the ruble stood at around 50 percent, that something could have been done. But these matters had to be resolved carefully and in conjunction with the prices of all goods and services. Rash moves could easily disrupt the monetary system, generating nothing more than a new and more powerful inflationary spiral.

In the mid-1980s, the authorities were afraid to tackle this issue on a broad front; valuable time was wasted as they waited for a miracle. In fact, our country's efforts to raise the living standard have almost always focused on the possibility of a miracle. We expected miracles from the revolution, collectivization, perestroika, the expanded planting of maize, land reclamation, and the concentration and specialization of production. And today we are hoping for a miracle from conversion, democratization, the privatization of farming, and much more, while at the same time doing little of practical utility to improve living conditions.

The next evening Gorbachev returned to Moscow. I remember that day well: it was my fiftieth birthday. In the plane's lounge at a high altitude, when Yakovlev and Razumovski drew Gorbachev's attention to this fact, Raisa sent for a bottle of red wine. It is worth pointing out that from the very beginning she had consistently opposed the new interpretation of the dry laws, declaring it utterly absurd to prohibit the consumption of wine.

I had always agreed with her and upheld the same policy whenever I could, although in those days I was denied the opportunity to do anything about this highly popular cause.

A wine known as Mukuzani was poured into glasses. Perhaps out of embarrassment in the presence of his subordinates, or possibly for other reasons, Gorbachev took a sip but did not drink. The conversation quickly turned to the results of the trip and the impressions it had left on his entourage.

All of a sudden Raisa said: "Let's drink to our cause, to loyalty to Mikhail Sergeyevich Gorbachev; I want you to swear that you will be loyal to him."

All those present were taken aback by this proposal. Yakovlev turned away, staring out the window; Razumovski unexpectedly laughed. Unable to believe that Raisa could really mean what she had said, and sincerely failing to understand the point of taking personal oaths, I tried to make light of the whole thing. After all, we were serving a cause and our country, but not any individuals or their spouses, and we did not live under a dynastic monarchy. Yet Raisa kept insisting, clearly with some purpose of her own in mind. Gorbachev raised his tall wineglass, but she persisted: "No! No! You must say 'I swear.'"

The episode was beginning to get out of hand, especially as it now appeared we were being required to swear loyalty to her, too. Imperceptibly changing the subject, Yakovlev made some remark about the experience of other countries, and the incident was allowed to come to an awkward close.

That glass of Mukuzani came to mind again several years later, when Razumovski, an old acquaintance of Gorbachev, was expelled from the

Central Committee. After Yakovlev had been summarily removed from the presidential council, he was assured that his benefits would remain unchanged. Those promises, however, turned out to be meaningless. In 1991 he complained bitterly about the way he had been treated: "After all, I asked for nothing and made no demands. They promised my benefits package would stay the same, but Gorbachev failed to keep his word."

That was one of the reasons for his resignation from the post of senior adviser to the president, though it was far from the only one. Articles in various newspapers had been severely critical of him, yet Gorbachev had done nothing to defend Yakovlev, although as general secretary of the Central Committee, he could have done a great deal. Gorbachev was reluctant to defend people, particularly if they were in trouble, and was quick to jettison those who had served him selflessly once they came under attack.

Demanding an oath of loyalty, even at 34,000 feet, was consistent with that same emphasis on personal dedication and with the princely habit of viewing people as one's personal slaves, required to serve not the principles and interests of the cause but rather individual figures, even if they were political charlatans. It was as if his subjects were expected to change their attire regularly to match the robes worn by their sovereign on any given day.

Time seemed to pass very quickly during those years. Gorbachev scheduled many meetings and frequently made speeches. And that meant we had to prepare all the texts, rewriting each one several times on his orders. By this time a whole brigade of speechwriters had been installed at the Central Committee's Volynskoye dacha, preparing reports, speeches, and remarks for the general secretary to deliver. International experts were also hard at work, as Gorbachev was acquiring a taste for foreign issues.

After his speech at Tselinograd on 1 September 1985, Gorbachev delivered a speech and some concluding remarks at a Central Committee meeting. The speech he was to make on French television on 30 September was being prepared. His October schedule included fifteen speeches, addresses, reports, and talks, not counting a number of others that were not published. In some months the total number of statements, including speeches, greetings, and published articles, exceeded twenty-two. Their number, however, was not the sole consideration: the trouble was that Gorbachev himself chose to become more actively

involved in the preparation of his speeches, rewriting texts that had been prepared for delivery, sometimes improving the original but more often mangling it. All in all, it was a very time-consuming process.

The sheer volume of Gorbachev's public appearances disrupted the normal arrangements whereby the Politburo endorsed the contents of his speeches. In fact, its members were beginning to learn of many of his initiatives and promises by reading about them in the press. Moreover, the fact that Gorbachev received so many foreign visitors left him with virtually no time for a thorough consideration of domestic problems and for talks with ministers, the first secretaries of Communist party Central Committees in the republics and of provincial and district committees.

All of this widened the gulf separating the general secretary from the members of the Central Committee, the first secretaries of parties committees, and the leaders of industry. They were all eager to go on helping Gorbachev, but contact somehow was lost. His tendency to avoid human contact was a grave flaw in his character. Gorbachev rarely called provincial officials or took any interest in what was going on. Alienation began to set in: local officials soon felt that meetings and phone conversations with the president were pointless. He began to lose interest in economic affairs; despite advice and requests, he stopped seeing ministers and directors of enterprises individually, tending instead to meet with them in large groups. He used these occasions to deliver brief pep talks, interspersed with heavy-handed criticism. Sensing alienation, people were reluctant to see him, doing so only in exceptional cases. After scheduled events, between ten and fifteen secretaries would be herded along to meet the general secretary. The tone of the discussion was formal, with Gorbachev doing most of the talking.

An old friend of mine, the first secretary of a provincial committee from Siberia, once told me of his disillusionment: "These political discussions really turn me off. I want to talk about specific issues, but I am treated to a standard political pep talk, the kind you get from the agit-prop lecturer at the local party committee. If you can, try to arrange for me to meet him face to face; otherwise I really wonder what this country is coming to."

Access to Gorbachev was controlled by his secretaries; I was unable and unwilling to regulate the process, as I did not consider myself to be his receptionist. Of course, when really urgent problems arose I would write a covering note requesting favorable consideration for letters from provincial committee secretaries or forward them to the receptionist for presentation to Gorbachev. Over the years, however, the number of such requests declined, and it became possible to reach Gorbachev without undue difficulty, indeed practically at any time, but now nobody came knocking at his door. Increasingly his visitors tended to be foreigners and representatives of the foreign press, people who wanted to bask in his reflected glory or be able to say casually to their colleagues that they had had a long conversation with the president of the USSR, and that he had supported their ideas and promised to help. Robert Maxwell, the British newspaper magnate, went to see Gorbachev with his own photographer, leaving shortly after pictures had been taken. He had no particular questions to ask, and since he and Gorbachev were both on the verge of bankruptcy, they were hardly in a position to help each other. But Maxwell nonetheless managed to turn the situation to advantage.

I was appointed assistant to General Secretary Gorbachev in the spring of 1985. After the preparation of his report to the 1984 conference, he had placed me in charge of ideological questions, though I realized it would not be for long. He appointed as his assistant A. P. Lushchikov, an experienced and sound man capable of resolving many issues. As chief adviser on Western international affairs, he at first retained A. Aleksandrov-Agentov, a former assistant to Brezhnev, Andropov, and Chernenko, who, despite his scholarly background, inevitably viewed the issues of the day from the standpoint of an earlier period. The man in charge of matters pertaining to the Socialist countries was V. V. Sharapov, later Soviet ambassador to Bulgaria. The Central Committee General Department was entrusted to Lukyanov, who was familiar with administrative matters, having worked, as he himself was fond of pointing out, with Molotov, Khrushchev, Brezhnev, Podgorny, Andropov, Chernenko, and Gorbachev.

One could hardly say that the thinking of the members of this team, or their approach to their work, was particularly harmonious.

At the time, Yakovlev was already in charge of the Central Committee Propaganda Department, and I failed to see why I should be moved to that post. It was not until later that I understood the reason. Smirnov, whom I had known since the early 1960s as the lecturer of the Central Committee, had been appointed assistant for ideological questions. He was well educated, calm, and even rather slow, capable of initiative only on rare occasions. Yakovlev, who had recommended him to Gorbachev, described him, fairly accurately, as a bull in a china shop. This was the motley crew that helped the general secretary formulate his thinking.

"LET THE BATTLE COMMENCE"

Gorbachev and his wife continued their travels around the country. We often visited industrial centers, such as large engineering and defense industry plants, collective farms, and state farms. He was scheduled to examine the situation in the Kuibyshev *oblast*, with its large engineering facilities, including the gigantic VAZ plant at Togliatti, some 500 miles southeast of Moscow. Even with such large-scale industry within its territory, the provincial leadership performed below par, while the authority of the first secretary sank to a low level. It seemed inevitable that such a situation would soon affect the entire province—as it in fact did, some time later. At the time, however, Gorbachev still hoped that his visit would bring about changes.

On the whole, the trip turned out to be quite interesting. Gorbachev and Raisa got a warm reception, but there was something about the television coverage of the visit that bothered Raisa. Smirnov, who was now responsible for such matters, relied on the TV crews and on A. I. Vlasov, who was first secretary to the deputy head of the Ideological Department under Yakovlev. At dinner one day Raisa raised the question of the visit.

"The people here are really wonderful and have given us a tremendous welcome," she said. "But the coverage in the media has been very poor. All that could be seen of Mikhail Sergeyevich was the back of his head; he has been shown cut off from his entourage, and yet there were masses of journalists, TV people, ideology experts from the Central Committee, and assistants assigned to this job."

Her remarks reminded me of an episode I had been involved in. I once heard exactly the same kind of reproach from Gorbachev himself, complaining of poor media coverage of the general secretary's first trip to the ZIL automotive plant. At Gorbachev's own request I, as organizer of the trip, had arranged for low-key, businesslike coverage. After all, this was to be a working trip on which the general secretary would familiarize himself with the situation at the plant and in one of the hospitals of the Proletarski region and visit a school, a shop, and the apartment of an "ordinary worker." Accordingly, few journalists were invited along, while "Vremya," the TV news program, was to show just a few shots. Gorbachev agreed to this arrangement. I personally believed, in any case, that unless trips were kept businesslike and serious, they tended to end up looking like publicity stunts.

The next day, however, I discovered that I was not only severely mistaken but I had also failed to understand what truly constituted proper coverage of the general secretary's visit and had failed to present it as an epoch-making event. Gorbachev, who only the day before had personally selected the shots to be shown on TV, was now complaining about the poor quality of the coverage. I took note of his remarks; yet after another trip I was rebuked again, even though I had gone to the trouble of involving experts from the Central Committee Agitprop Department. When Yakovlev found out about my mistake he remarked testily, after a few expletives, that the fact that Gorbachev had been shown from behind was utterly irrelevant. After all, anyone who has seen him can testify that the back of his head has an exceptionally noble, handsome profile, that he is unusual in that he goes to the hairdresser every day, and that many people would be proud if the backs of their heads were shown every day on TV. So what was all the fuss about?

As I pondered Yakovlev's words, I began to take a wholly new view of the question. I may, however, have spent too long thinking about it, or perhaps I just did not fully understand; but by the time I had figured out where to aim the TV cameras, I had been transferred to a new department, having been replaced by the experienced Smirnov, who was a corresponding member of the Academy of Sciences and former director of the Institute of Philosophy. Clearly there was no longer any need for me to worry about the back of Gorbachev's head.

The man in charge of enhancing the Soviet leader's image, Georgi Lukich, was seated at the table. While not addressing him directly, Raisa spoke of the ordinary people's love for the general secretary, of which there could be no doubt, and about the inability of TV to convey that love to the peoples of the USSR and to the rest of the world. Where the rest of the world was concerned, she may have been right. Whether prompted by some mischievous urge or by the memory of similar rebukes I had endured previously, I said: "In my opinion, not only was the trip a success but the coverage was also complete."

This response did nothing to calm the situation. Indeed, it triggered an even longer monologue, in which she shared her profound thoughts about agitprop and the ideological and professional skills of Soviet television cameramen. Eventually Smirnov, throwing his napkin on the table, strode off briskly to phone his team, which had come to cover the visit. His philosophical calm had been shattered. He issued orders for the general secretary to be shown only "full face."

The next morning Lukich and I were sitting in the hall, waiting to be summoned to breakfast (assistants were often invited to eat with the general secretary). It was getting late. He asked whether we had been forgotten or perhaps deemed unworthy of such an invitation. After a moment's thought, I replied that such a thing had never previously happened and that I was sure we would be eating very soon. To Lukich, who had had a serious stomach operation, regular meals were as important as medication. Eventually I grew impatient and asked the guard on duty in the corridor where Gorbachev was. I was told that the meal had been canceled and that Gorbachev, without summoning us, had gone on to the factory alone.

Shortly thereafter, Smirnov moved to a different department. For him, such a turbulent schedule was inadvisable. He was often sick and had grown accustomed to a moderate lifestyle, free from nervous stress and humiliation.

The turnover among Gorbachev's aides increased. When Aleksandrov-Agentov left, Gorbachev asked for suggestions to replace him. At the time I mentioned A. Chernyayev, whom I considered to be a capable and erudite man with good writing skills. His candidature, however, was not readily accepted. After meeting him on one of his foreign trips, Gorbachev somehow came to feel he would be unsuitable as an assistant. With the passage of time international affairs became increasingly important and when Yakovlev, as he told me, also mentioned Chernyayev, his appointment was practically assured. In my opinion Gorbachev never had occasion to regret his choice. The two men were practically twins.

Smirnov was replaced by Ivan Frolov, a well-educated and generally capable man with a broad cultural background. However, his poor health led to discord and inefficiency. This was doubtless one of the causes of the conflict at *Pravda* between the editor-in-chief and some members of the staff. And there were other new appointees as well, such as G. Shakhnazarov.

Petrakov made a meteoric appearance in our midst, before being elected to the Academy of Sciences. There were many other permanent and part-time advisers, assistants, assistants' assistants, and advisers' assistants, with all the attendant friction and conflicts that such a throng of political individuals inevitably generates. Each was eager to attract attention and to secure his own place in the sun. Intense infighting took place over the respective importance of advisers and assistants. Chernyayev and Shakhnazarov wrote a note to the president, pointing out that in the internal list of telephone numbers the assistants had been placed after the advisers. When the advisers learned of this, they contended that they belonged in a wholly different category and could not possibly be lumped together with the assistants. As often happens when people really have nothing substantive to do, petty disputes broke out. Many of them tried to blame me, claiming that the chief of staff unduly favored some, while underestimating the abilities of others. Why, they wanted to know, did X drive around in a brand-new car, whereas Yakovlev had been assigned an old car? Why had they not been given communication equipment, as Gorbachev had? The general secretary knew about all this bickering but took a philosophical approach, declining to inquire too deeply into the causes of the discord. Indeed, he told me not to waste any time over it, either.

Gorbachev spent the summer and fall of 1985 traveling abroad and around the Soviet Union. He did not have a complete picture of our country, its economic potential, the way people lived, or their concerns and needs; so he wanted to fill in the gaps in his knowledge and see more clearly what needed to be done. He was shaken by what he saw. He became aware of the vastness of the country and its huge productive potential and, of course, felt overwhelmed by the problems confronting him. There was good reason for him to react as he did: a system of economic management had been formed that could be destroyed only at the risk of bringing production to a halt.

Yet people were demanding change. Gorbachev still did not know what those changes would be, though he kept repeating, to his immediate entourage and in much larger gatherings, a phrase attributed to Napoleon: "Let the battle commence, and then we'll see."

One wonders whether it was necessary for Gorbachev to proceed so quickly to wreck all the country's productive and social structures. After all, he had declared his intention to pursue reforms and not to wage a devastating war on the economy, bringing ruin to his subjects. In any case, only Napoleon could afford to go into battle without a precise plan of action.

At the time, in order to launch into a socioeconomic battle, decisions would be needed not only from the Politburo and the Central Committee plenum but also from the party congress and the Supreme Soviet. Preparations were already under way for the Twenty-seventh Congress, which was to elaborate the strategy and tactics of reform and mobilize all the country's forces and resources to cope with vast and unusual challenges.

A meeting of the Central Committee Politburo appointed a team to draft the main report of the general secretary and other documents. It was headed by Yakovlev, head of the Ideological Department of the Communist party's Central Committee. We met at Volynskoye-2, situated in a small grove parallel to the Minsk highway, about a quarter of a mile from the Monument to Victory, not far from downtown Moscow. At the dacha, work started on the documents of the first party congress to be held since the dawn of the age of perestroika. As we discussed the main business at hand—the basic ideas to be included in the report and the structure of its main sections—we argued a great deal about where to begin. Traditionally one could start with domestic issues, but now it was suggested that we first take up international affairs and draft a statement of party policy on world developments. Yakovlev drew on the assistance of several members of the Institute of the World Economy and International Affairs, who promptly supplied a number of chapters and passages for the text. It was about this time that it occurred to him to map out a new approach to international problems, which later became known all over the world as the New Thinking. It is worth remembering that the notion of perestroika, together with all its basic components, was mainly the work of Yakovlev. Practically all Gorbachev's speeches were also based on Yakovlev's thinking. Now he had once more taken upon himself most of the hard work and was closely involved in the drafting of all sections of the report.

After covering international problems, the report was to turn to economic and social matters, which in a broad sense encompass virtually all aspects of perestroika. The formulation of this concept was being spelled out in greater detail, and again it seemed to me that we would end up by confusing people to such an extent that nobody would ever understand what exactly this word was supposed to mean and how it was to be put into practice. That is eventually what happened. Perestroika became the theme of many jokes and anecdotes. Indeed, it was gradually becoming a symbol of confusion and vacillation in all spheres of activity.

When we felt our version of the report was ready for a first reading, Gorbachev summoned Yakovlev and me to Pitsunda, on the Black Sea, where he was vacationing with his family. Though it was already late autumn, one could still walk around quite lightly dressed. Gorbachev proposed that our reading of the text should take place in a gazebo on the beach. With the surf rushing to and fro some 150 feet away, in a damp, piercing wind, Gorbachev, Raisa, Yakovlev, and I sat draped in blankets reading the report out loud. I recorded everyone's comments on a portable tape recorder I had brought with me, which was the cause of much mirth because the tapes could be played back only with headphones. The comments, which took up roughly three times as much space as the report itself, all had to be scrutinized and inserted in the text without displacing the substance of the original.

Gorbachev was becoming more and more directly involved in the drafting of policy theses. He had already mastered the subject matter fairly well, and his judgments on matters of substance were well founded. It was about this time that he began to take a more active part in the preparation of the most important documents, while inviting his closest associates to attend, but more as extras than anything else. Nonetheless, he still obviously needed the original draft, which embodied the most fundamental ideas, though he still made us write and rewrite the text several times.

We worked so hard at Pitsunda that by the time we returned to our quarters, located in a sort of cross between a hotel and a sanatorium, we were utterly exhausted. The dacha where the Gorbachevs were staying, which belonged to the KGB, consisted of three detached structures set in a world-famous pine grove. It was a pleasant and restful place to be, in the solitude of a huge nature reserve. Here, in a silence broken only by the sound of the waves sweeping across the fine pebble beach, relaxation came easily.

Gorbachev and his wife were staying in a two-story house with a wood-paneled interior, spacious rooms, and an office. Toward late afternoon we would move to Gorbachev's office and continue working there. Sometimes he would leave us to go for supper. The food here was as tasteless and monotonous as the food back in Moscow, and there was not much of it; so we often had another meal, of exotic Georgian dishes, when we returned to our own quarters. In any case, the atmosphere at Gorbachev's house was not particularly inviting. At ten o'clock the couple went out for their ritual walk, which they canceled only in the most exceptional circumstances.

Little by little our work advanced, as we proceeded to collect material. Soon we were able to return to Moscow with a pile of additions and comments. Then began the second phase of our work on the report to the Twenty-seventh Party Congress. By early January 1986 the text was ready for a final polishing by the general secretary, who proposed that the concluding stage take place at Zavidovo, a favorite vacation spot of Brezhnev and his closest aides. This military game preserve ninety miles from Moscow on the Leningrad highway had always been used by high-ranking marksmen, both from our country and from abroad. It is situated on a reservoir, not far from Konakovo station.

Some villas had been built here in the previous few years. Whereas Brezhnev lived in an apartment made of standard blocks of the sort used during the 1960s for the construction of five-story apartment buildings, the site was now occupied by a superb villa with expensive wood paneling and heavy chandeliers—a blend of peasant log cabin and contemporary Italianate residence in the grand style.

It was here that Gorbachev stayed. Yakovlev, Medvedev, and I were staying a hundred yards away, in a five-story apartment building with its own large pool and a sauna. Our house had a large dining room, a cinema, and a billiard room, and also contained hunting trophies and assorted memorabilia left by Brezhnev and his guests. Nearby were two more two-story luxury villas, built with imported fixtures and furnishings. They now stood empty.

About ten o'clock each morning all five of us sat down in the "peasant room" of the Gorbachevs' villa in large armchairs upholstered with boar and bear hides, at a small unpainted table, and started work. Raisa, who by now had become a fully fledged participant in the preparation of documents, discussed every line in minute detail. She was the organizer of our work and the custodian of the ideological purity of the text. Progress was slow, as most pages had to be dictated again, supplemented, and redrafted, while individual provisions needed to be developed.

At noon Raisa called a short break for refreshments, consisting of warm milk, coffee, candy, whipped-cream fruit mousse, cakes, and cream. She and Gorbachev took their coffee, which had been prepared from a special recipe, in Turkish glasses. After that, while the room was being aired out, we took a stroll to stretch our legs—and then back to the treadmill.

Both husband and wife had a remarkable capacity for hard work: they challenged Yakovlev and me repeatedly on points of our text, while we did our best to defend our handiwork. Only when we understood precisely what they did not like did we redraft various sentences, though they always had the last word. Even when we made a point of defending some particular piece of drafting, we found several days later that it had in any case been changed according to Gorbachev's preference. Only Medvedev was prepared to rewrite and provide a new draft for what he himself had already written, usually doing so on his own initiative. Yakovlev and I could somehow not help feeling that he had simply forgotten that at Volynskoye he had insisted on the existing language. Medvedev was also a relentless worker, who believed that the better was the enemy of the good, though the very next day he would find that the best was quite as certainly the enemy of the better. And then the whole process would start again.

At long last the report was finished and we were due to leave. We went outside to find the fields, trees, and ponds covered with a thick layer of snow. It was too cold to stand about, so we went for a brisk walk and got ready to leave. The domestic staff was already tidying up the house, and the security men were bringing our cars to the front door. We stood waiting for Gorbachev and Raisa. He came out first, followed a few minutes later by his wife. We shook their outstretched hands warmly. We felt like saying thank you, although we were perhaps not the ones who should have been expressing gratitude.

The evening before, there had been a farewell supper. We were served brandy, whisky, and wine, but the atmosphere was not particularly convivial, and there was little for us to talk to them about, apart from the events of the spring of 1985. People began to talk about the campaign to prevent Gorbachev from coming to power and force him out of politics altogether. The general secretary remembered everything very well, including names. He had clearly forgotten nothing.

Our party ended around midnight. My room was dark and depressing, and I had had enough of it by then. I gathered my papers. For the general secretary's report they had been sent here either personally to Gorbachev, or through me. The highly efficient Lukyanov, head of the General Department, knew how to keep documents on the move. He took his responsibilities to the general secretary very seriously, in keeping with tradition and the atmosphere in which he worked.

After Gorbachev had left, we drove to Moscow. I went straight to the Central Committee, as the documents had to be returned and the report had to be retyped. The next day it was to be reproduced and distributed to members of the Politburo and the Central Committee secretaries.

Now my work left me feeling increasingly dissatisfied. I had the impression that we were doing something wrong, concentrating on mere words—reports, speeches, statements. Tension was rising in society, while the party seemed to have lost its focus. The state of the economy was most disturbing. While the leadership was busy explaining what perestroika was really all about, performing a kind of moral striptease and heaping blame on its predecessors, people were increasingly wondering whether the leadership really knew which way it was headed and what needed to be done.

It might be hard to believe, but at the time nobody knew in concrete terms what needed to be done. We had entered a period of confusing and half-baked theorizing: one thing would be said today, another tomorrow, while yet a third would actually be done.

A Politburo meeting was scheduled the next day. The members had received the draft report and still believed they could substantively influence the ideas it contained. All members of the Politburo were supposed to be equal, but they began to speak in order of seniority or proximity to the president. I was dismayed by a tendency to give the greatest prominence to the reports and ideas of the general secretary. Now *everybody* seemed to be saying how well this or that part of the report had been drafted. The few comments and amendments that were made, even those on major issues, were treated almost as trivial afterthoughts. Gromyko, who had at first commented a great deal on substantive issues, soon lost heart and began to speak evasively and reluctantly, if at all. After the meeting Gorbachev, as usual, said: "Just see what you want to use—of course, not everything they said."

With instructions like those it would have been easy to disregard all comments, but we did try to incorporate any truly sensible ideas that improved the text. Two more days of hard work flew by, and the text was ready. Meanwhile the congress loomed ever closer. Indeed, the delegates were already assembling. Gorbachev shut himself off at home, reading the text out loud and figuring out where to pause for effect. He called us frequently, asking if there was any news and announcing that he had made changes that would oblige us to retype several pages. A few hours later he would call again, instructing us to retype a number of pages, usually ones he himself had amended only a short while before.

Together with Ligachev and Razumovski, Gorbachev drew up the membership of the future Central Committee of the party, a crucial part of the agenda for the congress. Most Politburo members simply did not know who would be elected and who would be dismissed. This secret, which was the basis of the leader's immense power, enabled him to decide the fate of the Central Committee and Politburo as he wished. Few people realized that this highly important decision was the result of personal reflections. Since the general secretary determined who was to be on the Central Committee, its grateful members then duly elected him as their leader. On some candidatures Gorbachev might ask Gromyko, for example, if he would object to the admission of a certain ambassador to the Central Committee. What could Gromyko possibly say, except that he had no objection?

Leaders are fond of talking about democracy, until it prevents them from making decisions. Even delegates to the congress who had been raised in the old traditions and were still mindful of the results of the Seventeenth Congress would never object and speak out frankly about candidatures. At best they might furtively strike out a name from the list, all the time quaking nervously at their own boldness. This, however, proved to be such a stressful experience that they would think twice before putting a line through someone's name. They would proceed more boldly when an order came from the delegation heads; but as it would be issued by the leadership, and only to trusted aides, it would scarcely be able to influence the outcome of the elections.

The hotels of the Central Committee and the Moscow City Council were gradually filling up with congress delegates, who were assigned to rooms according to their rank and delegation. All of them were engrossed in their own personal needs: they were anxious to buy large quantities of merchandise for themselves, their families, and friends, who had placed orders for so many things that it would be hard to transport them all back home, even by train. The Central Committee had a special postal section that mailed items back home. The Politburo had decided that the delegates to the Twenty-seventh Party Congress would receive more modest gifts, even though the total cost would still far exceed a million rubles. The gift sets included attaché cases, leather files, watches, pens, and various hard-to-get political books, in handsome editions prepared specially for the congress.

Moreover, each delegate could buy other things in the hotels, from special sections of the GUM department store, and in various food stores. Assorted ethnic foods had been sent from all the republics. The preparations for party congresses in those days were quite lavish. That, however, was the last congress at which the delegates enjoyed such privileged conditions. Thereafter those wishing to get a serving of sausage at breakfast had to stand in line with everyone else.

While Gorbachev was still at home studying the text, the delegates were studying their new leader. In those days his authority was at its height, though a barrier of insincerity and incomprehension divided the people from the leadership. These were the first fissures that eventually led to the collapse of the entire party, widespread social discord, and the breakup of the country.

The Twenty-seventh Party Congress commenced at 10:00 A.M. on 25 February 1986 in the huge and solemnly decorated hall of the Kremlin Palace of Congresses. It was always a magnificent spectacle. The members of the Politburo, the heads of delegations from foreign Communist and workers' parties, and virtually the entire leadership of the revolutionary and Socialist movements of the world assembled in the scarlet hall, bedecked with the symbols of the Soviet Communist party. The delegates rose to welcome the presidium.

Gorbachev walked to the microphone in the middle of the presidium table, announced that 4,993 of the 5,000 delegates were in attendance, and declared the congress open. This was the first time he had presided over such a large gathering in his capacity as general secretary. The delegates hung on his every word.

Numerous guests, diplomats, and representatives of the press were also present. Everyone was interested in Gorbachev's report. It was an exceptional event in the life of the party, the country, and the world Communist movement. The opening of the congress was in keeping with the best traditions, following a scenario that had been tested many times before. And it also ended as planned. Many people believed the report to be a success, and the speeches made during the congress had been focused and businesslike. The congress passed its own documents unanimously. The people Gorbachev had chosen were duly elected. Some moderate changes were made in the membership of the Central Committee, but many former highly placed individuals were allowed to stay.

The general secretary was also pleased with his dignified reaction to Eduard Shevardnadze's attempt to praise him. Allowing his emotions to cloud his judgment, or possibly failing to behave as expected in the age of perestroika, Shevardnadze delivered such a lavish, Georgian-style panegyric in honor of the general secretary that the hall instantly froze. For a few confused moments the fate of the whole of perestroika and the authority of Gorbachev himself hung in the balance. Had he remained silent at this point everyone would have thought that perestroika meant nothing more than a change of faces at the top, with the old principles and working methods left intact. Gorbachev quickly saw what was needed. He interrupted Shevardnadze and distanced himself from his words of praise. This could not have been easy, as the two men had been good friends since their Komsomol days. And while Gorbachev was on vacation at Pitsunda, Shevardnadze had been a frequent visitor, spending hours in conversation with the general secretary. Of course, later on Shevardnadze became Gorbachev's first nominee for the post of foreign minister.

"I've been thinking of appointing Eduard foreign minister," he said, in a tone that made it clear the issue was already closed. "Of course, we already have one Georgian. But Eduard is a capable and honest man. I hope he sticks to the policies we've already decided on."

I had formed a favorable impression of Shevardnadze and the state of affairs in Georgia. The only thing that bothered me was his lack of experience in international affairs, which I felt could create a poor impression. Gorbachev needed someone talented and obedient to execute his wishes, and clearly hoped for great things from his chosen candidate. Then came the incident at the party congress. The record of the meeting made no reference to it. Nonetheless, the number of those willing to praise Gorbachev in order to secure favors from him declined from then on. In later years such people were really necessary as a means of supporting the president, but at that time they remained silent for other reasons. Those who tried to mention his name were rebuffed by others. By the Twenty-eighth Congress the delegates were pleading with Gorbachev to dissociate himself from those who had praised and sought to ingratiate themselves with him, but now he remained silent.

The Congress adjusted the membership of the Central Committee, from which many former members were now excluded. Gorbachev's lengthy work on the list had borne fruit, as the Central Committee plenum had also altered the membership of the Politburo. New names now appeared: Lev Zaikov, former first secretary of the Leningrad *obkom*; Boris Yeltsin, one of the Central Committee secretaries; Marshal Sokolov; Nikolai Slyunkov, first secretary of the Belorussian Central Committee; Nikolai Talyzin, the chairman of Gosplan. The ranks of the secretaries now included Medvedev, head of the science section of the Central Committee apparatus; Nikonov, agriculture minister of the RSFSR (Russian Soviet Federal Socialist Republic); Razumovski, head of the party's organization section; and Yakovlev, head of the Central Committee's Propaganda Department.

There were now plenty of new, younger faces among the party leadership. The newcomers were credulous and eager to resolve all questions facing the party and the country. Generally speaking, they were not connected in any way with the past mistakes of the party and, indeed, did not fully understand them. Many of them, on the other hand, were not unduly burdened with broad political or economic experience, either.

After the Twenty-seventh Party Congress Gorbachev apportioned responsibilities among the members of the Politburo and the Central Committee secretaries. Ligachev became the second-ranking member of the Central Committee, presiding over meetings of the Central Committee Secretariat and, in Gorbachev's absence, those of the Politburo. By virtue of his new status he was in charge not only of the Central Committee Secretariat but also of the entire ideological sector. As such he was required to monitor the purity of Marxist-Leninist thought—a task with which he was already quite familiar. In the early 1960s he had headed the Propaganda and Agitation Department of the Central Committee's office for the RSFSR, performing his duties vigorously and, as usual, decisively. This, however, was a field in which Yakovlev, a newly elected member of the Central Committee, was also engaged. His appointment was a logical one, as he was by character and training quintessentially an ideologist, having spent many formative years since the mid-1950s in the Central Committee Propaganda Department. He was familiar with both the subject and the personnel involved in it, having been introduced to it early in his career. These two men, who had known each other well during the 1960s, now found themselves assigned to the same sector; a savage confrontation ensued.

Their divergent opinions on the same issue doubtless accounted for much of the wrangling, though it is hard to be sure. Matters were made worse by their strong wills and egos. One was forthright and resolute, with little time for subtle nuances and no penchant for maneuvering, while the other was mild-mannered, calculating many moves ahead. Their quarrel was damaging to the party, in that the schism it produced divided all the departments of the ideological front and their staff. Their feud eventually came to a dramatic end. Ligachev would schedule a press briefing one day, but Yakovlev, at another meeting with editors the next day or through individual contacts, would cancel everything Ligachev had said.

A week later the roles would be reversed. Both men were at the boiling point. Their differences spilled over into meetings of the Central

Committee Secretariat and into decisions on other issues. Draft decisions were needlessly withdrawn. Almost all the Central Committee secretaries were drawn into the conflict. I cannot remember a meeting of the Central Committee Secretariat or the Politburo at which the question of the ideological service and the mass media was not discussed.

In these circumstances Gorbachev took a rather flexible stance, trying not to get involved in the dispute. Occasionally in response to complaints from Ligachev he would tell him to hang in there—"Go right ahead and act. You have all the levers in your hands."

At the same time, however, he also supported Yakovlev, although he often said to him: "Do as we had agreed, but just make sure that they don't write anything stupid or deceitful. Talk to the editors, but stick to your guns."

The general secretary often lost his temper. After listening at length to some review of the press he would throw a tantrum in the Politburo, angrily and harshly cursing the editors and the press, and urging Yakovlev to restore order. On such matters, of course, he enjoyed the almost unanimous backing of the Politburo. While restoring order, however, Yakovlev gave Ligachev a chance to act, and he seized it with both hands, thereby storing up trouble for himself in the future, as the media turned him into a target for criticism. Broadly speaking, chaos and squabbling prevailed in the media during the second half of the 1980s, thus setting the stage for events that shocked a great many people.

THE MEDIA

It must be said that the role of the media, in Gorbachev's mind, was of special importance. He began to hold frequent meetings with creative intellectuals such as writers, journalists, artists, and people from the performing arts. All of them were invited to speak, and he himself spoke at length. They soon realized, however, that they were wasting their time, as not one of the problems they raised ever saw a solution. Writers complained about publishers, but virtually no changes were forthcoming. People talked about their professional needs, but theirs were truly voices crying in the wilderness. They spoke their minds about ways to improve the state of the economy, culture, education—all in vain.

Writers and journalists of my acquaintance would come up to me, shyly at first, as if asking for advice, and then complain about the futility of the whole exercise. At the time I did not understand what was happening. After wondering whether the meetings could be a kind of relief valve, to allow steam to escape from an overheated intellectual boiler, or whether Gorbachev was really powerless to help, I concluded, to my own regret and that of many intellectuals, that it was a bit of both.

Unfortunately, as time sped by, many assurances and promises remained unfulfilled. The euphoria generated by a belief in the new leader's miraculous powers began to fade, to be replaced by rumblings of discontent. Gorbachev was deeply hurt by any criticism. He had never previously been criticized at all, given the kind of jobs he had held and the absolute power he had wielded in Stavropol. True, some anonymous letters about him were sent to Moscow, but all of them were sent back to him. For this reason the first public opinion surveys showing a decline in his popularity ratings made him furious. I well remember his pained reaction to a survey conducted by *Moskovskiye Novosti* (*Moscow News*) among passengers on a train: he flew into a violent rage, lambasting Yakovlev for the laxity of the press and saying that the survey was not representative and was wrong to conclude that his ratings were falling. Yakovlev then acted to redress the situation.

A short while later, however, another newspaper, *Argumenty i Fakty*, published similar findings. More angry scenes followed. Finally, at a meeting with intellectuals Gorbachev lost his temper and publicly blasted the newspaper, vowing to dismiss its editor. Judging by his reaction, one would have thought this was the ultimate crime. The response to his threats stopped him dead in his tracks: other media representatives stood up for the paper. Being so indecisive, Gorbachev would no doubt have done nothing to the editor of *Argumenty i Fakty* in any case. But now he was frightened. Thereafter he remained subdued for a long time and began trying to ingratiate himself with the press.

Although they valued Gorbachev's perestroika, journalists, writers, academics and people from the world of the arts nonetheless knew what kind of man they were dealing with. Mounting disrespect for the leadership manifested itself in the form of anecdotes, parody, and caricature. On the face of it Gorbachev did not seem too upset and adapted to criticism and ridicule, while apparently content with the few sources of satisfaction remaining. When the strain caused him to lose his patience, and he lacked arguments with which to rebut his critics, he often threatened to resign from one post or the other. I knew, however, that he was merely trying to frighten the waverers and had no intention of ever quitting, as he was far too fond of his positions of authority.

Raisa, if anything, was more upset than he. She frequently called to inquire about the mood of the intelligentsia and the attitudes of individual writers or cultural figures toward her husband. She wondered what people in the performing arts were saying and who could be counted on for support. I had little information to give her, as such matters were now the purview of Frolov and other aides, whose duty it was to safeguard ideological purity and propriety and to monitor attitudes among the intelligentsia.

All of these clashes occurred gradually in the period after the Twenty-eighth Party Congress, in July 1990, but they became increasingly dramatic with the passage of time. Immediately after the Twenty-seventh Party Congress, however, in February 1986, the mood in both party and country was upbeat and creative. The congress had put forward a program of radical reforms in virtually all spheres designed generally to accelerate the socioeconomic development of the USSR. It soon became evident, though, that it would be extremely difficult for us to move ahead fast without profound changes. Moreover, certain forces were far keener on wrecking the existing political system than on accelerating the pace of scientific and technological progress. The obscure term perestroika evidently served as a camouflaged vehicle for such forces, while the vague explanations of its meaning that had been proffered shed little light on its possible consequences. The word itself was not a newcomer to the Russian vocabulary. It had been in widespread use in the mid-1950s and 1960s. I well remember how the arrival of Brezhnev shook up many government structures, so much so that officials joked about it, in the form of a rhyming couplet: *Derzhis stoiko—Nachalas perestroika* ("Hold tight—perestroika has begun").

This did not seem to bother Gorbachev, though it is possible he simply may not have known that the entire history of postrevolutionary change in the USSR has essentially been perestroika. He brought the word back into circulation, this time at an official level. Slowly it became something of a household word, evidently symbolizing global change in the country. The general secretary began to test the word on one of his first trips to Siberia and the Far East. He trotted it out twice during a speech in Vladivostok, where, as it happens, he mentioned Dmitri Yazov, who was serving in the region. Then, in Khabarovsk, he gave a broad description of perestroika in the country, though here he was referring to it in the sense of the acceleration of socioeconomic development.

Gorbachev kept on deciphering the notion of perestroika, whose essential tenets had been formulated by Yakovlev, throughout his time in office. His interpretation of it changed constantly, in both time and coverage. When the promised results began to recede from view, Gorbachev enunciated the concept of perestroika as a process taking place within a given historical period. That would probably have made sense, were it not for the fact that many cardinal structures guarding society against chaos and anarchy had already been demolished. As in Brezhnev's time, the public heard words that, though uttered distinctly, had no binding force or practical significance. Things were getting worse: the party's self-flagellation for its past sins and its inability to rectify the situation had caused people to turn away from it and to view it as the focus of all evil. The collapse of the power structure was accompanied by the formation of new factions that loudly and boldly denounced both past and present, while failing to offer clear-cut solutions of their own. The situation became extremely tense. Perestroika had brought the country virtually to the brink of revolution. All that was needed was an excuse, and that appeared in August 1991.

As the country sank deeper into difficulties and confrontation, Gorbachev began to reduce his plans for domestic travel, which exposed him both to personal danger and to the sight of angry crowds. His focus shifted increasingly toward international relations and foreign visits. The greater the tensions within the Soviet Union, the louder the chorus of praise from abroad. In fact, Western adulation of the general secretary had reached the point where he was idolized as one who had achieved something beyond the powers of any military or other forces. Gorbachev's unpopularity at home was compensated to a great extent by such flattery from his Western supporters, though that compensation took other forms as well.

4

FOREIGN VISITS

Once again the rattle of keys, the grating and squeaking of the door, the hard sound of heels on the floor: I have to collect my things and move to another cell. There's a search going on. They're checking everything, looking through all my things and frisking me. An hour later we're in a new cell, with the same dark blue walls with the same concrete and ceramic finish that we're afraid to touch, let alone write on; the iron bunk beds; a table welded to the floor; and the same peephole, the eye that watches you twenty-four hours a day. Actually at night, when their superiors are not around, the young guards often whoop it up out there, keeping me awake with their laughter, arguing, and loud footsteps. Sometimes I get so weak that I doze off briefly, but I cannot sleep.

Our memory churns up all that happens in our lives. Actually my life seems to have consisted of just one thing: fourteen or sixteen hours of backbreaking, relentless work every day, all week long, including Saturdays and usually Sundays as well. I was like a locomotive, pulling loads that should really have been shared by several people. Why did I do it? Because I saw it as my duty; I wanted my long-suffering country to climb out of the mess it was in. In all those years I had not made any money; in fact, I had to borrow money in order to make ends meet. When the market economy came along, I realized that it would eventually make my children and grandchildren, if not me, the hirelings of those shrewd individuals who had been smart enough to get rich, while I was writing speeches for Gorbachev about the transition to socialism with a human face and a Communist perspective.

Gorbachev's hard-currency accounts, amply furnished with funds by his foreign trips, made life much easier for him. And he certainly liked to travel. While still first secretary of the Stavropol *kraikom*, Gorbachev and Raisa managed to see a number of European countries. After moving to the Central Committee, he at first organized his own trips, such as those to Canada in May 1983 and to Great Britain in December 1984. It was not long before our ambassadors tried to lure this rising star to the country to which they were accredited. After the start of perestroika and the implementation of his policy of New Thinking and his peace initiatives, invitations came pouring in. An active foreign policy made it necessary for him to meet a variety of foreign leaders.

PROTOCOL

Whether in or out of the country, Gorbachev almost always traveled with Raisa. They began their preparations long before each trip. In the early years of perestroika, decisions related to each visit were discussed at meetings of the Politburo. It was customary for members to receive copies of the invitations that had been received, together with the opinion of the Foreign Ministry and the Central Committee's own International Department about the advisability of each trip and the chances of concluding any agreements and starting negotiations that seemed likely to lead to practical solutions.

After the Politburo had heard Gorbachev's assessment of the possible outcome of the visit and statements from the foreign minister and other Politburo members, it would decide whether to go ahead. Various organizations and organs were instructed to report on the political situation in the country to be visited, on trade and economic contacts, and on other issues that could arise from the trip. The Defense Ministry, KGB, embassies, and institutes concerned with the country in question also stated their views. Gorbachev referred the matter to one of his aides—at first Aleksandrov-Agentov and later Chernyayev or Sharapov—with instructions to produce a synopsis of all material thus presented and to arrange with the Foreign Ministry and embassies the program for the trip and possible meetings with political leaders, businessmen, academics, and scientists.

A special program was drawn up for Raisa, usually consisting of meetings with academics, scientists, and people from the fields of culture and education and visits to exhibitions and museums. She was also invited to tea and held tea parties of her own. This was the tricky part of the visit, with frequent mixups, false starts, and even outright fiascos from a protocol point of view.

The protocol section at the Foreign Ministry and the security service also worked hard to prepare for the visits, contacting their counterparts abroad and making the necessary complex arrangements so that the visit would go smoothly. They figured out the time and place of each meeting and the list of those who should attend, who would provide security for the Soviet head of state, whether the bodyguards would be armed or whether the host country would assume responsibility for security. These questions were thoroughly discussed and the size of the general secretary's entourage amended accordingly. One thing that hardly ever changed was the need to arrange for shipment to the host country of our own limousines, usually ZILs, containing special communications equipment enabling the general secretary to contact Moscow from virtually anywhere on earth. They were elegant vehicles, with good built-in protection. From the standpoint of contemporary automobile construction, however, they were rather antiquated. They had a capricious engine, with the bad habit of stalling at the most crucial moment.

On one of Gorbachev's visits to the United States, the Americans, who were interested in our ZIL and rather liked its appearance, asked whether it was a British car. They found it hard to believe that they were looking at a Soviet car; in fact, they stood there for a while, shaking their heads, as if to say: "Come on! We're not that dumb!" In the Federal Republic of Germany, on the other hand, they did not doubt that these were Soviet cars, especially when they failed to start promptly; to a chorus of exclamations and offers to lend a hand pushing, everyone agreed that they were our own Soviet-built wonders. Our security men, of course, did their best to downplay the mechanical failures of the ZILs, saying that hot weather made gasoline volatile, so that it would take time to pump it through the system. Sometimes other arguments were adduced. All in all, though, I must say that they were handsome, reliable, and powerful vehicles, with beautiful interiors, that could survive a confrontation, if not with a tank then at least with an armored personnel carrier.

Documents, speeches, and statements were not the only focus of attention during preparations for a Gorbachev visit, though he certainly worked on them with meticulous care, especially at the beginning. His appearance and image were also important. New suits, appropriate for the climate of the host country and the various parts of his schedule, were ordered long before his departure. Those intended for wear on official occasions were dark, whereas during the journey itself he preferred to dress in lighter shades. Assorted shoes, ties, and shirts were also carefully chosen. As we have seen, in this respect the general secretary looked much more resplendent than the people he was visiting. The more modest apparel worn by foreign leaders might, however, have been more in keeping with current notions of propriety. Not all statesmen would consent to appear dressed like a tailor's dummy. A slight casual touch conveys a much more solid impression than extravagant jackets that look as if they have just been pressed.

Raisa's clothes were a matter of special concern. She always dressed quite stylishly, drawing on an extensive wardrobe, and had outstandingly good taste. She did not like to wear the same thing twice. This was particularly true of her jewelry, though I did notice that in several countries she wore the same large, white metal bracelets, rings and earrings. She had a fine array of footwear, bought somewhere in the West, and some elegant fur coats and hats. I cannot tell which animal's fur went into the manufacture of these items, though the overall effect was certainly impressive. Such attire must have seemed extravagantly expensive to some people, but one wonders how it could have been, since the general secretary's salary was never very high. How Raisa could afford such finery is a secret known only to her, to security chief Plekhanov, and to God. In any case huge numbers of suitcases, boxes, and special packages for storing outer wear were loaded onto the plane.

Gifts, both official and personal, were another concern of the Gorbachevs. On the third floor of its main building, the Central Committee kept a well-stocked warehouse precisely for this purpose, crammed with objects of great beauty that were expensive in those days and by now must be priceless. Like Aladdin's cave, it was accessible only to those wielding a magic lamp, in this case the Central Committee's chief administrator, Kruchina, who accompanied me on my first visit with one of his deputies. I beheld paintings and sculptures by the great masters, exquisite painted boxes of the Palekh school, hand-inlaid weapons from Tula, a set of hunting rifles, handmade porcelain and crystal tableware, albums containing rare postage stamps, numerous clocks—in short, everything that could be made to special order in the Soviet Union. Besides objects made from precious metals, the warehouse also contained jewelry, jewelry cases, and other objects of stone and semiprecious stone.

When on closer inspection I found that it also included items left over from the days of Brezhnev, which had originally been kept in the state storage facility, Gokhran, I advised Kruchina to send them back. And he did return a nineteenth-century silver samovar and, I believe, some cups. I was also amazed to see the extraordinarily low prices on most of the articles. In those days appraisals were distinctly on the low side, so that an antique gold clock could be had for between thirty and fifty rubles.

Shortly before the couple left on a foreign trip, the staff of the Department of the Administration of Affairs would lay out, in a room adjoining the general secretary and president's office, various samples of gifts intended for foreign leaders and their wives and senior government officials. Gorbachev and Raisa always inspected them, choosing those most suitable for that particular trip. At first they spent a long time trying to make up their minds; later on, when they had familiarized themselves with the contents of the storeroom, they would choose much more briskly. I remember asking Gorbachev, when he was about to choose what I felt was an inordinately expensive gift, whether there was any real need to choose these gifts with such care, pointing out that in other countries official gifts were habitually surrendered to the state, anyway. With a laugh he replied that the practice applied only to official gifts, and that personal gifts were quite another matter.

The spouses of foreign officials also got presents. Gorbachev once told me: "We already have a present for Mrs. Thatcher, so just pick out something for her husband, in line with his inclinations." From what Gorbachev himself had told me, the Iron Lady's husband inclined toward drinking. With the general secretary's agreement the gifts were chosen: a hunting set, consisting of a dagger in a silver case, a silver-gilt cup, a hatchet with gold inlay—and, apparently, a few bottles. For this purpose there was a wine cellar with bottles of various shapes and contents, to which they added a "gentleman's set," consisting of the best Soviet caviar, crabmeat, and vodkas.

The wives of presidents and prime ministers usually got crystal or porcelain sets, one-of-a-kind tableware, a variety of jewelry and other articles made of semiprecious stones, large and exquisite lacquered boxes of the Palekh school, and much more. Kruchina once told me that when he discovered that Gorbachev intended to give Ronald Reagan a handsome leather saddle, made in the best traditions of the art, he tried to dissuade him, arguing that it could be misconstrued. But he was overruled.

Gorbachev felt greatly flattered by his admission to the club of world leaders. He talked a great deal about the lives, customs, foibles, and passions of presidents, prime ministers, and monarchs, offering his own appraisals of them and their entourage and telling funny stories about them. He was particularly amused by Reagan's penchant for Russian proverbs and anecdotes, and several times asked for a manual on the subject to be prepared. Raisa was fond of making known her views of the women she had met. First ladies in many countries, she seemed to be saying, had no taste in dress and could hardly string two words together.

A great deal of mystery and secrecy surrounded the ceremonial exchange of gifts. The precise nature of the gifts we had given and received were a big secret for parliament, let alone the general public. Despite the New Thinking, certain instincts perpetuated this ancient practice of mutual gratification. Virtually all those accompanying the general secretary received gifts, whose value varied according to the person's rank: from a keychain, watch, and camera to the kind of gift that was kept in the greatest secrecy. As far as I know, however, Kruchina and I were practically the only ones who surrendered our presents to the state. When the time came to submit a memorandum listing the gifts returned to the storeroom after visits abroad in the previous few years, not even half a dozen names appeared on it. After returning from the Federal Republic of Germany I surrendered a small cup I had received there. A representative of Gokhran (the state treasury) later sent a note saying that a silver article weighing a certain amount had been received from so-and-so. And that was all. Something tells me the general public would have been unhappy with this procedure had they known about it.

On a trip to the United States I once received a small wooden box from President Reagan. I opened it slowly and, finding it empty, stared at it for a long time. It then occurred to me that it must have been symbolic, in the sense that I had to fill it myself, so I was satisfied. I imagine that in many countries such gifts are treated as symbols, with no commercial implications, though the value of gifts seems to vary inversely with the wealth of the country whose representative is giving them. In this respect we were certainly far ahead of everyone else. However, by comparison with what happened under Brezhnev, today's presents were certainly far easier on the public purse.

Preparations for the visit would then shift into the next phase. Raisa, when informed of the schedule, would bury herself in books on the country in question. She would watch its movies, read its classics, study its culture and art, and learn about its museums and exhibitions. On the rare occasions when I spent time with her I noticed her evident pleasure at being able to talk to her hosts about their country, its ancient monuments, and various other sights. For their part her hosts, whether from tact or ignorance, listened to her attentively. The merits of her approach are open to debate, though it is certainly better than finding oneself staring for the first time at some cultural site one has never even heard of.

When everything was ready for the trip, the composition of the president's entourage would be established, or rather confirmed. The Gorbachevs liked to travel in the company of a large retinue of people from the worlds of art, culture, literature, and journalism. The couple's chronicler, Uralov, also went along, as a rule, to record their doings on videotape. Chernyayev began to draw up a list of members of the president's party long before the trip. It usually consisted of two parts: the immediate entourage and a group intended to provide ideological support and embellishment. The first group included members of the delegation, usually the foreign minister, the representative of the Central Committee's International Department, one or more heads of republics or the Supreme Soviet, and our ambassador. Besides aides and advisers to Gorbachev, his personal secretaries and typists, and the security detail with its chief, Plekhanov, this group also included aides to the members of the official delegation and interpreters. All of these persons flew in the president's plane.

The second group left earlier. As we have seen, it included writers, academics, and scientists, other prominent figures whose presence in the president's entourage was deemed to add luster to the visit. At least that was how things were in the beginning. After a while I noticed that some of those invited to travel with Gorbachev excused themselves on various grounds, thus upsetting Gorbachev and particularly Raisa, who had devoted much energy to the formation of her husband's entourage. Frequent changes occurred, with some names being removed and others added to the list. Anyone known to have made disparaging remarks about Gorbachev stood no chance of being invited to travel with him. Some people were never invited at all, either because they were too independent-minded or because they were unwilling to take part in the Gorbachev road show. Some of them whom I knew well phoned me to ask whether their absence would be taken the wrong way, while I know that some of them used sickness as an excuse for not going.

When preparations were complete, a departure time was set. The Gorbachevs loved to be seen off by a large group of acquaintances. Mikhail Sergeyevich established a system whereby that group included the members of the Politburo and the Central Committee secretaries, their aides, and the heads of key government departments, principally Boris Pugo, Kryuchkov, Yazov, and Baklanov or their predecessors, regardless of whether or not they occupied a rung on the party ladder. Initially that had also been the case on trips within the Soviet Union. As Gorbachev also insisted on television and press coverage of his departures and arrivals, hundreds of letters began to arrive, condemning those who spent all their time at the airport either seeing the president off or welcoming him back from a trip.

Gorbachev soon agreed that only his foreign trips should elicit a full turnout at the airport. Those trips abroad, however, were so frequent that the torrent of letters continued unabated. Here, however, the ritual was observed scrupulously. The send-off party soon included the members of the Presidential Council and then the Security Council, though the number of Central Committee members taking part declined, eventually being reduced to only Ivashko and Shenin. The membership of the send-off party was always ordered by Gorbachev, who added or subtracted names as he saw fit. Only persons invited by him, sometimes over the phone, came to the airport.

The members of the send-off party would gather at Vnukovo-2, the special air terminal for dignitaries, long before the presidential plane took off. While they were waiting they coalesced into groups in which various problems were discussed and quite often resolved, as if they had been continuing their formal meetings. After the general secretary's arrival, he would take part in the discussion, if time allowed, issuing instructions and voicing preferences. The entire party then walked over to the steps leading to the plane, where the ritual farewell took place. The airport party lined up in three rows, with Lukyanov, Pavlov, and Ivashko in front, members of the Politburo or the Security Council behind, and all other aides, ministers, and the rest in the back. Hands were shaken, at length in the front row, more briefly in the middle row, and fleetingly in the back.

The president and his wife then climbed the steps, turning to wave sadly at the crowd before disappearing into the cabin. The members of the farewell party then waved their hands vigorously in the air, smiling blissfully all the while—in accord with the dictates of television. They used to put on the same performance even in the old days, when kisses were exchanged on the tarmac before takeoff, though in Gorbachev's time kissing became less common. The rapid turnover among the members of the leadership apparently disrupted the inbred ritual of leave-taking. The farewell ceremony, during which the party on the tarmac stood hatless, continued until the plane had taxied out of sight, to the end of the runway. Everyone looked forward to that moment. They then went into the terminal building and waited until the plane was airborne, it being considered improper to leave before the takeoff. Khrushchev's plane once had to make an unexpected landing shortly after takeoff; the farewell party, however, had vanished without a trace. Ever since that incident the members of the farewell party waited until an Aeroflot representative announced that the plane was in the air and the flight proceeding normally before leaving the airport. It was touching to see how attached they seemed to one another's company, especially since they were practically certain to meet again in an hour or less, at some meeting or other.

While the farewell party was on its way home, the presidential plane was bustling with activity. It took about thirty minutes for everybody to find their seats. Gorbachev and Raisa began to settle in and change in the first cabin, which accounted for about half the length of the aircraft. It contained a bedroom that served also as an office or a lounge, and a large room with two tables and comfortable armchairs, a television set, a telephone, and other equipment. The furniture was all made of exotic woods. Adjoining the lounge was a well-stocked kitchen capable of satisfying the most demanding passengers.

Chernyayev, the foreign minister, and several other members of the presidential party shared with security men Plekhanov and Medvedev a small lounge, with tables, behind the kitchen, which was designed to accommodate eight people, and was most uncomfortable. Everyone was crammed in so tight that our knees would touch. Sleeping on transoceanic flights was particularly difficult.

Besides the security detail, the third lounge contained the doctors, domestic staff, and typists, who were more comfortable despite the long time they had been on board waiting for the delegation to arrive.

After takeoff people began to take out papers and newspapers, while others waited for tea and desserts to be brought around. Forty or fifty minutes later Gorbachev sent for the foreign minister, his assistant, and occasionally a few other people from his party. It was hard to work properly in such a noisy environment, so after repeated discussions of various documents, the talk would turn to more general topics.

When I flew with Gorbachev, which was not often, I had no particular function to perform, being considered rather like a piece of furniture or a suitcase that could conceivably be needed but probably would not. Naturally I did not enjoy this arrangement and tried tactfully to decline, pointing to my heavy work load. Gorbachev, however, plainly expected me to view the invitation I had received as a boon or an incentive. Yakovlev had the same experience. Shevardnadze made all the decisions and took part in negotiations, while he, as a member of the Politburo, felt out of place in the midst of statesmen.

Some of those working in the presidential lounge stayed there for dinner, while the rest of us were served at our seats. In the lounge occupied by the security men, doctors, and stenographers, however, food was served in the usual Aeroflot manner, on small tables attached to the seats in front. There was usually plenty to eat: hors d'oeuvres of fish, meat, caviar, crabmeat, and vegetables, followed by consommé or fish soup, with a hot main dish of fish or meat. Then came coffee or tea, milk, chocolates, pastries, ice cream, and fruit. Liquor was also available, though few people seemed to want it on the outbound leg, at least not in lounge No. 2. When we were homeward bound, however, that was another matter.

The president and his wife usually stayed either in the Soviet embassy or in an official residence provided by the host country. As far as I remember, however, they stayed only in the embassy. Perhaps that merely shows how rarely I traveled abroad with them.

Then came the official talks, meetings, lunches, and working breakfasts—which I found quite tedious, as they required me to stay rooted to the spot with a serious look on my face while various agreements were being discussed. I knew all along, of course, that everything had already been agreed, and that all that remained to be done was the signing of various documents; if any points were still in dispute they were personally resolved by the leaders with trusted senior officials from the Foreign Ministry.

GORBACHEV AND REAGAN

I particularly remember the trip to the United States during which Gorbachev met Reagan and signed a number of important agreements. He and his wife stayed at the embassy, for which purpose a certain amount of reconstruction was needed, along with the rearrangement and renovation of furniture. High-level visits always prompted "renovation" of this sort. In fact, our embassies looked forward to receiving the head of state, as they took advantage of the occasion to make requests for extravagant amounts of money for sprucing up their premises and buying new sets of cutlery and tableware. Projects that had been pending for years could come to fruition as a result of a single visit. Some of the acquisitions thus made possible, however, were not really needed for the visit itself.

The rest of the party stayed at the superb Madison Hotel, almost directly opposite the embassy, where the service and cooking were both excellent. Even by Western standards my suite was big, consisting of two rooms that could be turned into three. I was particularly struck by the fact that each room had its own toilet, bath or shower, and television set. All I did in these luxurious surroundings, however, was sleep.

Downstairs in the hotel the delegation and perhaps other members of the presidential party had access to a smorgasbord, from which one could pick whatever one wanted to eat. This was another facility that I was practically unable to use, as my time was taken up with assorted official functions: breakfasts, dinners, and talks.

I went to the White House for the first time on 8 December 1987, at the beginning of our talks. Our delegation found itself in a building resembling a rather small Russian country mansion, with lots of small rooms. Only on the second floor was there a room capable of accommodating around a hundred people. The White House library, the conference room of the National Security Council, and, indeed, the president's office were so small that it was hard to imagine fitting more than fifteen or twenty persons in any of them.

Before the start of the joint meeting, the two presidents spent some time alone in the Oval Office, while everyone else strolled around the rest of the building.

I sat and talked with Vladimir Kamentsev, the vice chairman of the Council of Ministers, in the conference room of the National Security Council, where we discussed matters of substance as well as our impressions of the White House. Looking around the room, figuring out who sat where and who had previously sat where, we agreed that only tradition could oblige the leaders of the nation to meet in this tiny ground-floor room, situated practically on the same level as the lawns. Thinking back to our own offices in the Kremlin, we sympathized with President Reagan: Kamentsev's office was twice as big, though, unlike the president of the United States, he did not have his own wing occupying half an entire floor.

Gorbachev continued his talks alone with Reagan. The rest of us wandered about, as did the American participants in the negotiations. As the hours passed it was obvious there would be no big meeting; there was time left only for us to return to our hotels and change for dinner. Gorbachev did not like large meetings. He soon emerged and got into his limousine, whereupon the whole motorcade left for the residence.

In mid-afternoon the ceremonial signing of the INF (Intermediate-Range Nuclear Forces) Treaty was held. The cream of American society had been invited to the official dinner at the White House, which began at seven o'clock: high government officials, businessmen, academics, people from the performing arts. The seating arrangements were unusual in that husbands and wives sat at different tables. The congenial group at my table included the leaders of the Democratic party, as well as my compatriot Natasha Simes, who had emigrated to the States years ago, married, and eventually become quite rich. The conversation was rather general. The Americans carefully collected the menus from the dinner and asked for each other's signatures.

By our standards the dinner was sufficient but not extravagant. Hors d'oeuvres consisted of salmon, lobster, and salad with various dressings. Then came finely sliced filet of veal and fruit. A light white and a red wine were served with the hors d'oeuvres, and champagne with the ice cream and coffee. My dinner companions were saying how important it was to be fit and to avoid putting on weight; I must say they looked exceedingly trim and fit. Overeating had clearly caused some of those present to put on weight. President Reagan and the general secretary each made speeches, and everyone raised a glass and applauded.

Dinner did not last long. Music, mixed with the sound of loud voices and laughter, could be heard coming from the hall, so everybody went out to join in the merriment. The atmosphere was cordial, the wine having put everybody in a good mood. The pianist Van Cliburn then gave a recital in a small room, playing a Brahms intermezzo, some études by Rachmaninoff and various pieces by Schumann, Liszt and Debussy, finishing with "Moscow Nights." A perfect end to a wonderful evening.

Before flying home Gorbachev also gave a dinner at our embassy, inviting the best-known people in America, some of whom came all the way from California and other far-off states for the occasion. In keeping with our tradition, vodka was served. At first some of the guests did not take caviar, which the waiters served with spoons from silver bowls, but they eventually asked for a second sampling; it is possible they may have found it slightly different from the American variety. They liked our black bread, to the point where their waistlines became a secondary consideration. Next came lightly pickled fish: different kinds of smoked salmon and sturgeon, followed by hot meat, mushroom, and crab appetizers. The guests tasted the vodka, and many of them were delighted with its quality. Some, however, perhaps seeking to dispel lingering doubts about its merits, tried more than one glass. There was then a choice of fish soup, clear beet soup, or consommé, followed by trout, hot roast beef, and finally cakes, ice cream, chocolates, wines, champagne, coffee, and brandy.

I was pleased to see that our guests plainly enjoyed our cuisine, although it did occasionally run afoul of their dietary principles. Seating was in the American style, with spouses sitting apart. Only Reagan and Gorbachev, seated on the high table, what we would have called the presidium, sat next to their wives.

Dinner was accompanied by music, including a performance by the famous mezzo-soprano Yelena Obraztsova, who was given a rapturous reception. Everybody sat down with drinks and coffee, engaging in lively and good-humored conversation, and having such a good time that the performers could, at times, scarcely be heard.

Such informal socializing impressed me most favorably. It seemed that relations between our two countries were reaching a watershed, though substantial changes were still a long way off. Festive dinner parties were not, of course, an ideal way of judging such things.

Gorbachev summed up the visit and answered numerous questions in a press conference at the end of our stay in Washington, held in our new embassy. Two hours later the delegation was at the airport. After an uncomfortable night we landed in Berlin, where the heads of state of the Warsaw Pact were briefed on the documents that had been signed with Reagan and on the results of the visit in general.

On the way back home the Gorbachevs normally invited the principal members of their entourage in for a drink—wine, Armenian brandy, and, for those so inclined, whisky. Everyone reminisced about various episodes in the talks. Little alcohol was consumed, however, as some people merely clinked glasses during the toasts. We were all severely under the influence of jet lag on flights back from the United States, and in a much jollier mood when returning from Europe. On these occasions Gorbachev almost unfailingly spoke of the time when he had fought his way to the top, mentioning the names of those who had stood in his way. Some individuals still provoked an allergic reaction in him.

Back at Vnukovo we were met by the same happy, smiling faces that had seen us off; everyone told us how they had watched the whole thing on television and congratulated us on our success. In our country good people are reluctant to upset others by pointing out that they simply do not understand a given decision, or wonder why no agreement had been reached on it. Because of the unlimited power wielded by the men at the top, everyone had learned that obedience and praise were the proper course.

I often wondered why they behaved that way, as they found many of the general secretary's actions questionable and impulsive. Sometimes I was reminded of a story by the writer Aleksandr Yashin in which several Communists from a collective farm had gone to a party meeting and, while waiting for a quorum, talked about the calamitous situation on the farm, where animal feed was in short supply and the grain harvest was poor. They were convinced that if they supplied more than the plan called for, they would be forced to slaughter livestock, thereby weakening the farm's performance the following year. Such frank discussions were perfectly normal among ordinary people, worried by the state of their local economy. Then, however, the meeting started and those same people, speaking from the podium, promptly asserted that production exceeding the requirements of the plan was an honorable duty to the Fatherland, and one that the *kolkhoz** should fulfill by delivering more grain to the state.

Many of us evidently share that paradoxical frame of mind. People often come to their senses only when faced with extreme adversity. Yet I remember similar behavior at the airport, when those in the reception

---

Kollektivnoye khozyaistvo, a collective farm.

party spoke only of the success of the general secretary's foreign travels and how we had managed to solve many issues that had eluded our predecessors for many years.

THE COLLAPSE OF
THE SOCIALIST COUNTRIES

The Gorbachevs also made official visits to the Socialist countries, where they were received by the heads of state and party, old friends of Gorbachev like Yanosh Kadar, Erich Honecker, Voichekh Jaruzelski, Todor Zhivkov and Nicolae Ceausescu, who had been involved with him in party work for many years. I well remember their amicable, trusting relations, frequent phone conversations, and regular exchanges of gifts and best wishes on both official and private occasions. It had always seemed to me that although some of them were not entirely comfortable with the new general secretary, nonetheless, as old friends, they initially supported his policies and did much to enhance his stature in their own countries.

The leaders of our countries were, of course, not alone in their embrace of Gorbachev. Hundreds of thousands of Soviet citizens enjoyed fraternal relations with the people of eastern Europe. We had a single defense alliance, closely interwoven economic relations, and well-established relations between towns and enterprises. Gorbachev's visits to those countries were accordingly well organized and smoothly conducted. Both he and Raisa often talked of the warm, heartfelt welcome they had received in eastern Europe.

"You know something, I've never had a reception like that, anywhere," Gorbachev would say after such a visit. "The whole country turned out; people were ready to pick us up bodily in triumph."

They certainly were; and equally certain was the fact that in his speeches Gorbachev, when referring to the USSR, proposed changes in the entire Socialist commonwealth, even though not everyone in those countries was yet ready for such changes.

During private talks attended by both leaders' spouses while on a trip to Romania, Gorbachev had a very heated and important discussion with Ceausescu, who told him that switching to a new political course was all well and good, but that it needed to be done first in one's own country, that other leaders should at least be kept informed of the purposes of such changes, and that it was wrong to incite other peoples to follow suit. Gorbachev was also reminded that the establishment of Communist regimes in Romania and the GDR had not been the initiative of those countries themselves, but of the Soviet Union, which had needed a post-war buffer between East and West. It was the Soviet Union that had insisted on the need for armies, military bases, and the like, in order to withstand the pressure of the West during the cold war. Gorbachev's answers to these points did little to restore mutual understanding between the two leaders.

Frank exchanges in a similar vein doubtless took place with other eastern European leaders. But at the time the general secretary was riding the crest of a wave of euphoria. Propelled by the situation back home, he proceeded to sow the seeds of changes among his neighbors.

The results were not long in coming. Velvet revolutions occurred in one eastern European country after another, sweeping away parties and all the established power structures. The last one was in the GDR, where the Gorbachevs had been welcomed by vast throngs of demonstrators, and where they effectively helped bring about a situation leading to the country's collapse. Expert analysts have found that the Soviet Union derived no advantages from these changes, and did not even take the trouble to protect Soviet property in that country. The continued division of the German state was clearly difficult to sustain any further, but simply pulling out while neglecting many of our interests was just plain wrong—a point repeatedly emphasized at Politburo meetings. The Soviet public wrote vast numbers of letters inquiring about the terms on which our troops were being withdrawn.

Both Gorbachev and Raisa were really shocked and horrified by the death of Ceausescu and his wife. As we have seen, Gorbachev was already being driven around in an armored-plated ZIL limousine. More-over, security had been considerably tightened and more guards assigned to his protection. Pay for the security personnel was raised, though it is doubtful that this had much effect, as pay raises for his immediate entourage caused resentment among those who performed a vital though inconspicuous role in other services.

Events in the neighboring countries were moving so fast and so chaotically that Gorbachev's friends in the Communist movement soon found themselves in disgrace, out of a job, and, in many cases, awaiting trial. Tragically, though, the general secretary did nothing to help or defend them at the time of their greatest difficulties. His failure to act was profoundly disturbing to many people. The political leaders were not the only ones in an unenviable position: the military, intelligence agents who had performed valuable services for the security of our country, party leaders, ministers, and the directors of large industrial and agricultural enterprises suffered a similar fate. As most of them were sincere friends who had studied in the Soviet Union, betraying them now meant that we were abandoning not only our friends but the principles of decency as well. Neither we nor the United States had ever done this before. The Americans took great risks in order to extricate their friends, but felt it their duty to do so, as they felt nobody would ever cooperate with them again if they did not. Besides being a question of party ethics and morality, this is the morality of common sense.

Why was it that nobody, at virtually any level of the power structure, raised the alarm over the dismantling of the military, political, and economic alliances of the Socialist states?

The main reason was that people in the Soviet Union had long been accustomed to a situation in which their leaders did their thinking for them. It was known even in the Politburo and the government that international affairs were the prerogative of two or three people, and chiefly the general secretary. *Nobody* dared venture into the sphere of international relations, unless invited or instructed by him to work on a given subject.

Apart from that, Gorbachev and the foreign minister had a virtual monopoly over information about the processes taking place in the world at large, particularly in the public mood and the political leadership of the Socialist countries. The situation in this regard was the same as in Stalin's time, and the present general secretary intended it to stay that way. If anything it got worse, as many notes on talks between the general secretary and foreign leaders were not circulated at all. The Foreign Ministry and the Defense Ministry were obliged to forward the most important coded telegrams to a single addressee: Gorbachev. On certain issues telegrams were also forwarded to Ryzhkov, Yakovlev, and sometimes other members of the Politburo, as appropriate. Run-of-the-mill political information, in the form of a review of the international press, was sent to all members of the Politburo and frequently to the nonvoting Politburo members and the secretaries of the Central Committee. This meant that neither the party nor the state leadership was fully informed about events in the former Socialist countries.

As we have seen, both Gorbachev and his wife were thrilled by their trips abroad, from which they would return in a buoyant, ecstatic mood. Their pleasure derived more from contact with the public than from their high-level meetings with government and party dignitaries. I once accompanied the general secretary to Poland, where I could see for myself the warmth of the welcome extended to him by the people, particularly in Szczecin, where he confirmed that the city was and always would be Polish. Raisa, who represented her husband at his request at a meeting with miners, I believe in Katowice, was also given a tumultuous welcome. The Poles were convinced that here was a leader who could help them escape from their harsh living conditions and find a new path to socioeconomic development. At the time, of course, they did not know that what awaited them was a step backward, into a past with which they were only too familiar.

When Gorbachev announced on his return from Berlin in October 1989 that Honecker's days were numbered and that we should start thinking about the reunification of Germany, there were no particularly strong objections. Interest in the subject was so faint that nobody bothered to find out about the terms of German reunification and, consequently, of the withdrawal of our troops. Gorbachev and Shevardnadze made no effort to inform anyone about it, and there was no thorough discussion of it at the meetings of the Politburo. The publication of a long letter by chemist Nina Andreyeva in *Sovietskaya Rossiya* in March 1988 viciously attacking Gorbachev's policies, on the other hand, was debated for two whole days. International affairs had long been firmly in the hands of Gorbachev, Shevardnadze, and Yakovlev, although the latter was largely precluded from making decisions. When disarmament documents had to be prepared, experts were brought in from the Foreign Ministry and the Defense Ministry. The Supreme Soviet and its commissions knew little about the substance of proposed agreements, and the handling of important decisions sometimes seemed more like rubber-stamping than a thorough and critical consideration by the deputies.

The monopoly on information and power, and the absence of democratic principles in the work of the general secretary and the Politburo, meant that all the changes in the former Socialist countries took place quietly and imperceptibly, with no clashes of opposing views and no impassioned political debate. Being in charge of the Politburo, Gorbachev decided state policy as he saw fit, to such an extent that the national interests were often overlooked, becoming little more than a vehicle for the high-stakes game playing of the leaders.

The Soviet public naturally understood that a divided Germany was not entirely conducive to peace in Europe, and that sooner or later the question would have to be tackled head-on. There was time for thought, as our former allies in the anti-Hitler coalition were in no hurry, while some of them, while not actually opposed, had grave doubts about the need for such haste. Yet even if, as Gorbachev contended, the time had come to act, it should have been done after thoroughly taking account of public opinion throughout the country. The Foreign Ministry, the Politburo, and the president were not morally entitled to resolve this problem behind closed doors, especially as the terms for reunification and for the withdrawal of troops had not been properly drawn up and were not based on consultations with our former anti-Fascist allies.

The major changes in the countries of the former Socialist commonwealth were never discussed in any forums whatsoever, large or small. As far as I recall no serious attempt was made to raise the matter in the Politburo, the Presidential Council, or the congresses and the conference of the Communist party. There was no corresponding item on the agenda of the Supreme Soviet. The fact that the general secretary's report to the Twenty-eighth Party Congress contained only two or three paragraphs on the subject demonstrates the absence of any serious opposition, shortly before the congress, to our policy toward the former Socialist countries. As Gorbachev remarked during the congress, all the criticism consisted of nothing more than reproaches: "We're being reproached for leaving without a fight."

Each time Gorbachev returned from a foreign trip he would brief the official welcome party at the airport on various impressions he had gathered, but he did not really present anything like a balance sheet. Even the Supreme Soviet, as the delegates complained, knew little about the nature of his talks with foreign leaders and the agreements that had been reached.

In later years foreign travel and the reception of Western leaders in Moscow made up the bulk of the president's work. Western public opinion saw in Gorbachev a new breed of man, not wedded to the dogmas of his predecessors, outwardly open-minded, and, when necessary, charming. Sensing that he was working toward peace and the destruction of the previous totalitarian system, people supported him wholeheartedly. Before long, Gorbachev had become an idol in the West. He was constantly being given monetary awards and gold medals, named Man of the Year, and featured on television and in newspaper and magazine articles, all of which subtly played on his vanity. Westerners did not realize that it was easier to criticize the past and demolish existing structures than to create anything new. They could not understand why Soviets were so ill disposed toward the general secretary, and why, after he had begun to do such commendable things, he found himself the target of a barrage of criticism in his own country.

That criticism, of course, was not gratuitous. Since 1987 the country's financial and economic situation had deteriorated sharply. The Soviet public knew this all too well, as they faced increasingly severe shortages of sugar, meat, and many other foodstuffs. Many consumer goods had simply disappeared from the stores. Tensions were rising throughout the country, as many people began to question the wisdom of perestroika and the ability of their leaders to find a way out of the crisis. Senior officials in the party organizations and committees began to show signs of disagreement and even profound disenchantment with the general secretary.

5

GLASNOST: A TURN TOWARD DEMOCRATIC REFORMS

It is hardly surprising that Gorbachev knew of the new mood of the Soviet people. Their former idol now stood increasingly alone, as those once inclined to heap lavish praise on him now cursed his very name. The people's love turned out to be fickle, indeed. From this point on, a dispirited general secretary found himself battling not only conservative forces but the ordinary people, whose loyalty was a thing of the past.

He and I frequently talked about this. As he scanned the mail, and particularly negative letters, Gorbachev consoled himself with the thought that these could be viewed as confirmation of the merit of his chosen course: "You can't make real changes without treading on someone's toes, somewhere in society. It's nothing—it's really not so bad. I'll show the letters to everyone. Circulate them among the members of the Politburo," he would say.

Plans for domestic travel were nonetheless reduced. There were periods when he spent more time abroad than inside the Soviet Union. He received ever more frequent briefings on current events from the statistical organs, the KGB, the departments of the Central Committee, and conversations and meetings with people's deputies during the sessions and congresses of the Supreme Soviet. The state of the country began to be discussed at meetings of the Politburo, where members pointed out that decisions of the party congress were not being implemented and action on even the easier issues was at a standstill. There were demands for tougher discipline and greater control and accountability where deci-

sions of the congress were concerned. It became common to hear proposals for measures that would have been meaningful some three or five
years earlier. The qualitative shift that had occurred in the mood of the
party and the whole society was so substantial that the need for tough
measures to enforce strict discipline was no longer taken very seriously;
yet few people realized that this was the case.

Officials from the party, industry, and agriculture tended less and less
to take any notice of the authority of the Politburo, the Central Committee secretariat, and the Council of Ministers. The General Department of the Central Committee was supposed to monitor not only the
progress of documents but the implementation of decisions. More and
more, I was told that Politburo decisions were not being carried out on
time; sometimes bureaucratic formality and even outright lies would take
the place of a proper report on action taken pursuant to those decisions.
I frequently had occasion to report on my findings to Gorbachev and the
Politburo, but the general secretary was quite unperturbed. Whereas he
had originally circulated the information received from the General
Department in the Politburo, now he could find time for no more than a
glance at the memorandum. Everyone was aware of the general secretary's attitude; it soon became evident that monitoring the implementation of decisions was simply pointless. Documents were ignored. Eventually they became so vague and so full of exalted abstractions that no
one saw any point in monitoring their implementation at all.

The weakening of authority at the highest levels of the Communist
party opened the fissure that later led to the collapse of all its governing
structures. Portentous speeches were still being made, and many decisions adopted, but people now realized that the new leader and the Politburo were no longer in control and could not impose the kind of
accountability the situation demanded. Many people saw the need for a
new way to stir the masses, account for failures, and involve everybody in
the solution of economic problems. Yet the alienation that now existed
between the general secretary and the executive organs was insurmount-
able.

Gorbachev avoided meetings with members of the Central Committee apparatus and the Council of Ministers, to whom he referred in
highly disparaging terms. Whenever he wanted to voice his displeasure
with a particular person, for example, he would say: "There's another
apparatchik." Coming from a man who had spent his entire life working
in the apparatus of the Komsomol and party, such reproaches sounded

strange indeed. Unlike him, the members of the Central Committee apparatus had previously worked in industry, construction, collective and state farms, research institutes, or the media. They knew a hundred times more than the general secretary, the top-ranking apparatchik, about people's working lives. Even so, he used the apparatus skillfully and to good effect, compelling its staff to prepare analytical documents and monitor the implementation of decisions. Inwardly, however, he remained hostile. He was fond of recalling how, when he was already a member of the Central Committee, and a *kraikom* secretary, he had been obliged to sit in the offices of the instructors and the section heads and listen to their advice and, from time to time, their moralizing. The fact that he had had to submit to such an indignity, at the hands of an instructor, filled him with rage. Throughout the whole of his tenure as general secretary, he was never willing to address the Central Committee apparatus, in which there were many educated and highly qualified experts, though he several times sent word to the Communists of his intention to speak at the general party meeting of the Central Committee apparatus.

Toward the end of January 1987, at a plenum of the Central Committee, Gorbachev delivered a report entitled "Perestroika and the Party's Personnel Policy." Its purpose was to reemphasize the heritage that had been passed down to Gorbachev in all spheres of society. He began by criticizing the ideological organs and those academic experts who had wound up in a theoretical dead end in politics, philosophy, and political economy, continuing to repeat the basic tenets of the 1930s and 1940s. Sociologists, he noted, had failed to offer a constructive analysis of the state of affairs in the country or to propose new ways out of the country's difficulties. The planning organs and the machine-building sector came in for some sharp criticism, as did those responsible for providing moral and material incentives.

The main focus of his remarks was the democratization of society, as the one vital prerequisite for progress, and the problems it posed. Targets were set for the expansion of glasnost, criticism, and self-criticism, the use of democratization in industry and agriculture, and worker participation in management. The report also suggested other major ways of using democratic principles in the development of society. The Central Committee members endorsed the basic proposals in the report, broadening the notion of democratization under perestroika. This was an achievement for which Gorbachev, the Politburo, and the plenum deserve credit.

January 1987 saw the beginning of a new phase in the struggle to extend democratic principles into all sectors of society. Many people understood this broadening of democracy not as a means of enhancing productivity but as a weapon in the fight to uphold personal and social freedoms. Glasnost went to people's heads. It was now possible to release pent-up thoughts that long years of enforced silence had suppressed, without caring about who heard them, and to criticize anyone, including those who had previously been feared. The wind of freedom swept across the country, as people did whatever they pleased. Their boldness astonished even the radicals of Western democracy. There was certainly plenty of opportunity for such expressions of opinion: the party itself had opened the door to unlimited glasnost by criticizing itself and its past and present errors.

Glasnost, as we have seen, frequently ran into serious obstacles, some of which were caused by objective factors such as the cavalier attitude of the media to the factual accuracy of published material and the deliberate distortion of events. But there were other reasons, too. Hardly anyone liked criticism. All of this was evident to Yakovlev, since he as head of the party's Ideological Department had to deal directly with all the consequences of freedom of the press. Discussions of these issues had convinced him of the need for both broad democratization and a press law. He persuaded the general secretary, who had gradually come to understand the need for democratic reforms, to support his position. Thereafter Gorbachev discussed the matter more frequently. He would invite some of his associates around, after the tensions of the day's meetings had subsided, to review current events and talk about the ineptitude of certain Central Committee members and the inadequacies of the Union and republican Supreme Soviets, the local councils of people's deputies, and other governing bodies. Democratization required changes in their structure and activities.

As the seventieth anniversary of the October Revolution approached, a comprehensive report had to be prepared for the occasion. Some of the speechwriters assigned to the task suggested that it should contain extensive coverage of those impending democratic changes. After some hesitation, Gorbachev agreed. Then began the long and intensive job of drafting texts on the principal tenets of democratization and the improvement of the political system. In the jubilee report democratization was assigned a cardinal role in the development of society and subjected to unprecedented analysis.

Such difficult problems could not be tackled without the firm backing of the members of the Central Committee, the Secretariat, the Politburo, and the secretaries of party committees. But was Gorbachev confident that these innovations would have such support? The speeches, replies, and talks he held on the subject seemed to suggest that he was not.

Only a few months after the Twenty-seventh Party Congress, he found to his regret that the changes in the membership of the Central Committee had been insignificant. Then, when drawing up lists of the participants in the Central Committee plenum, he was guided by the need for continuity of policy and for quiet evolutionary change. At this point he felt the old guard had him bound hand and foot.

This was no mere impression. It was widely felt that it would be dangerous to embark on democratization in a crumbling economy, as it could only hasten economic collapse and incite separatist sentiment in certain segments of the population, both in the constituent republics of the USSR and in the autonomous republics of the RSFSR. By now, however, the general secretary was more inclined to interpret expressions of alarm over the methods and pace of democratization as threats to his own authority. This in turn made it necessary for him to crush dissent in the Central Committee. Documents prepared for the Twenty-seventh Party Congress contained provisions allowing for the holding of party conferences. He now sought to use those provisions to overhaul the composition of the Central Committee.

"You can tell that these people are over the hill, they're dead wood," he would say. "They can't even understand which way to steer the party in today's circumstances, and how we should be working. Mark my word: the party's being criticized mainly because the people carrying out perestroika are the same ones who were in charge during the period of stagnation."

To a large extent he was right. The presence in the Central Committee of so many old-timers—many of whom, however, were progressive and talented—was increasingly criticized in the press and at formal meetings. The wholesale dismissal of all those elected by the congress was unwarranted, especially when one considers that Gorbachev himself was an old-timer. Yet he kept looking for a way to rid himself of undesirables.

At the time the Central Committee included many of his associates who had helped him become established and had supported and acted on his initiatives. Now they seemed to him not only unnecessary but an actual impediment, a liability; so he decided to persuade some of the members of the plenum to quit the Central Committee of their own free will and to announce their decision publicly. This was not an easy move, and Gorbachev laid the groundwork for it most thoroughly.

He began by ordering the staff of the party's organization section to draw up lists of those who were on a pension or were very old. He then sat at his table examining them carefully. Razumovski took it upon himself to negotiate with various comrades with a view to securing their voluntary departure, arranging for them to help persuade any waverers. It was all done so smoothly that when the *komikadze*—the Central Committee members volunteering to quit for the sake of party unity—assembled in the Secretariat conference room, there was no problem at all. They even began to justify the reasons for their resignations.

Gorbachev addressed the meeting, speaking at length about the needs of the moment and arguing in favor of an overhaul of Central Committee membership. With the exception of Y. E. Slavski, the minister in charge of the nuclear industry, who was unwilling to attend the meeting, he managed to talk everybody into accepting the decision he needed. Later on, he was embarrassed by what he had done. He realized that he had expelled his own associates, who, despite their years, had always supported him, even in the most adverse circumstances.

His move backfired, however, when the new members who replaced them proved to be intransigent and critical of him. I felt he regretted his decision. He once said: "Well, we got our replacements all right, I tell you. Another bunch like that, and the Central Committee will be out of control."

Two meetings were held, as it was felt necessary to proceed in two stages: a first group, whose willingness to quit was not in doubt, and a second, which was expected to cause trouble. But everything went off without a hitch. All of them, being accustomed to party discipline, unanimously volunteered to leave the Central Committee and signed a collective message to the Politburo and the plenum of the Central Committee to that effect. There was no precedent for such a mass collective action in the history of the Soviet Communist party or, for that matter, in other parties as far as I know.

Addressing that meeting of the Central Committee, in the presence of many former ministers, Gorbachev promised that their social benefits would remain unchanged, so that the pensions, medical care, and everything else needed to maintain their living standards would be preserved. Unfortunately it was not long before these people, who had given long years of service to the state and endured the hardship of war, accumulating debts rather than assets in the process, found themselves evicted from their dachas and deprived of much more besides.

The general secretary's inability to keep his word disturbed many members of his team, not only because it weakened his authority but also because it suggested an unwillingness to help his associates once he deemed them unnecessary. I drew his attention to this aspect, and did all I could to rectify the situation, but to no avail. He lost interest in people once they ceased to be necessary. Gorbachev's secretaries simply erased those names from the lists of those to whom greetings were to be sent on special occasions, while they also apparently vanished from Gorbachev's memory. It amazed me that a man of such high rank could so effortlessly switch images and opinions and disown associates as soon as they came under fire. Yet astonishingly, if such a person ever rose again or acquired a new post, he would forget his former hostility and ask me to send greetings to him.

He also bore a grudge against anyone who had ever contradicted him or argued his own case, let alone those who had, deliberately or otherwise, offended or humiliated him. Such individuals found their paths blocked. This is what happened to someone I'll call VVK, a talented young economist well versed in agricultural matters, who had shared a state prize at the age of twenty-five with Academician Nesmeyanov for studies on the use of cybernetics and mathematics in the economy. VVK, who worked in the Compilation Department of Gosplan, was once invited to meet Gorbachev at a time when the latter was still engaged in the agricultural sector. Gorbachev was one of the many speakers addressing the meeting and boasted of the enormous role of agriculture in the Soviet economy and the high proportion of peasants employed in the economy. He expressed his delight with the high proportion of the national income attributable to agriculture. The next speaker was VVK. Among other things, he pointed out that there was no particular reason to boast of the large proportion of peasants employed in the economy and the prominence of agriculture, as both were evidence of distortion and underdevelopment, as well as the agrarian character of the economy.

He saw a need for industry to become dominant, and for agriculture to employ not 20 percent but 5 to 7 percent of the population, as was the case in most developed countries.

Gorbachev, feeling that his grasp of economics was being depicted as less than adequate, flew into a rage. He let loose a barrage of ferocious criticism, never forgave VVK for his remarks, and effectively blocked his career. But when Tikhonov, chairman of the Council of Ministers, appointed VVK as head of one of the all-union committees, he suddenly began to be solicitous and had me send him greetings. On rising to the position of general secretary, however, he again turned on VVK, requesting the inclusion in the Politburo's agenda of an item on the work of his committee and then subjecting him to a veritable character assassination. Later on the general secretary saw to it that he was denied promotions. When V. P. Mozhin, one of the senior members of the Central Committee's Economic Department, offered VVK a job, Gorbachev moved to stop him. All my attempts to intercede on behalf of a talented man, whose sole fault was that he had told the truth and shown his superb grasp of economics, ran into a solid wall of bitter hatred.

Gradually Gorbachev discarded what he called "deadwood" in the Central Committee and replenished its ranks with active supporters of perestroika. One immediate effect was that it became easier to move around the plenum conference room, since the ranks of the veterans had been much thinned out. But did such a weeding-out process in the Central Committee satisfy the critics? Not significantly, I suggest. If anything, it sharpened the appetite of the general secretary's opponents and prompted them to step up their demands.

Quite frankly, my knowledge of the inner workings of the decision-making process suggests that the depth and progressive character of decisions did not depend on the size and composition of the Central Committee. It is my considered opinion that if the objectives of perestroika and the need for new methods had been cogently explained to them, the members of the Central Committee would have voted unanimously in their favor. They would have done so, first, because they were experienced managers from industry and agriculture and party workers who had long known what was wrong with the development of the USSR, and, second, because their trust in the Politburo was so great as to preclude doubt about the projects put before them. Eventually the election of young party workers to the Central Committee did not make it more loyal and obedient, as some of the newcomers criticized Gorbachev's plans and were not afraid to oppose the ones he proposed to the party and the country.

Having castigated the apparatus of party, Soviet, and economic organs for exceeding their powers and for their dictatorial treatment of representatives elected by the party and the people, and also having rid themselves of the oldest members of the Central Committee, Gorbachev and the Politburo now began to broaden the democratic foundations of the work of the party, state, and organizations and to advocate fuller freedom of dissent. The Soviet constitution was amended to abolish the Communist party's monopoly over power. Of course, this happened in response to massive pressure from the people's deputies and the public at large. A press law greatly extending glasnost was adopted. All of this led to radical changes in the traditional methods of government and expanded opportunities for economic development based on new principles.

The most substantial and far-reaching decisions on the need for democratization and political reform were adopted at the Nineteenth Party Conference, in June 1988. The general secretary's report was permeated by ideas such as the broader participation of the people in government, greater freedom for the development of each national group, the strengthening of socialist legality and law and order, and the demarcation of the functions of party and state organs.

WHO'S IN CHARGE?

So who was really in charge of twenty million Communists and a state with two hundred million inhabitants?

For almost seven decades this function had been performed essentially by the Secretariat and the Politburo of the Central Committee. They defined domestic and foreign policy and, through the Council of Ministers and its organs of local government, ran the economy and controlled the ideological side of society. They also contributed to the Soviet Union's rise to great power status and to the sometimes tragic mistakes from whose consequences the Soviet people are still suffering.

Tuesday is traditionally the day when the Central Committee Secretariat holds its weekly meetings. At 4:00 in the afternoon the Central Committee secretaries and the heads of departments and of the party's

Ideological Department meet to resolve issues influencing not only the party but the whole of society.

In theory the duties of the Secretariat include current issues affecting the work of party organizations and committees, the work of the ideological organs, the implementation of instructions from the Politburo and the Central Committee plenums, and monitoring the implementation of their decisions. However, the Secretariat frequently went beyond its official terms of reference and supplanted the Politburo and the Council of Ministers. In a formal sense there was some justification for this, as the party organizations operated throughout society. They were present in industry, both collective and state farms, the armed forces, the militia, the KGB, the media, theaters, and museums. The Central Committee Secretariat often generated agenda items having to do with the activities of party organizations in the railroads, construction sites, and oilfields.

The consideration of items at the meetings of the Central Committee Secretariat also depended on the preferences of the Secretariat heads. Andropov gravitated toward problems of the administrative organs and international affairs, while Chernenko emphasized ideology and Gorbachev agriculture, the economy in general, and youth. The Secretariat's investigation of the activities of Sputnik, the international youth organization, was widely publicized. The abuses discovered caused a severe shake-up among senior officials of the Komsomol, some of whom lost their jobs.

With an agenda that went far beyond the scope of party and Komsomol organizations, Secretariat meetings were tantamount to a second Council of Ministers, more authoritative, powerful, and tough than the real thing.

The fact that the Secretariat discussed socioeconomic problems naturally provoked resentment on the part of the Council of Ministers. For instance, as soon as Tikhonov learned that a given item was being readied for discussion in the Central Committee, he would hastily convene a meeting of the presidium of the Council of Ministers and take certain steps. Ryzhkov often complained to Gorbachev about encroachments on his sphere of activity.

All of this, however, came later. Before 1985, when Gorbachev was in charge of the Secretariat, there were difficulties of another kind. Chernenko and his aides had the last say on the agendas for meetings. Many items that had been prepared at the meeting were not circulated, and therefore could not be brought before the Central Committee secretaries for discussion. For this reason, despite Gorbachev's best efforts, he performed his role within a certain framework that had been established for him. It often happened that the Central Committee Secretariat placed on its agenda and made decisions on more important issues than the Politburo. Of course, Gorbachev was motivated by the gravity of the issues at hand, but also to a significant extent by a desire to show the party and the Central Committee apparatus that he could rise to the height of the No. 1 man in the party, whose purview included every single issue of concern to society. Moreover, Gorbachev's ability to resolve issues far exceeded that of Chernenko.

Under Gorbachev, the Central Committee Secretariat, in contrast to previous custom, used to meet for several hours. Practically anyone wishing to take the floor could speak. Large numbers of people attended these meetings. The first item to be dealt with was usually personnel questions, such as the appointment of cadres of the Central Committee Secretariat nomenklatura—the first secretaries of *obkoms* and *kraikoms*, the editors of newspaper, magazine, and other ideological organs. The appointment of members of the nomenklatura, particularly the *obkom* secretaries, was discussed extensively. Candidates were nominated by the party Organization Department of the Central Committee. The situation in each *oblast* and *krai* was described in great detail; the reasons for failure were explored and ways of remedying the situation were suggested. Newly appointed officials were given every possible support at the beginning of their tenure; resources were assigned to aid the *oblast*, and everything possible was done to ensure that the candidate should receive the support of the party organization and earn the respect of Communists and the entire population of the *oblast*, *krai*, or republic.

In some instances the Central Committee Secretariat concluded, after considering the issues and the situation in a given *oblast* or *krai*, that the time had come for a change of the leadership there. The Central Committee secretaries discussed such matters behind closed doors, before referring them to the general secretary for a decision. The *obkom* or *kraikom* secretary was then summoned to the Central Committee and invited to tender his resignation. Provided he was not too decrepit and was only partly to blame for the failures in question, he might be sent to work in some ministry or other or to an embassy abroad, perhaps even being appointed ambassador somewhere in Africa or southern Asia.

The Central Committee apparatus devoted much attention to the deployment of Communist cadres to key posts throughout the country. In fact there was practically no meeting of the Central Committee Secretariat that did not consider these questions. In a single day, between thirty and fifty new officials could be voted into their new posts. Many attempts were made to reduce the number of posts belonging to the nomenklatura, as well as the size of the governing apparatus, though the final result in both instances was an increase. A story is told about Anastas Mikoyan, who held high government office without interruption from Lenin to Brezhnev, who is said to have managed "to last from one Ilich to the other without heart attacks or paralysis": *(On trudilsa ot Ilicha do Ilicha Bez infarkta i paralicha)*.

He once likened bureaucratic growth to crows on the branches of a tree: when you alarm them, they fly off in all directions; but if you look up a few minutes later, you find that they are back and in even greater numbers. This is what happens with attempts to curb the growth of the governing apparatus.

Some progress was made, after repeated efforts, but the reductions in the size of the nomenklatura were quite modest. When the Secretariat concluded that a change of leadership was in order, a new candidate for the post of first secretary would soon appear at a meeting. The appointment and removal of cadres was a powerful lever with which to influence the situation in any *oblast* and *krai*. The extremely grave consequences of failure to carry out Secretariat decisions had a deterrent effect in maintaining discipline and order.

While almost all Secretariat meetings started with a discussion of personnel issues, they ended in quite different ways. It often happened that a number of items were removed from the agenda and discussed in the presence of only the Central Committee secretaries, with perhaps one or two departmental heads. This part of the meeting dealt with certain particularly delicate questions such as the conduct of Central Committee members, heads of *obkoms* or *kraikoms*, breaches of internal party ethics, and abuse of privilege. Excessive entertaining or irregularities in the apportionment of apartments were among the most common items of this sort. The decisions made after such deliberations were often drastic, although in earlier times they had been given scant publicity.

The most complex and substantive matters considered at Secretariat meetings, primarily those within the purview of the Council of Ministers and other government bodies, were later forwarded to the Politburo, where a final decision was reached.

The chairmen of Secretariat meetings varied in their style and working methods. Gorbachev conducted the proceedings briskly, though he tended to waver when difficulties arose, often retreating and adopting a decision that had no binding effect at all. Some time before his election to the post of general secretary, someone raised the idea of allotting land to city dwellers, especially in areas whose inhabitants had moved elsewhere. I wrote a memorandum and handed it to Gorbachev. Our analysis had shown how many people nationwide were eager to tend orchards and vegetable gardens and how many vacant plots and villages existed. It clearly demonstrated the merits of allotting land. Other speakers made the same point. Gorbachev, in the heat of the debate, said: "This certainly needs to be done. People should have a chance to work on the land. There's no shortage of land, is there? In fact, it's getting overgrown with trees, and not being put to use."

The next speaker, however, was the representative of the Central Committee's Agrarian Department, who pointed out that it was not quite that easy: the farm directors would object. He argued that as a result of the proposal, city dwellers would go into the countryside and relax in their hammocks, while the peasants would toil away in the fields on both Saturday and Sunday from dawn to dusk. Farming would suffer. The future of the collective and state farms had to be considered. Eventually the time came to make a decision. By now Gorbachev's tone was milder, his voice and words more hesitant. He was prey to conflicting emotions. What if publicly owned farming were to be destroyed? And another thing: Andropov was against the building of dachas. On the other hand, the city dwellers need to be placated. Then came the final decision: "Wherever possible, land should be allotted," said Gorbachev, "but we must not harm the interests of the farms and overlook the morale of those who till the soil."

These remarks were pure, vintage Gorbachev. As a result of this compromise the matter was left dangling in midair, as if it had never been discussed. Needless to say, nothing was done. Unfortunately, in those days there were plenty of such half-baked, hesitant decisions. Later on their number increased.

When Ligachev began to preside over meetings, his personality made its mark on the proceedings. He was fond of railroading items through the Secretariat, using all available means to secure his goals, sometimes riding roughshod over the members in the process.

Gorbachev jealously monitored Ligachev's performance. He was anxious to know how the Secretariat meetings were going, what was being discussed, and what decisions were being made. He would often delete one or more proposed agenda items, claiming that the Politburo was the proper place for them to be discussed. However, they were also kept off the Politburo agenda. There was the usual, perfectly human petty squabbling, as Gorbachev sought to prevent encroachments on his turf and to remind everybody that he was very much in charge.

The impulsive, outspoken Ligachev committed many excesses. Finding that Razumovski was bypassing him in the selection of cadres, he began to apply tremendous pressure, often calling him into his office, where he would grill him relentlessly about impending personnel changes and insist on being told why he had not received timely notification. Razumovski often complained about the gulf of incomprehension that separated him and Ligachev. Yet it is hard to see what else he could have done, since Gorbachev's instructions were that personnel matters should be reported to him alone. Tension among the secretaries soon led to a calamitous episode, followed by additional severe turbulence later on.

Relations between Ligachev and Yakovlev, as we have seen, were increasingly strained. It was not long before they reached the breaking point, due to differences over the activities of the media. Yakovlev's support of liberal publications such as *Ogonyok*, *Moskovskiye Novosti*, and a number of literary journals was matched by his hostility toward *Nash Sovremmenik*, *Molodaya Gvardiya*, and other conservative publications. These differences led to the use of different working methods and weakened control of the ideological sector. Both men reported on this state of affairs to Gorbachev, who seemed, however, quite unperturbed. His life was easier when his associates were at each other's throats, thereby weakening each other. This may have been done deliberately or may have resulted from his lack of guile; it is hard to say.

The nasty part came when the conflict spilled over into the Politburo, where Yakovlev found himself under fire at every single meeting. Ligachev or Ryzhkov would lead the attack by referring to certain press articles; then came a barrage of criticism from many quarters, drawing attention to the impotence of those in charge of the Ideological Department. After the liberal *Moskovskiye Novosti* and *Ogonyok* published articles directly or indirectly critical of Gorbachev, Yakovlev was doomed. The general secretary, seeing that the majority of Politburo and Central Committee members opposed the position taken by Yakovlev, began to seek a replacement. Now that he no longer enjoyed support and trust,

Yakovlev himself felt the time had come to move to some other field. He used to say: "Let's face it, I have never been given a single job where I could be my own boss. Why is that? Let Ligachev handle agriculture, where things are pretty bad. Why do they have to put two bears in the same ideological den?" Even in international affairs, where Gorbachev shifted him next, he found himself under Shevardnadze's thumb.

Yakovlev was unquestionably proud and influential; time and time again, practically every speech Gorbachev made would float one or more of his ideas. Yet his relations with the general secretary were not always smooth. Gorbachev always found ways of cramping Yakovlev's capacity for initiative. He employed similar methods with almost all his subordinates, rarely allowing them to act independently, except in the case of some unpopular action.

Yakovlev could not understand why he was never allowed to address the solemn meetings in honor of Lenin's birthday and on the eve of the Great October holiday, and he asked me to intercede on his behalf. This was something he had always wanted to do. When I reminded Gorbachev, as I often did, of who had spoken at such events and who had not, suggesting that Yakovlev's turn had now come, he would say nothing for a while and then remark that it was still too early. Yakovlev never did get a chance to speak.

The only possible explanation is that Gorbachev did not want Yakovlev to deliver an address whose ideas and format might overshadow Gorbachev's own effort. Yakovlev and I also concluded that there might be another explanation: on assuming the post of general secretary, Gorbachev had invited him to serve as an aide, but Yakovlev had refused. That, I suspect, is the kind of thing that Gorbachev never forgave. No matter what field he was working in, Yakovlev thereafter found himself confined to the role of speechwriter, supplier of ideas, aide, or adviser; his status as such was eventually recognized when, after the disbanding of the Presidential Council, he was appointed as a senior adviser to Gorbachev.

Throughout this period the atmosphere in the Secretariat remained tense, especially because the Central Committee secretaries could see that their decisions no longer carried their former weight. Documents were being adopted that they could not—or would not—implement. The Secretariat, once a powerful, influential organ, had turned into a debating society. Ivashko, who was elected deputy general secretary of the Central Committee Secretariat and was in charge of the work of the

Secretariat, was unable to rectify the situation, as a number of crucial links had been removed from the once solid chain of party influence. The entire many-layered structure began to sag, on its way to eventual collapse. The party could not influence economic affairs as it once had, while the media, as a consequence of glasnost, were now beyond its control altogether. The advent of competitive elections had eliminated any chance of directing personnel policy. Time after time, the Secretariat would appoint one man as *obkom* secretary only to find that the Communists, at their conferences and plenums, had elected someone else. Seeing what was happening, local officials throughout the country carried out Secretariat decisions merely as a matter of tradition, out of respect for what had once been a mighty and influential organ of the Communist party.

THE MAIN ARENA FOR
POLITICAL INTRIGUE

The Central Committee Secretariat dealt primarily with the party's organizational and ideological affairs, although its purview had also been extended to cover many economic issues that had been the concern of party committees. The main political organ of the Communist party and the entire USSR, however, their nerve center and brain, was the Central Committee's Politburo, which handled all substantive questions of domestic and foreign policy. It was Politburo decisions that sent troops into Hungary, Czechoslovakia, and Afghanistan and approved proposals concerning frontier demarcation and disarmament, space flights, the development of the virgin lands, the construction of the Baikal-Amur Railroad, price rises and price cuts, monetary emission, the sale of precious metals and precious stones, and much more.

The membership of the Politburo traditionally included the most highly placed leaders of the party and the state, and authoritative figures from the field of international affairs. The members of this areopagus of wise men had in the past tended to be fairly old, at times nearly ancient. This select group of men made everybody very nervous and commanded respect and interest both at home and abroad.

The size and composition of the Politburo were not always the same. At various times, for example, its members did not include the minister of foreign affairs or defense, the chief of the KGB and Gosplan, or the republican leaders. Over the past two decades the number of members had hovered around eleven or twelve. After the Twenty-seventh Party Congress twelve members and seven candidate (nonvoting) members were elected. Its membership included Gorbachev, G. A. Aliyev, V. I. Vorotnikov, Gromyko, Zaikov, Dinmukhamed Kunayev, Ligachev, Ryzhkov, Solomentsev, Victor Chebrikov, Shevardnadze, and Shcherbitsky, as well as candidate members Pyotr Demichev, Vladimir Dolgikh, Yeltsin, Slyunkov, Yuri Solovyov, and Talyzin. The elected membership changed between congresses, depending on a variety of circumstances, both domestic and international.

There was no precedent for the membership of the Politburo after the Twenty-eighth Party Congress in July 1990. Besides a number of Central Committee secretaries and heads of economic organs, it also included the first secretaries of the Communist parties of the republics, most of whom were also the presidents of those republics.

The Politburo traditionally held its meetings on Thursdays mornings. For about half an hour before the meeting convened, the militia cleared Kuibyshev Street of all traffic. The ponderous ZIL limousines, with a security escort, then carried their important passengers, who held the country's fate in their hands, from the Central Committee building to the Kremlin.

Meetings were usually held on the third floor of the government building, over the office once used by Stalin. The general secretary's Kremlin office, a gloomy, cavernous, and uncomfortable place, was located on the same floor. It was roughly forty feet long and twenty feet wide, with windows along its length; its shape was determined by the presence of a load-bearing wall dividing it from the corridor. Behind the office was a lounge, though it is hard to imagine anyone lounging restfully in there; Gorbachev admitted that he never went in there to relax, even when he was not feeling well. The general secretary's office had recently been renovated and refurbished with new Italian furniture. There was a handsome desk made of dark cherry wood, with a massive top and a solid wraparound base. Anyone sitting in either of the two adjacent leather armchairs and gazing up at the general secretary inescapably felt very small. On the side closer to the door was a conference room capable of seating only six people. In one corner was a low table with easy chairs, where Gorbachev was fond of taking his coffee. A small bookcase stood at one end of the room. The floor was covered with beautiful carpets, and huge crystal chandeliers illuminated the office and its domed ceiling.

One entered the office through the reception area, past Gorbachev's personal secretaries and bodyguards. The reception area was cramped, dark, and gloomy, like the rest of the building. It also led into the Walnut Room, so named after the color of its wood paneling. Here the members and candidate members of the Politburo and the Central Committee secretaries used to assemble before the start of their meetings. No one else was allowed in. The Walnut Room was where all confidential issues were discussed—that is, everything that only the tiny group of men at the pinnacle of power needed to know. From there the Politburo members would proceed through yet another door into the conference room, often having already made up their minds on a number of issues discussed in the Walnut Room.

Most issues, however, were discussed in the Politburo conference room. It could seat eighty people, though not with ease. In the middle of the room was a large table covered with green cloth, perpendicular to the chairman's table, on which stood an inkstand, a clock, a bell, and the control panel for a series of maps hidden in a special wall. The seating arrangements were based strictly on status and seniority.

To the right of Gorbachev sat Ligachev, in the seat permanently occupied by the No. 2 man in the party—a seat that Gorbachev himself had once fought so long to achieve. Facing Ligachev was Ryzhkov; then, in the following order, came Gromyko, as chairman of the presidium of the Supreme Soviet and the oldest member of the Politburo, followed by Solomentsev, Shevardnadze, Slyunkov, and Yazov. Beyond them were Yakovlev, Medvedev, Kryuchkov, and, after them, in a similar order, the candidate members and the Central Committee secretaries. Members of the government, when invited, sat behind these. Everyone knew his place, and it would never have occurred to any of them to sit, as it were inadvertently, in someone else's seat. The head of the General Department and his first deputy sat at a table to the left of Gorbachev, where they kept a record of the proceedings and determined the order in which participants would be invited to attend.

The chairs along the wall and the window were usually occupied by aides to the general secretary and those who had a standing invitation to these meetings: the head of the Ideological Department, the chief editor of *Pravda* and the first deputy head of the party's Organizational Department.

Finally there was a small reception area, beyond the conference room, where invited participants waited until their particular agenda item came up for discussion. Many of them found this an uncomfortable place to wait, so they strolled up and down the corridor.

Preparations for Politburo meetings started with the drafting of the agenda. Gorbachev received a list of the documents that he had previously circulated among members. These originated in the Council of Ministers, of either the Union or the Russian Federation, the Foreign Ministry, the Ministry of Defense, or other government bodies, and required a decision by the Politburo. The members of the Politburo then examined these documents; their aides assessed them from the standpoint of political expediency and the interests of the government department concerned. Such a thorough scrutiny enabled the Politburo to judge the merits of each issue objectively and in depth. Written comments were submitted on many of the draft proposals, and additions and amendments were included. As each question was analyzed in great detail, the Politburo was able to make well-founded decisions.

The agenda usually contained one or two major issues requiring extensive examination, plus a number of small matters that often never came up for discussion at all; instead, the members of the Politburo, having read the drafts, would just agree to them without further ado. For major items, those sponsoring the draft proposals were usually given from ten to fifteen minutes to make an introductory statement, depending on the complexity of the item in question. After that Gorbachev would call on other interested parties, particularly those with comments or objections to make. Meetings devoted to the consideration of such items sometimes lasted between three and five hours, though their length was not necessarily an advantage. In fact, it could be a nuisance. Before Gorbachev became general secretary, Politburo meetings were over in thirty or forty minutes, whereas in later years they went for up to ten hours. Gorbachev used to boast about it, saying that now we were really doing our job. But the members were tired and working less efficiently, and the business of the Politburo was not getting done.

Like the members of the Politburo, I too failed to understand the real reasons for such lengthy meetings. If an item had been prepared, action could be taken on it; if it had not, it should be sent back to its sponsors for further work. As it was, everyone was becoming exhausted; Gromyko, Slyunkov, and several other members with cardiac problems tended to be short of breath and found it particularly stressful. Gorbachev, afraid he might catch cold, asked for the air-conditioning to be turned off. After several hours of uninterrupted work in cramped surroundings, the atmosphere was hazardous even for a healthy person. This or that member would turn to me from time to time, hinting through gestures at the need for air-conditioning. I would issue orders for the air-conditioner to be turned on, only to be told that it was already working.

In the beginning, of course, with the Chernobyl disaster of April 1986 and the sinking of the passenger liner *Admiral Nakhimov* in the Black Sea in September of the same year, there was plenty of work and no time to waste. An unkind fate seemed to have decreed that Gorbachev was to be dogged by man-made and natural disasters and loss of life. Many of those disasters never reached the floor of the Politburo for discussion at all, as he increasingly sought to delete them from the agenda.

THE POLITBURO:
TOPICS ON THE AGENDA

The first official reports about Chernobyl that reached Gorbachev made it clear that there had been a disaster of epic proportions—an assessment borne out by Western sources. It was already obvious that the human toll was monstrous and that the economy would have to bear a huge additional burden. Yet the magnitude of the disaster was not immediately disclosed. Information that found its way to the press was carefully sifted, but total secrecy was out of the question. Ryzhkov was put in charge of a special commission made up of scientists, experts, and high-ranking representatives of the military, industry, and agriculture. The Politburo frequently met to consider the state of affairs around Chernobyl, hearing reports from Ryzhkov and its deputies about the elimination of the consequences of the disaster.

Some experts tried to lay the entire blame for the accident on the staff of the nuclear power station, while others found fault with the scientists, arguing that the reactor unit had been wrongly designed. The meteorologists provided reassuring weather forecasts, but with the passage of time it became increasingly evident that the zone of heavy radioactive contamination was spreading and now encompassed not only parts of the Ukraine but Belorussia and parts of the Russian Federation. Long-lived radionuclides were being observed in areas far from Chernobyl. Clearly, radioactivity had contaminated enormous areas, some of which would be unsuitable for human habitation for many decades, if not centuries. For a number of reasons these facts were not considered in depth.

Of course, in such a disaster only a powerful state, such as the Soviet Union, can muster the vast material and technical resources needed to alleviate the tragedy. One wonders what would have happened if Ukraine or Belorussia had had to cope with such a calamity on its own. All the time, the winds were scattering radioactive particles into many regions far from the site of the accident. Several European countries, particularly those in which vegetables and fruit had been contaminated, sought damages from us. The winds also carried the dust from Chernobyl to the Caucasus and the Trans-Caucasus, into parts of the Russian Federation. This was the disaster of the century. It showed that any use of nuclear weapons would be dangerous.

The Politburo devoted a great deal of attention to the case of Matthias Rust, who flew a light aircraft from the Baltic frontier to Moscow in May 1987 and landed next to Red Square, in the very heart of Moscow. I well remember the overcast day when it happened. I saw a small plane circling around the Kremlin. As helicopters and planes had been flying over the downtown area frequently for the past few years, shooting footage for historical and documentary films, I thought nothing of it. A few minutes later, however, I got a call from the Interior Ministry and the KGB saying that a German sports plane had landed next to the Kremlin and that its pilot, of German nationality, had explained that he had come to visit Moscow. It all seemed so implausible that I asked for confirmation.

Gorbachev was out of town at the time. I seem to recall that he was in Berlin and arrived back in Moscow the next day. As soon as he emerged from the plane, he began a discussion of the incident with the members of the Politburo, who had gone to the airport to meet him. The underlying political cause of the Rust flight seemed obvious enough. Raisa at once judged it to be an attempt by the military to humiliate her husband. Gorbachev scheduled a special meeting of the Politburo on the matter and asked the defense minister to report in detail on what had happened.

The landing of a German plane right next to the Kremlin left the Soviet people deeply shaken, as they had been proud of their anti-aircraft defenses, on which they had lavished billions of rubles. It certainly damaged Gorbachev's standing in the eyes of the general public and, I feel sure, in the eyes of many of his foreign admirers as well. The general secretary interpreted the incident as a premeditated move by the military against him personally. Previously he had viewed the military with some misgivings, but now he was filled with savage hatred for them and never forgave them for their little "joke." Long afterward he had still not forgotten; in public and in private he did his utmost to denounce the military, creating an atmosphere of animosity and feeding them to the media and the parliamentarians of the Union.

The explanations offered by the military at the meeting of the Politburo were none too convincing. There can be no doubt that it is difficult to spot a slow, low-flying, single-engine plane, but a flying object did show up on a number of radar screens in various places. First it was detected by the border defense units, which notified the anti-aircraft defenses. They, however, did not spot Rust's plane. Soon he appeared on military radars, though the image was blurred and, as representatives of the air force explained, looked like a flock of migrating birds. When fighters were sent up for a closer look, the pilots saw a plane in a clearing between the clouds. Mindful of the Korean Boeing 747 incident, they decided not to shoot it down. They then lost sight of it, as it was traveling at a different speed. Rust changed speed and course frequently; just outside Moscow he was practically invisible as he flew along a railroad line. Meanwhile, in Moscow nobody knew anything about any flying object.

Many Politburo members took the floor on this matter, and the military was hard-pressed to account for the incident. The final outcome was harsh: some officers were put on trial, and others were forced to retire. Defense Minister Sokolov was dismissed. This may well have been the only time Gorbachev actually took drastic steps; but he did so primarily because he viewed the incident as a personal attack on him by the military.

At first the discussions were—or at least appeared to be—thorough and collective, though as time passed problems were given a more superficial and hurried consideration. Gorbachev was increasingly inclined to impose his views, limiting the time allotted to speakers, including Politburo members, and sometimes cutting them off altogether with an utter lack of tact. The harsh and imperious manner in which Gorbachev conducted meetings of the Politburo was accentuated by his growing belief in his own infallibility.

As he gained in strength, Gorbachev was increasingly disposed to part company with his associates at the first sign of disagreement or the first hint of criticism of his performance and his life in general. There was far less circulation among Politburo members of the reports and speeches he delivered at meetings and later at Central Committee plenums. The sacrosanct principles of collegiality and consensus had been flouted. At times he would describe the general content of a forthcoming report and invite members to endorse the concept embodied in it, but this habit became more rare. A dictatorship of sorts now prevailed at the Politburo meetings. Members would exchange fearful glances, to express their amazement at these innovations, but they said nothing.

These trends were much in evidence during the discussion of Nina Andreyeva's scathing letter to *Sovietskaya Rossiya* in March 1988. Gorbachev had found nothing wrong with it; indeed, the sentiments it expressed may well have been favorably reviewed in his family, where the press was subjected to a distinctly biased interpretation. One evening, while looking through some documents and issuing instructions on their contents, he casually asked me whether I had read the 4,500-word letter. I replied that I had started it but had not yet finished.

"Well, it looks all right to me; but there's such an awful fuss being made over it," he replied.

I thought nothing of it at the time, but later felt obliged to read it through because of Yakovlev's highly negative feelings on the subject. A few days later Gorbachev's opinion had changed sharply: he now found it to be an assault on perestroika. What caused him to change his mind is something of a mystery, but at the next Politburo meeting the letter was on the agenda. Most members of the Politburo had either been unaware of it or had attached no importance to it. Some of them simply endorsed what it said—and made their views known.

Late in the day, as this frank but by now sluggish debate drew to a close, Gorbachev suddenly burst into action, saying that the item was highly substantive and that we would have to state our position on the ideas contained in the letter. Before adjourning, he announced that the discussion would continue the next day. This emotional outburst was incomprehensible and inexplicable.

The Politburo continued its meeting the next day, but this time in the Central Committee conference room. Gorbachev was in a fighting mood. Once again he began by stating his opinion of the letter and then invited comment. The speaker's list in the Politburo usually followed the order in which members were seated, starting with those next to the chairman and then proceeding to the Central Committee secretaries. Despite Gorbachev's masterly groundwork there were divergent views, though, broadly speaking, speakers tended to find fault with the letter. At the same time many of them agreed with what it said about our history and about the achievements that had been made possible by the toil, sweat, and blood of our people. Plainly irritated by what he was hearing, Gorbachev gradually abandoned parliamentary etiquette, occasionally treating the members of the Politburo with outright disrespect. After the meeting he said: "Now I realize the kind of people I've been working with. You can forget about perestroika with people like that."

By then respected members of the Politburo were bending their views to match those of the general secretary. Gorbachev started heckling the speakers and heaping sarcasm on anyone who found even the slightest merit in the letter. Every now and then I found myself wondering how those people could allow the general secretary to impugn their loyalty to the chosen policy and trample on their self-esteem. Everyone is entitled to form his own judgment and hold his own opinion, and the very idea of switching positions in response to the cracking of an oratorical whip should be out of the question.

In the press and in my conversations with Western politicians, I have often heard it said that Gorbachev is a well-mannered, cultivated man of sound character. He could certainly create the right impression when he wanted to, as I could certify. However, I and many others knew that certain other traits and habits lay hidden deep within his character. Gorbachev could be rude, insulting and humiliating his subordinates.

After spending the entire day explaining their positions, the members of the Politburo eventually found themselves simply swearing loyalty to the general secretary, forgetting the original purpose of their meeting, which was to discuss what Nina Andreyeva had written. Gorbachev increasingly resorted to similar techniques whenever controversy arose over the situation in the Soviet Union or the Socialist countries during the concluding phase of debates in the plenums and in many other instances. The sound of members swearing loyalty soon became commonplace. In fact, it reminded me of that flight from Tselinograd to Moscow on my fiftieth birthday when Raisa invited Yakovlev, Razumovski, and me in for a drink and then demanded that we swear our undying loyalty—not to certain ideas and principles, or to the Soviet people and nation, but to its leader in person. At the same time, the stronger the public's criticism of his failure to act and his wrong decisions, the more he emphasized the need for obeisance. He would often raise his voice during discussions if he noticed that someone was not listening to him attentively, and abruptly cut off speakers, especially Lukyanov, even threatening to have them expelled from the room. Everyone pretended not to notice such tactless behavior, which only a short while before would have been unheard of.

It did not even occur to me at the time, but how is one to explain the fall of Ryzhkov, overcome by a grinding work load and even more by the browbeating he endured at Gorbachev's hand and the deterioration and near-collapse of their relationship? The outcome in his case was a severe heart attack—and he was not the only one. After a merciless drubbing in the Politburo, Geidar Aliyev wound up in the hospital with another severe heart attack and was out of action for two years. In his case, of course, there were certain grounds for criticism; but why was he shamelessly hacked to pieces at a meeting where respectful criticism, where warranted, had previously been delivered in a comradely spirit? Aliyev was forced to resign. During the Central Committee plenum Gorbachev paid tribute to his work, yet had those complimentary remarks expunged from the record of the meeting when the time came for its publication.

Ryzhkov was also forced out of office, on the dignified pretext of "ill health." His illness and the reasons for it, however, developed gradually. I remember when relations between Gorbachev and Ryzhkov had been most cordial. It was Gorbachev who originally persuaded Andropov to make Ryzhkov a Central Committee secretary, and then recommended him for the post of chairman of the Council of Ministers. Ryzhkov always supported and helped Gorbachev, working between fourteen and sixteen hours a day. In those difficult times, however, the system proved incapable of adapting quickly to the new set of rules, having itself been formed in quite different circumstances. Failure to give effect to one resolution of the Council of Ministers led to a whole chain of failures and reduced the effectiveness of its work. The consequence was criticism of the government, which the presidium of the Council of Ministers, and Ryzhkov personally, found most disagreeable.

Ryzhkov worked hard to implement a number of major economic reforms he had proposed. Yet adequate help was not forthcoming; instead, he found himself on the receiving end of criticism from all directions. Under increasing nervous strain, he tended to side with those speakers who felt that unfounded press attacks on the government's actions only made matters worse. He also spoke out against the self-destructive trend in the ideological sector, thereby getting himself into further trouble.

In the Politburo he often inquired: "Can someone tell me why the government is being subjected to such ignorant and foul-mouthed criticism, while not one article explaining the truth is to be found anywhere in the press? What kind of glasnost is that?"

He might as well have spared himself the effort, however, as such remarks only provoked even heavier criticism. At a press outlet for the opinions of ministers and other economic officials, he proposed the establishment of a weekly government newsletter. Unfortunately few people read that publication, particularly during its first few months, as it was not well known, did not have a big print run, and was inexpertly produced.

Nikolai Ryzhkov's relations with Gorbachev began to change perceptibly after his visit to Armenia, where there had been a powerful earthquake in December 1988. His performance there favorably surprised many people. He worked vigorously to solve the problems created by the earthquake and made a number of competent appearances on television. After this visit Ryzhkov's rating soared, much to the dismay of Gorbachev, whose own authority was already sliding downhill.

"Nikolai is quite a populist, isn't he?" Gorbachev said at the time. "He's going into politics, but he should be getting on with his job and do something about the economy."

Ever since they first met, Gorbachev had called Ryzhkov Mikola or Nikolai. He addressed almost everyone, even complete strangers, with the familiar form (ty). He was afraid of Gromyko, however, and never risked such familiarity with him.

Ryzhkov's new independence may well have deepened the fissure between the general secretary and his prime minister, though there were other reasons as well. Even then, Ryzhkov was demanding more resolute action to restore order and tighten discipline in the country. Smarting under these implied rebukes, Gorbachev eventually came to see Ryzhkov and various other members of the Politburo as his personal rivals and adversaries, and lost no opportunity to criticize them. Ryzhkov's ill health and resignation soon brought to an end Gorbachev's relations with an associate who helped him greatly in his ascent to power.

Gromyko originally supported all Gorbachev's proposals and statements in the Politburo. Rather like a commissar, he was the first to climb from the trenches, eager to defend the general secretary's position even on issues with which he was not familiar. Eventually, though, he began to fall silent. His age made it difficult for him to work, especially under that particular general secretary. Normally, as chairman of the presidium of the Supreme Soviet, Gromyko should have been involved, *inter alia*, in international affairs, a field in which he was an expert. Yet he was denied such an opportunity from the very beginning, and was virtually shut out of foreign policy altogether. In any case he was unaware of many details of Gorbachev's meetings and talks with foreign leaders. The general secretary sent notes on these talks to Politburo members less and less often. The government, including the Cabinet of Ministers and many others, including the Ministry of Defense, the KGB, and the foreign trade services, were kept in the dark about many negotiations and agreements. The members of the Politburo and the Security Council, as well as the heads of the constituent republics of the Union, were not fully informed about the foreign policy activities of the general secretary. I do not know where these notes wound up, but they reached my desk with declining frequency.

It was not long before Gromyko, now visibly aging, gave up the fight. I could see the fatigue and illness in his eyes. He surveyed the scene around him with anguish and pain, clearly tormented by his involvement in the tragedy taking place in the country. As we have seen, he took the floor in the Politburo less and less frequently, tending to focus, when he did, on the hardships the ordinary people were facing and on his own reminiscences. Gorbachev would glance at members, winking as if to say: "You see the kind of people we have to work with." He originally had assured everyone that he would not repeat the mistakes of Brezhnev and certain others who had held two posts at the same time. Nonetheless, he forced Gromyko to resign and was soon head of the Supreme Soviet. I had long been aware that if the man at the top says no he should be understood as meaning maybe and perhaps even yes. Gorbachev was the master of his word—he could both give it and take it back.

Toward the end of Gorbachev's tenure then, the agendas of Politburo meetings changed substantially. Important substantive issues were now much less likely to be referred to the political leadership for discussion; the atmosphere was tense, with some speakers angry and others apathetic. My phone started ringing more often, with requests for information about how to apply for a pension, about the possibility of keeping one's medical benefits, about the amount of the pension, and so on. Pensions for Politburo members had previously been standard, and they had been allowed to keep their medical benefits; they also were entitled to a dacha and a chauffeur-driven car. Yet I was unable to provide them with definitive information, as pension rights were increasingly precarious.

There was much contentious debate in the Politburo, and appraisals of current events were widely divergent. On most issues, Ligachev tended to disagree with the policies of the general secretary, but they saw eye to eye on the need to implement perestroika. While everyone acknowledged that change was necessary, they disagreed over the timetable and over Gorbachev's policy of reducing the power of the army, the military-industrial complex, and the party structures. Most of all, they could not understand the discrepancies between the general secretary's words and deeds, his frequent deviations from agreed policies, or his attempts to win favor alternately with the left and right wings. A number of Politburo members were therefore either critical of the general secretary or silently refused to accept certain decisions.

Ligachev was outspoken in defense of his ideas. Many members of the party or the Politburo either sensed or knew of his disgreements with the general secretary. Support for him was widespread. Gorbachev viewed him apprehensively as an emerging leader, capable of uniting various factions behind him; and that was something he was determined not to allow. Ligachev soon came under fire in the press, and was wrongfully accused of taking bribes. For such a prominent politician these charges were unprecedented, and called for an immediate response. Gorbachev, however, was unwilling to intercede on behalf of his closest associate, though he did once tell me: "I don't believe Yegor took bribes. It's somehow not in his character. He might have done all sorts of things, but not that."

Gorbachev did not publicly refute these slanderous attacks, and Ligachev was allowed to drain his cup of undeserved disgrace to the dregs and to fend for himself unaided. While he no longer feared him as a potential leader, Gorbachev limited his sphere of activities. Whereas he had previously presided over meetings of the Politburo in the general secretary's absence, Ligachev now found such opportunities rare indeed. Instead, those meetings were not held regularly, and all serious business was omitted from their agendas. Before long, Ligachev was also unable to conduct as many Secretariat meetings as he once had. Gorbachev used to say: "Do we really need two parallel organs? The Politburo will make whatever decisions are necessary."

Secretariat meetings began to be held less frequently. Ligachev found himself isolated as a potential leader—which was exactly what Gorbachev and those accusing him of bribe taking wanted.

6

BEHIND THE SCENES IN THE COMMUNIST PARTY

Fyodor Kulakov, a bon vivant who, like Gorbachev, was from Stavropol, was the head of the Politburo's Agricultural Department. In 1978 he died from an overdose of alcohol while recovering from stomach surgery. By creating a vacancy in the Politburo and the Central Committee Secretariat, his untimely death became the prelude to many dramatic events in the Soviet Union. Without that tragic event, Gorbachev would never have been able to rise so swiftly through the hierarchy.

With his background in Stavropol politics Gorbachev became a member of the funeral commission and uttered some appropriate sentiments about the deceased from the top of the Lenin Mausoleum. That was when I first set eyes on this man, whose external attributes left me with some conflicting impressions. Though not yet old, he was, to put it mildly, a little heavy for his age, with severely thinning hair. His speech was laden with local dialect and littered with misplaced tonic stresses, thus identifying him as a provincial. That was all I remembered at the time, though I must say that I did not take a close look at this newcomer from the distant southern steppes. It never occurred to me that I would ever have any dealings with him, still less that he would one day be head of the party and the state.

He evidently thought otherwise. After delivering the eulogy atop the mausoleum and placing Kulakov's ashes in the Kremlin wall, Gorbachev waited anxiously to see who would be appointed head of agriculture in the Politburo. Then fate smiled on forty-seven-year-old Mikhail Sergeyevich Gorbachev, first secretary of the party's Stavropol *kraikom:*

he was chosen to take Kulakov's place in the Central Committee apparatus. As we have seen, many of the top party figures already knew him, although for others his appointment was quite unexpected. Andropov had recommended him, and he was a familiar figure to Suslov and virtually all the high officials who used to visit the sanatorium at Mineralniye Vody for recreation and treatment. Certain factions, however, sought to impress on Brezhnev the merits of their own candidate, F. Morgun, secretary of the Poltava *obkom* in the Ukraine. Both prospective candidates arrived in Moscow at the same time to be considered by the leadership. Yet when the time came for Gorbachev to be presented, Brezhnev was nowhere to be found. There was a distinct possibility that Morgun could be driven to Brezhnev's dacha first. Had it not been for Chernenko's secretaries, the outcome would have been very uncertain. But some ingenious detective work on their part saved the day. They managed to find the driver of the car in which Gorbachev had driven off, thus making it possible to find him before it was too late. Brezhnev supported Gorbachev's candidacy, thus strongly influencing the outcome. Gorbachev was elected a secretary of the Central Committee, and before long a candidate member of the Politburo. He became a full member during the Twenty-sixth Party Congress in October 1980.

The arrival of this energetic and assertive young Central Committee secretary upset the tranquility of the Politburo, where it was immediately evident that some members did not accept the impudent young man from Stavropol. He did not get on well with Kosygin, and there was tension between him and senior members of the Council of Ministers, including a few ministers. In those days membership in the Central Committee was taken very seriously. Very few members took the liberty of acting independently, and even when they did, one assumes they first checked with the chairman of the Council of Ministers.

Relations between Gorbachev and Dinmukhamed Kunayev, first secretary of Kazakhstan, also got off to a poor start. For a long time Kunayev did not recognize "this young man," never went to see him while visiting Moscow and, I presume, never phoned him either. Whenever some matter relating to Kazakhstan came up, Kunayev would promptly contact Brezhnev, with whom he was well connected, and always got what he wanted. When necessary he would turn to the Politburo, which would not dare decline a request from the head of such a large republic. Kunayev had long enjoyed close relations with Ustinov,

Chernenko, Suslov, Gromyko, and Andrei Kirilenko—an impressive array.

Kunayev naturally changed his tune when Gorbachev was elected general secretary, but by then it was too late. In September 1985 he flew to Tselinograd during Gorbachev's visit to the *oblast*. It was harvest time on the golden landscape of northern Kazakhstan. The new general secretary traveled to the regional center, Shortandy, to see Academician Barayev at the All-Union Grain Farming Institute, where he spent half a day studying advanced farming techniques and methods for combating wind erosion. Though seriously ill, Barayev showed him what he could and reported on the work of the research institute. Gorbachev then inspected the fields where the combine harvesters were at work, chatting with their operators.

He also talked with Kunayev, but no mutual understanding came about. They said goodbye after breakfast on the morning of Gorbachev's departure. Kunayev had brought traditional Kazakh gifts: two dark-green velvet dressing gowns adorned with Kazakh embroidery and trimmed with sable. There was also a Kazakh sable hat with velvet top. The second gown was intended for Raisa. Gorbachev accepted these gifts, though the scars in the two men's relationship did not heal.

In December 1986 rioting broke out in Alma-Ata, incited, as Solomentsev informed the Politburo, by nationalist sentiment. As a result, and also because he had accepted gifts from subordinates, Kunayev was expelled from the Central Committee. As he left the building the guards took away his identity pass. This long-time party member and republican leader ended his political career in humiliation and disgrace.

Gorbachev's relations with Vladimir Shcherbitsky were also strained. The irrepressible and independent "Uncle," as many then called him, took a dim view of the youngster in the Politburo. Yet he did call from time to time, and made Gorbachev ecstatic when he went to see him in Moscow once. Gorbachev often mentioned this visit, which clearly made their relationship somewhat smoother; rough edges still remained, however, and soon made themselves felt. Shcherbitsky did not attend the Central Committee plenum at which Gorbachev was elected general secretary, claiming that it had been impossible for him to fly back from New York in time. Gorbachev and his advisers later concluded, however, that he could in fact have returned in time for the meeting.

The two men clashed during Gorbachev's 1985 visit to the Ukraine.

In a speech to party members Gorbachev sharply criticized the republican leadership for numerous shortcomings—something no previous general secretary had ever done or even countenanced.

Shcherbitsky's many enemies in the republic promptly reared their heads, responding to this signal from on high. "Uncle" realized that the time had come for change. Thereafter he was much less belligerent at Politburo meetings, although it is only fair to note that he was never devious or underhanded, merely frank. He spoke less, though, and soon retired for reasons of ill health when a new team was appointed.

Gromyko seemed to me an independent figure, detached from mere earthly concerns. He enjoyed widespread respect as an erudite and skilled diplomat who had defended Soviet interests well. His authority had been enhanced by his extensive appearances on television. Being engaged in foreign policy, consorting with Brezhnev, Ustinov, and Andropov, and later formulating that policy virtually single-handed, he hardly noticed Gorbachev—at least not as much as the young man would have liked. In fact, it was not until Gorbachev was made second secretary of the Central Committee, in charge of the Secretariat, that Gromyko began to focus on Gorbachev's personality.

About that time the Western media had already singled out Gorbachev, among the ranks of the doddering party leadership, as a young man of what they called "a new generation." After his meeting with Margaret Thatcher in London in 1984, he attracted the attention of virtually every politician in Europe and the United States. His successful British trip greatly enhanced his stature, making him more assertive and confident. Back home, however, few people were aware that he had been to Great Britain at all.

The Soviet news media, which received reports on visits made by Central Committee members, followed a long-standing tradition whereby the successes of only one of them—the general secretary—were given prominent coverage. The same rule was observed at the Foreign Ministry, which often sent the reports of its ambassadors on such visits exclusively to the general secretary. If the need arose for more information about the outcome of the visit, it was couched in cold and impersonal terms, wholly lacking in adjectives, lifeless as stone.

On several occasions, on the initiative of either Western or Soviet intelligence agencies, high-ranking Soviet political figures on visits abroad had found themselves embarrassed by sudden revelations or, conversely, delighted by extravagant praise. Once the suspicions of the general secretary had been aroused in this way, the individual concerned, ignorant of the devious machinations going on around him, could easily find his career ruined.

Gromyko sent many telegrams about Gorbachev's British trip only to Chernenko, while withholding some of them altogether. There was nothing about his successful visit in any newspaper. So the inexperienced and troubled Gorbachev concluded that factions opposed to him in the Central Committee and the Foreign Ministry had planned the whole thing. He was all the more inclined to think this way, because he had been in the same situation in 1983, when he visited Kadar in Hungary. He thought it very important for the press to publish a brief report on his reception by the Hungarian leadership, as it would have acknowledged his status as a leader of the world Communist movement. But the report was delayed. Moscow may not have attached much importance to it, although, on the other hand, hostility to Gorbachev may have been a factor. I was also present during Gorbachev and Raisa's visit to Hungary and, like them, was upset by the indifferent attitude of the Soviet press toward Gorbachev's reception by the Kadar government. I took part in efforts to secure the desired press coverage. Justice triumphed, but not until he had returned to Moscow.

Gromyko watched all the skirmishing from the sidelines. Only at the last minute, being himself a master of the diplomatic volte-face, did he change his attitude toward Gorbachev. He easily came to terms with him and eventually, as we have seen, sponsored Gorbachev's rise to the top, thereby demonstrating an impressive flair that helped extend his own career. Gromyko and Gorbachev, as it turned out, needed each other. Both before and slightly after his election as general secretary, Gorbachev showed the utmost respect for the veteran diplomat. Soon, however, as his own power and authority grew, the post of head of state became increasingly attractive. At that point his attitude changed.

PROBLEMS IN THE
CENTRAL COMMITTEE

Gorbachev's arrival in the Politburo did not immediately prompt Dmitri Ustinov to pay undue attention to the new secretary. Although they already knew each other, theirs was very much a teacher-pupil relationship. Gorbachev saw Ustinov as a strong, key player in the Politburo. He would often call him, particularly when help was needed during the all-out effort to bring in the grain harvest, when the army traditionally dispatched motorized battalions to the eastern part of the country.

Ustinov must also have noticed the young man's capabilities, as close and friendly relations quickly developed between them. I was present when Gorbachev, after Andropov's death, said to Ustinov: "How about it, Dmitri, there's work for you to do! We'll support you for general secretary." Ustinov declined the offer. He once pointed out that the job was not for him: "I'm getting on now, and my health hasn't been good. Chernenko can do it."

This remark upset Gorbachev, who realized that he would not be sitting in the general secretary's chair anytime soon. Of course, he did not know at the time that Ustinov, while discussing the appointment of Chernenko, had extracted from him an assurance that Gorbachev would be given the second-ranking post in the party. And Chernenko kept his promise, strictly speaking, by nominating Gorbachev as head of the Central Committee Secretariat. Lacking true support and many of the attributes of power, however, Gorbachev was unable to perform his duties in that position to the full.

As soon as Gorbachev was admitted to the Politburo, all the factions opposed to the "crafty young man" began to mobilize against him. The existing membership did not trust Gorbachev, fearing that his rise to power would disrupt the entire leadership. Accordingly, someone nominated Grigori Romanov as a contender for the top post. He was definitely "one of them," tried and tested as head of the large Leningrad party organization. His candidacy made sense: apart from his experience in Leningrad, he was quite a prominent figure and was familiar with the defense industry. His backers worked hard on his behalf, but he was not ready for such lofty responsibilities. Having worked for so long at the level of one *oblast*, Romanov could not bring himself to think as a statesman in charge of an entire nation. He was neither an outstanding politician nor a brilliant speaker and tended to say little at meetings of the Politburo and Central Committee Secretariat. He also had one private though inescapably noticeable vice, found fairly commonly in the Russian Federation, which often caused him to feel a bit sluggish after lunch. Some subtle backstage scheming, and the floating of various rumors, did not help his cause.

According to one particularly damaging rumor, Romanov had allowed the use of an aristocratic mansion and czarist tableware for his daughter's wedding. This was, of course, a deliberate but clever falsehood. In any case it circulated for a long time in the corridors of power and the apartment blocks of the public. When a parliamentary commission of the Russian Supreme Soviet investigated the allegations, they found that the wedding party had consisted of twelve people, that it had been held at Romanov's dacha, and that, because of some family quarrel, he had spent most of the time upstairs alone, in his office. The story about czarist tableware, taken from a museum, was a complete fabrication.

But the press was unwilling to publish the true facts once they became known. Gorbachev heard about this from senior officials of the Supreme Soviet of the RSFSR; I also spoke to him of the need for verification and suggested the text of a draft press release for the purpose. The general secretary was not interested. The party leader no longer wanted to uphold the truth where his comrades were concerned. In this way Romanov retired in disgrace, having been wrongfully humiliated, and without fighting the slander that had plainly been circulated by some masterly hand. As I gained a deeper understanding of the process of political intrigue, I came across new facts that shed light on the high-stakes secret maneuvering for the top positions, and particularly for the general secretary's throne. In the mid-1980s a number of factions were contending for the key posts. This was a game in which the players did not abide by the rules. And there is always the possibility that Soviet lobbyists were not the only ones involved in removing one aspirant or another. Romanov may have been an accidental victim of the collision of powerful rival forces. I could hardly recognize him when I met him at his dacha in Zarechiye in the summer of 1991: he looked old and limp, with sunken cheeks. He was clearly overwhelmed by injustice and exhausted by illness.

Another candidate for the post of general secretary was Dolgikh, who was sponsored by Chernenko, Tikhonov, and virtually all the senior members of the Council of Ministers. He had worked in various major branches of the economy, such as fuel and energy and machine building, and was influential in the industrial sector generally. He had served as director of the famous Norilsk plant, and had worked his way up the industrial and party ladder. When he joined the Central Committee he was first secretary of the Krasnodar *kraikom*. Tikhonov supported him vigorously, and invited him to take part in discussions of many questions on the agenda of the Council of Ministers. All this made Gorbachev very jittery, and strained his relations with Dolgikh to the breaking point. A secret war was being waged, eventually ending in the defeat of Dolgikh. He retired with vast amounts of unspent energy that could have been put to good use.

After retirement Dolgikh often came to hand me letters he had written to Gorbachev asking for permission to work, as he was under some financial strain. None of them was ever answered. "He's really crafty, isn't he?" Gorbachev would say. "He was careful to hedge his bets, obviously afraid of backing the wrong horse. Well, now he can sit back and take it easy." Gorbachev could not forgive Dolgikh the torments he had endured when it seemed that power might slip from his grasp.

Gorbachev had good relations with Andropov, when he was in charge of the KGB, and received valuable help from him, but his relations with Chebrikov were always poor. He knew that Chebrikov, as an obedient bureaucrat, diligently served Chernenko and kept him fully informed about the relative strength of the various factions. When he phoned Gorbachev he was simply going through the motions, rather than conveying much useful information, since he feared that whatever he told Gorbachev might somehow get back to Chernenko. On the other hand he was afraid *not* to call Gorbachev, since he was uncertain which of the contenders in the current power struggle would eventually replace the ailing Chernenko. Gorbachev duly took note of his every move; then, after he had become general secretary, he looked for ways to remove Chebrikov from his position as chairman of the KGB. He got his chance when he managed to have Lukyanov moved to the Supreme Soviet.

Chebrikov was ousted from the KGB system and, like Antaeus, lost his strength. As a Central Committee secretary he lacked his former status and quietly faded away, stripped of influence, power, and information. As soon as the first reorganization took place, he was forced to retire. On the recommendation of Yakovlev, who had known him for several decades, Kryuchkov was appointed chairman of the Committee for State Security. It was with him, as with Yazov, that Gorbachev made the most confidential decisions.

Gorbachev also disliked Grishin, who doubtless felt the same way about him. The powerful Moscow secretary, who wielded tremendous influence, was allied with the Chernenko camp. This made it all the more necessary to weaken him. An opportunity soon came along, when a number of commercial aides were found guilty of corruption in a widely publicized trial. It became obvious that Tregubov, the powerful head of the city's commercial management, was involved in bribe taking. The investigation into these cases worried Grishin, who realized that he was the real target. In 1984, just after his return from vacation, he discovered to his indignation that the Central Committee was investigating possible links between the staff of the Commercial Department and the party apparatus. I heard him tell Gorbachev over the phone: "The party organization of the Moscow City Council cannot be held responsible for every single crook out there; I reject out of hand these insinuations about the leadership being personally connected to Tregubov and others high up in the Commercial Department."

Gorbachev tried to calm him down by saying that the investigation was not an attempt to discredit the authority of the party committee and its secretaries but that the truth had to be established. "He sounds worried," said Gorbachev, putting down the receiver, "I'll bet there's something fishy going on over there. There must be a full investigation."

Ligachev became involved in the closing stages of the affair, as new evidence of criminal mischief and bogus invoices continued to surface. Ligachev started to unravel the matter of bogus invoices in the construction industry. A variety of rumors, some of them implausible, were making the rounds in Moscow. Promyslov and Grishin were now both thought to be compromised. As a result the city's leadership was reduced to helplessness.

Chernenko often lent Grishin a helping hand, but the secretary of the Moscow City Council now stood no chance at all of rising to become general secretary. Grishin in turn was most helpful to the ailing general secretary, remaining loyal to him to the very end. His provocative relationship with Chernenko, and the resulting desire to redeem himself, may explain why he was one of the first to support Gorbachev's nomination for the post of general secretary. It is hard to say to what extent this prolonged his tenure in the Politburo. Soon, however, Gorbachev invited Grishin in for a chat, after which Grishin went into retirement, pursued by even more news reports compromising the senior officials of the Moscow City Council. Public opinion was regaled with a variety of details of the case for some time to come. Gorbachev also distrusted and suspected certain other Central Committee secretaries and candidate members of the Politburo.

During Gorbachev's tenure, the Politburo and the Central Committee Secretariat did not work creatively and harmoniously. From the outset the members of the Politburo and the Central Committee secretaries viewed each other in a spirit of rivalry and distrust, which sometimes degenerated into veritable showdowns and threats of resignation. Gorbachev apportioned the duties of the Politburo and the Secretariat in such a way that clashes between the party leaders would inevitably occur. Such conflict, as we have seen, occurred between Ligachev and Yakovlev, Ligachev and Nikonov, and Shevardnadze and Yakovlev. While dealing with the same issues, these people had equal powers vested in them and were unwilling to yield.

I remember once being in Gorbachev's office when Lev Zaikov showed up asking to talk to him on an urgent matter. I got up to leave, but Gorbachev stopped me. He may have felt that in my presence Zaikov would be less candid and therefore unlikely to stay long, or he may have wanted me there as a witness. For whatever reason, the general secretary had a habit of conducting confidential talks in the presence of a member of his staff. This time I was an involuntary witness to an outpouring of emotional complaints about the state of affairs in the Secretariat and the relations between the chairman and certain other Central Committee secretaries. Zaikov was terribly agitated and upset. He was practically in tears as he described how the chairman of the Central Committee Secretariat had been shouting at him, making his life difficult at work, and interfering in matters he knew nothing about. Razumovski had complained to Gorbachev in a similar vein.

The tensions between Ligachev and Yeltsin, which were well publicized, did much damage to the party and the nation. Ryzhkov complained endlessly about interference by several Central Committee staff members in economic affairs. He was at loggerheads with Ligachev and, later on, with Slyunkov. Other senior officials asked Gorbachev to relieve them of their duties on account of the discord prevailing in relations between members of the Politburo. Such widespread tension greatly hampered the business of government. In any other organization tension and quarrels might not have had such a lamentable impact on performance, but the party and the Soviet Union as a whole could not afford the kind of surreptitious squabbling that went on among members of the Politburo.

Gorbachev had a unique and astonishing ability to generate bickering and feuds among those he worked with. I never could understand whether he deliberately sought such strained relations as a way of enhancing his control over the Politburo or whether his own personality and lack of experience were to blame. The result was the same: at Politburo meetings people would talk at cross-purposes, thus making consensus impossible. There were heated arguments all the time, some of them quite nasty. Gorbachev tended to stay behind after Politburo meetings to argue with Ryzhkov; he would later say, "Nikolai just doesn't understand what perestroika is all about." Ryzhkov may not have understood perestroika, but then neither did Gorbachev, as he maneuvered this way and that, confusing the entire power structure and even his own associates as he did so.

Not surprisingly, Gorbachev accelerated the turnover rate among his subordinates. By 1987 virtually the entire membership of the Politburo had been changed, only to undergo another overhaul in 1990. From then on the Politburo turned into a gathering of representatives of the republics and the central government that was utterly incapable of deciding or uniting anything at all—a sure sign that the collapse of the organs of government and of the entire party was imminent.

In the early years the Politburo discussed many aspects of the work done by the Foreign Ministry. Members would sometimes gather in small conclaves after the adjournment of the formal meeting to consider the most confidential matters, especially personnel policy. Shevardnadze began to restore order in what had become an exclusive hunting preserve, but his efforts amounted to little more than a rearrangement of the furniture, leaving a number of corrupt officials in place. He was, of course, faced with a herculean task. After years of neglect, family dynasties had become more pervasive in the Foreign Ministry than in any factory.

With the passage of time, as we have seen, the role of the Politburo began to decline: meetings were convened more rarely, the summary records filled fewer and fewer pages, and decisions were made more hastily, at times by a single man. Months could go by without any decisions at all—a fact much deplored at the plenums of the Central Committee. The members of the Central Committee could see their once powerful party bleeding to death; they knew that they were witnessing the demise of an organ without parallel in the history of their country. The paralysis of power was increasingly evident. Gorbachev refused to hear what Ryzhkov, Ligachev, Slyunkov, and later Shenin and others had to say about the Politburo's impotence, though they doubtless expressed themselves more tactfully.

V. Gaivoronsky, an electric welder at the Azovmash factory in the Donetsk *oblast*, and a member of the Central Committee and the Secretariat, put it bluntly: "At meetings of the Secretariat we used to defend the chosen policy line, and we couldn't have cared less about how the top party leaders reacted to anything we said. I must point out that, unfortunately, Mikhail Gorbachev, the general secretary, showed up at Secretariat meetings only twice."

By the early summer of 1991 the Politburo had not met for three full months. Addressing some other meeting, Yuri Prokofiev, first secretary of the Moscow *gorkom*, had this to say: "If the Politburo doesn't meet soon, I shall demand its abolition at a plenum of the Central Committee. As members of the Politburo we should not be held responsible for decisions made individually by Gorbachev."

On 17 July Gorbachev was attending a meeting of the Group of Seven in London. I spoke with Oleg Shenin, a member of the Central Committee, saying: "I've been talking to a lot of people, in and out of the party. Journalists have been probing me for information, thinking that as a member of the Secretariat I would surely know something about what went on in London. But I don't." He replied: "Listen, Valentin, I'm a member of the Politburo, and I don't know anything either."

I then realized that we had taken that first fateful step toward the creation of yet another Supreme Leader.

The general secretary was the kind of person who loses all sense of proportion after rising to great heights; success goes to such people's heads, so that, without realizing it, they become detached from reality and prepare their own downfall. He had not entirely lost his sense of danger, however. Gorbachev was afraid to rely on the party, which had become discredited by its inconsistency in dealing with problems, and for other reasons. At the same time he knew that divorce from the party was tantamount to political death.

The death throes of the Politburo began after the Twenty-eighth Party Congress. The party's chief political organs met only a few times. There was no discussion of serious problems, even those pertaining to the party's own activities.

PLENUMS

The Central Committee plenums played a prominent role in the work of the party, essentially defining both current and strategic policy for the entire country. They made all major personnel changes in the party and its highest organs. Gorbachev's arrival on the scene renewed the vitality of the plenums by restoring certain Leninist principles of democracy and banishing formalism, among many other ways.

I well remember how it all began.

Participants in the plenum welcomed the new general secretary, a congenial and energetic young man, with a standing ovation. Gorbachev smiled, waiting for the applause to die down. He then requested permission to open the plenum and invited the members of the Politburo to conduct the meeting. The members of the Politburo and the Central Committee trusted the new general secretary and agreed that the plenum should be opened and conducted as he suggested. As long as the situation improved, they were ready to agree to lots of things.

The decision of who should preside over the plenums had always been decided in a collegial manner. Even Stalin requested permission to preside, and the conduct of the plenums was not always placed in his hands. Democratic procedures were followed then more diligently than they would be later on.

The plenum then opened, and the details of attendance at the meeting were read out. Toward the end of his tenure Gorbachev introduced the custom of inviting the commanders of the branches of the armed forces; the secretaries of *obkoms*, *kraikoms*, and the republican Communist parties who were not members of the Central Committee; government ministers and public figures; and eventually deputies from the Central Committee and members of the presidium of the Supreme Soviet. The one group he did *not* want to admit to the meetings was the staff of the Central Committee apparatus, even if they were needed to perform certain functions. Gorbachev would scrutinize the list of those invited to attend, striking out those he deemed undesirable. I occasionally managed, at the last minute, to include certain individuals on the grounds that they were needed for the record of the meeting or for some other purpose. Apart from the general secretary, Ligachev and Ryzhkov usually presided over these meetings, calling on speakers, including Gorbachev, in the normal manner. Occasionally, however, Gorbachev gave himself the floor and then walked to the podium to address the assembly.

During his early years, much careful thought went into the preparation of his speeches. Later on, however, they were disjointed and loosely worded. They also incorporated some highly questionable notes he had received from various sources, which, on close examination, turned out to be far from the truth. At the beginning, though, the participants in Central Committee plenums were charmed into accepting his ideas.

Constructive discussions took place, in which members of the Central Committee spoke as and when they wished, and not in accordance with some preordained list. As requests for the floor were registered and then placed on Gorbachev's table, new speakers' lists were prepared. Admittedly, Gorbachev himself did the choosing, so that the first one on the list could quite easily speak last or not at all. Several members of the Central Committee complained to the presidium, wanting to know why they were never given a chance to speak.

Despite these shortcomings, the meetings now took place in an unfettered atmosphere, in which one could voice whatever views, critical or otherwise, one wished. Some speakers did find it harder, from one plenum to the next, to express their views, especially those who could be expected to call for tighter discipline nationwide and fuller information for Central Committee members, or to ask why the ideological organs were standing idly by and allowing criticism of everything and everyone, including some things that the Soviet people held to be sacred.

As time went on, criticism of the Ideological Department became particularly severe. Speakers vented their anger at Yakovlev and, after his resignation, at his successor, Medvedev. Newspaper editors were also criticized, among them Ivan Frolov, who was accused of allowing *Pravda* to espouse fundamentally wrong principles and of stirring up trouble among his staff.

Whereas in Gorbachev's early years Central Committee plenums focused on concrete solutions to specific problems, they eventually came to engage in political debate for its own sake. In later years the party no longer dealt with practical problems: it was at war, and personal, parochial interests held sway.

Gorbachev realized what was happening and often, under pressure from critics, he began to change his position, developing a sharp edge to his voice as he did so. But this was merely the typical kind of zigzag course he steered in the hope of cooling things down or keeping everyone off balance. In 1990 and 1991, when cornered by the members of the Central Committee, he fell back increasingly on his own homemade ploys. Sensing that his opponents were about to discharge a new volley of criticism, he would himself unleash a torrent of emotions on those present in the hall, intimidating them with threats of resignation. This certainly made an impression, throwing speakers off their stride and blunting criticism. Once this method was exhausted, Gorbachev would begin to meet with the secretaries of *obkoms, kraikoms,* and the republican Central Committees before the start of the plenums, giving them a chance to speak their minds and let off steam, thus reducing tensions.

I did not always understand the significance of his maneuvers. It seemed to me that if he wanted to remain general secretary, he should have explained to the Central Committee members, in a calm and reasonable manner, how he saw the situation developing, what the future role of the party would be, and what the secretaries and party organizations should do. Such candor would surely have induced the party to throw its weight behind his efforts. Instead, he showered his audiences with verbiage, laced with mysterious foreign words like *consensus* that meant nothing to his listeners. They were like brightly colored candy wrappers, with no candy inside.

Central Committee members frequently complained that the general secretary had mastered the art of waffling to the point where it took them several hours to realize that, instead of food for thought, he had actually given them a pacifier.

Gorbachev did not like other speakers to present reports to the plenums, although such presentations had long been a party tradition. He did agree on one occasion to let Ligachev address the plenum on educational issues, though he followed with a speech, which really amounted to a formal report, on questions of ideology. The result was that the discussion on Ligachev's report was virtually derailed, and all subsequent speakers found themselves focusing, though without preparation, on the party's ideological issues.

This jealousy and determination to do everything himself did nothing to improve the atmosphere in the Central Committee or the Politburo. People turned indifferent, finding themselves relegated to a third-rate role. Therein lies one of the reasons Gorbachev's associates became alienated and less active politically.

Plenums were rarely over in a single day, as Gorbachev allowed the maximum number of speakers, each of whom, under the generous rules of procedure, could take the floor for fifteen minutes. Every two hours there was a break, and people went downstairs for a buffet. In Gorbachev's early years, this consisted of a wide range of dishes, sandwiches, and fruit. At lunch there were hot sausages, soup, and baked goods. All this originally came out of the party budget; members were required to pay only in later years. While eating, members continued to discuss and argue the main report of the day and the speeches they had heard. Many *obkom* and *kraikom* secretaries used their time at the plenums to take care of their own pressing needs, such as securing industrial hardware and other resources.

Gorbachev used to ask the secretaries and department heads, and his aides, about the mood of the meeting, either while it was still going on or just after adjournment. They, however, found it increasingly difficult to tell him what he wanted to hear. Members gradually stopped coming to see him, so he often went home as soon as the meeting was over. The *obkom* and *kraikom* secretaries no longer bothered to contact him or the members of the Central Committee apparatus. A disturbing atmosphere of mutual incomprehension and dissatisfaction developed.

Toward the end of his tenure the changed mood was illustrated by the lack of applause when the general secretary entered the plenum hall; nobody stood up, and many people just continued talking or wandering around the room, taking no notice of him at all. To get their attention, Gorbachev had to call for order in the room. The members of the presidium would take their seats without being invited to do so by the plenum. Some of the people sitting up there were complete strangers. Everyone was wondering who they were, why there were two Politburo members from Estonia, and who were those people from Armenia and Georgia. They were astonished by the new arrangements for the election to the Politburo of all the first secretaries of the republican Communist parties. The situation changed so fast that I sometimes suspected Gorbachev himself could not always remember who was who.

The men sitting at the presidium were mere shadows of the party's past greatness. Most of them must have sensed the approach of disaster, though they could do nothing under that particular general secretary and merely waited for their terms of office to expire. Even if the clock had been turned back, they would still not have been able to act.

The Twenty-eighth Party Congress, in July 1990, marked the beginning of the end for the Politburo and the Central Committee plenums. The Politburo met less frequently, and angry scenes erupted regularly in the plenums. The blind were now debating the deaf. The brain of a once great party had died, poisoning the entire organism.

From the spring of 1985 onward, the party found itself looking for guidance in the voluminous collections of Gorbachev's selected works and the records of its plenums and Congresses, in which the party's ultimate doom was writ large.

DOCUMENTS AND LETTERS FROM THE PUBLIC

Early in 1987 Lukyanov was elected to the post of Central Committee secretary in charge of the State and Legal Department of the Central Committee apparatus. He was not unhappy to be moved from the exhausting General Department that he had directed since 1983. In his new office a vast new field stretched before him, ranging over the army, KGB, MVD,* the Procuracy, and all the administrative and law enforcement organs. His transfer to this new post coincided with the end of my service as an assistant to Gorbachev.

One day after a plenum, I was unexpectedly summoned to the conference room, where members of the Politburo and the Central Committee secretaries used to meet during coffee breaks. I arrived in the middle of a freewheeling discussion of the meeting, details of the report and the various speeches, worthwhile or otherwise. Gorbachev interrupted the conversation and said: "Here is my replacement for Anatoli Lukyanov. You all know Boldin; I'd like you to confirm him as the head of the General Department."

I was taken aback. Two months previously Gorbachev had vaguely suggested such an appointment, but I turned it down, claiming ignorance of paperwork and saying that if my services were no longer needed I should go back to *Pravda*. I told him: "It's like a merry-go-round in there. I won't be able to handle all those papers; I'll just wear myself out."

"You make it sound like a death sentence!" said Gorbachev in reply. "I really need the job done, and I'd like you to help."

The subject was not raised again, either because he was offended by my reply or because he had not made up his mind and was simply floating a trial balloon. At any rate I opposed the idea as firmly as I could; every ounce of me rebelled at the thought of that kind of incomprehensible work and the danger of being permanently stuck to a desk—something I had never experienced. I preferred to be my own boss: it was part of my character, and also what I had been used to. Then I suddenly found myself called in and introduced to the Politburo members as if I already had the job. The members voiced their approval of Gorbachev's choice, whereupon he promptly signed a formal decision on my appointment, apparently drafted by Lukyanov.

Adapting to this alien job, which I hated at first, was a painful experi-

---

Ministerstvo Vnutrennykh Del—Ministry of Internal Affairs.

ence. Whereas I had previously left for home around nine in the evening, now I was lucky to get out by midnight.

What exactly was the General Department, and what were its functions?

Its structures were first formed back in the early 1920s under Stalin. It grew out of a special section of the Central Committee and served the Politburo, the Secretariat, and the plenums of the Central Committee. It also transmitted documents, letters from citizens to all the departments of its apparatus, and handled all the material produced by those departments for the party's highest political organs and its local committees and organizations. The volume of documentation was enormous. Toward the end of Gorbachev's tenure, the Central Committee received more than one million letters in one year from the general public, tens of thousands of different documents and other material dealing with issues currently on the agendas of the party, government, and economic organs, as well as assorted information on local conditions around the country. A similar mass of mail was sent to the republics, the *krais*, *oblasts*, and individual districts.

This torrent of documents reached the Central Committee through a single gateway—the General Department. The mail was promptly distributed to the appropriate Central Committee departments and was also sent to the Central Committee secretaries and the members of the Politburo. A record was kept of each piece until the corresponding decision had been made and a reply sent to the applicant.

As time went by, Gorbachev grew more and more irritable when documents were sent to him for comment. Fatigue was doubtless preventing him from reading them and issuing instructions as vigorously as he once had. Sometimes he kept them for a long time, and even sent them back unopened. On most days when he was preparing material for congresses, plenums, or the Supreme Soviet, the mail just had to wait, although he did look at some of the more sensitive items without delay.

Letters from the public accounted for a colossal amount of mail. As I have said, more than a million such letters were received in a single year, and in 1987 the total was 1.2 million, most of them addressed directly to the general secretary. As many as 300,000 or 400,000 of the total number came from abroad. Later on the flood rapidly turned into a mere stream; and when Gorbachev's popularity waned after the start of the debates in the Supreme Soviets and Congresses of People's Deputies of the USSR and the RSFSR, it shrank to a mere rivulet.

Gorbachev once phoned, asking me to collect and show him all the letters received by the Central Committee in a single day. Placed in boxes and arranged in one of the large empty offices on the fifth floor, they occupied all the tables and chairs, and even much of the floor. Three thousand of them were addressed to him personally. He leafed through them, reading a few here and there; later on, in the Politburo or at his meetings with the public, he spoke of what he had found in them. These letters, in which people had sent their requests, complaints, proposals, and wishes to the Central Committee, made up a gigantic human document. Many of them were profoundly disturbing and frightening. People wrote about dreadful living conditions, lawlessness, and the hardships of everyday life. The ones that upset me the most were those describing sickness in the very old and the very young. It was like a desperate scream for help from people who were dying as a result of indifference and the shortage of medications. Just thinking about it was painful. The people in the department did everything they could to help old people in need, but there were limits to what we could achieve.

When criticism of his performance came to predominate in these letters, Gorbachev lost interest in them. Every day, however, I gathered some twenty letters and put them on his desk. It was unpleasant for both of us, but especially for him.

THE PRIVILEGES OF THE NOMENKLATURA

Yet another day fades away. It must be a fine day, with the sun low in the sky, still warming the city. Sometimes in the late afternoon its rays shine through the thick steel blinds and land on the iron bars and on the hand I have placed next to the narrow crack; then I feel the living warmth of the late summer. But the shadows quickly lengthen, the sunlight fades, and the dark sky wraps the earth in gloom. After dinner I somehow feel the approach of winter, coupled with a grim foreboding that will not leave me alone. Today I have spent about three hours standing where the window is supposed to be. It has been covered over with thick glass blocks, leaving only a narrow strip visible through the blinds to suggest that there is sun, earth, and sky. But I cannot see them.

Lights out. I lie with my eyes open, as my thoughts turn again to home and to the women whose fate is still on my conscience—my ninety-year-old mother, my wife, my daughter and granddaughter. I have never had anything but my salary and the proceeds of a few jobs I did while still working for Pravda. But the investigators made my wife and daughter forfeit that money. What are they living on now? My wife's 180-ruble disability benefit? The 100-ruble allowance my daughter gets while she's on maternity leave? Why are they and my five-month-old granddaughter suffering so?

I think back to my home and try to visualize my family and the baby's crib. Lenochka must be asleep. In two days she will be five months old. Shall I ever set eyes on her? I am overwhelmed by feelings of bitterness, warmth, and tenderness. I never imagined that my little granddaughter would ever mean so much to me.

My little sunbeam! When I think of you the whole cell radiates warmth and light. I reach out to touch you, but instead my fingers feel the rough cell wall. I have not been able to do my duty to these women, and now it seems I never will. That is what torments me more than all the physical suffering.

How will you get through the winter? How are you going to survive being cast adrift on a stormy ocean? Will you be strong enough to make it? I search for answers but find none. If your well-being depended even a little bit on me, I would let you have all my lifeblood, drop by drop.

I have thrown your lives into turmoil and brought you grief and suffering because I deeply love my homeland and cannot bear to see the anguish of millions of refugees fleeing their homes, the suffering of my brothers, now at war, and the blood of innocent people. Am I right to feel this way? I ask myself these questions, while asking also about my wife, my daughter, Lenochka, but I get no answer. Even the floors and walls are silent, but for the sound of the guards' heels outside the door.

Is it possible, while serving one's country, to be led to the scaffold because of the collapse of that country and its army and because of fratricidal war? I believe it is. But it is wrong to love one's country in return for privileges. I have no doubt that for many people they meant very little. They were certainly not what caused me to work for Gorbachev. I was the first member of his entourage to refuse to drive around in a Chaika,* and I stayed in the same densely populated dacha I had been given ten years before, though my rank gave me access to much better living conditions. Nor did I use the special clinic, although working fourteen or sixteen hours a day with virtually no days off or normal vacations took a heavy toll on my health.

---

*The luxurious Chaika was the status car of the Soviet nomenklatura in the 1960s and 1970s, predecessor of the Zil.

Privileges there were, however, and they were used to the full. Information about them has been both distorted and understated. The understatement was, of course, intended to deflect criticism away from those who really did enjoy every benefit they could get their hands on, virtually free of charge.

How did this system come about? Why did it survive so long and collapse only under a barrage of criticism?

A HIERARCHY OF PERQUISITES

The system of material incentives in the Soviet Union has never been based on principles of equality. It is well known that during the early years of the revolution some state employees had access to special restaurants serving a wide variety of high-calorie foods. The explanation for the opening of such establishments was that the working day of government employees was not regulated, and that, unless such services were provided, it might be difficult to attract highly qualified experts into government service. The therapeutic restaurant on Granovski Street, used by sick and anemic staff members, was opened on the initiative of Lenin. The system was gradually extended to cover party workers. And although industrial workers and government employees received practically the same pay, the government apparatus did provide numerous and varied privileges. These compelled the employees to value their work highly, not to disclose industrial or state secrets, and not to get involved in illegal operations. In those circumstances the existence of a number of privileges was clearly justified. Like any breach of principle, however, they degenerated and began to be hidden from the rest of society.

Special restaurants and stores also operated in the capitals of the various Soviet republics and in a number of big cities. Some Germans once came with a view to borrowing from our experience in the establishment of such a system. They inspected the restaurant on Granovski Street and found the principles on which it was based to be excellent. Their only comment had to do with what they felt must surely be a national characteristic: even in special stores closed to the general public, Russians managed to make people wait in line, sometimes for hours. They were right. Anyone wanting to pick up a pound of sausages sometimes had to wait for two hours. I remember seeing famous academics, industrial designers, artists, and others prominent in culture and science standing in line during normal working hours. These people's time was so valuable that it was a crime for them to waste it on such things. Not until Andropov became general secretary did these daytime lines disappear; thereafter it was possible to get whatever was in stock without a long wait.

The privileges accorded certain party members and government employees fell far short of those to which those at the highest echelons of power had access. Until 1987, at least on paper, the members of the Politburo, including the chairman of the Council of Ministers, earned 800 rubles a month. This was not a large amount, but it did not determine the living standards of the top leadership of party and state. Exactly who was entitled to what was set forth in a number of secret decisions of the Politburo and the Council of Ministers, some of which were known to only three persons. In addition to their salary, for example, Politburo members were entitled, free of charge, to 400 rubles' worth of food from the warehouse of the KGB's Ninth Directorate. Central Committee secretaries actually working in the Central Committee apparatus also enjoyed free breakfasts, lunches, and dinners, along with fruit and whatever else they wished to order.

I often saw security men, staggering under the weight of boxes or briefcases, accompanying their lords and masters to their cars, before delivering them and their rations to their dachas. One of the secretaries, working in foreign affairs, was particularly greedy. This indomitable fighter for world revolution and the universal triumph of communism was not averse to grabbing extra portions of goodies, which he would then take home to his large extended family. When I saw what he was doing, I began to take a dim view of our bright future.

The party's chief administrator, Nikolai Kruchina, often came to show me a thick wad of bills recording the colossal daily expenditures of the members of the Politburo and Central Committee secretaries on official hospitality and on their own households. These were expensive pleasures, especially since some of the food in question ended up at their dachas. In those days many highly placed party officials were costing the party thirty, forty, and sometimes fifty rubles a day, which is equivalent to the monthly pension payable to many veterans.

"Now you tell me what can be done about all this," Kruchina would say.

"Why don't you tell Gorbachev and try to get the practice changed?" was the best advice I could offer.

Without a word he took out Gorbechev's bill, number 001. It showed an amount of such magnitude that I no longer felt inclined to offer advice on the matter. I was also disturbed to see that wad of bills. Campaigns against privileges were being waged all over the country, but our leaders were the only ones who seemed to be out of touch with the times and with the actual living conditions of the ordinary people. In the summer of 1991 I proposed to Gorbachev that there be a fixed allotment for official hospitality and that everything else should be paid for. But that did not apply to the general secretary.

The system of privileges for the top leadership was not confined to higher pay and free supplies of food. The state or party budgets also financed apartments, dachas, automobiles, and much more. Most such apartments were located in comfortable buildings, with security guards and servants laid on as needed. By Western standards, of course, the apartments were fairly modest. Moreover, considering the huge burden of responsibility borne by their occupants, they can hardly be described as extravagant. The senior party and government officials in question tended to spent little time in town: as far as I know, Brezhnev, Andropov, and many others of comparable rank did not live regularly in apartments in Moscow, as there was no need for them to do so.

Dachas were quite a different matter. They were located in an area west of the capital, along the Moscow River. Most of them were superb modern villas—in fact, architectural masterpieces—usually on as much as 120 acres of coniferous woodlands, complete with greenhouses, aviaries, and enclosures for other wildlife. Swimming pools and saunas were added in later years.

Government dachas had a large household staff, cooks, maids, waitresses, cleaning ladies, gardeners, and security guards. When a friend of mine, on being elected to high office, was allotted such a dacha, he came to me looking quite distraught: "Look, I can't live in a dacha like that," he said earnestly. "I wouldn't be able to relax there. There are servants everywhere, and you could easily get lost in those luxurious apartments. I intend to give it up and tell Gorbachev about my decision."

Shortly before this incident, I had had a similar conversation with another newly elected Central Committee secretary who was also worried about the prospect of living in such high style, surrounded by servants. He wanted to ask his superiors to let him stay in his previous Central Committee dacha. All I could do was advise him take his time about deciding. People have an unfortunate, or perhaps fortunate, habit of getting used to the good life. After a while the issue comes to seem irrelevant, and people living in such surroundings begin to feel more important; their status begins to show in their appearance, gait, and speech, as the gulf between them and their former friends sharply widens. For that reason, and also because I knew that Gorbachev himself assigned dachas to Politburo members and Central Committee secretaries, I was in no hurry to offer any advice at all.

Besides the dachas just outside Moscow, there were villas and mansions dating from czarist times available for summer vacations, in various resort areas. Virtually every family had its own dacha in these areas, but new ones were being built all the time. Gorbachev continued to work on plans for new villas in the Crimea, along the Caucasus coast of the Black Sea, and in Kislovodsk and other regions of the Caucasus. This kind of construction appealed to him, and he liked to incorporate his own ideas about both design and landscaping. He was unwilling to take summer vacations in the residences previously used by former general secretaries or by the members of the Politburo. So one of the general secretary's residences was built by the sea in Georgia. As Gorbachev pointed out, a number of senior Georgian officials had impressed upon him the merits of the local climate, with its blend of sea air and the rich scent of Caucasian mountain conifers. Construction proceeded briskly and on a grand scale; in fact, sand for the beach was trucked in from over a hundred miles away. Gorbachev's residence at Foros was built even faster, as thousands of military construction personnel were put to work on it.

Gorbachev's major construction project, however, was his new residence in the suburbs of Moscow. Few people apart from the builders and the security guards were in a position to describe it in detail; but what I heard from the experts, and from Gorbachev himself, suggested that what the security people called his *Wolfschantze* (or "wolf's lair") was a pretty lavish place. It contained everything necessary for the operations of government at any time.

I believe the leader of a state like the Soviet Union needs a residence of this sort, but that decisions about its design features should be left up to the Supreme Soviets and the people's deputies, since its cost runs into hundreds of millions of rubles. No doubt the construction of summer residences should also be under the control of the people, so as to keep costs within reasonable levels. After all, party leaders are not Arabian sheikhs, and extraneous imperial flourishes should not be financed from the public purse. Even the czars used their own personal wealth to buy land and build residences. Unfortunately Gorbachev's passion for architecture and construction was not limited to suburban residences.

THE SAGA OF THE APARTMENTS

Sometime toward the middle of the summer of 1987, Kruchina called me to request an urgent meeting. A few minutes later he arrived, looking distinctly unwell. He had high blood pressure and had been taking pills and having injections ever since his stroke. He was obviously distressed over something, yet he remained silent for a while. Then, wiping the sweat from his brow, he told me he could not make up his mind about certain issues that had come up.

"Gorbachev invited me in and presented a few ideas for me to think over, so that I could give him a preliminary report on the best site for a new house for the general secretary," Kruchina said after a long pause. "I set about finding a suitable spot, but I guess there'll be no need for that now. I've been ordered to build it in the Lenin Hills, not far from the university."

I listened to him without saying a word, quite as astonished as he was by such a decision. No predecessor of his had ever decided to build himself a special house. Each of them had simply moved into vacant apartments, in the same buildings as dozens and even hundreds of other families. The buildings in which those apartments were located were naturally of good quality; but even if they found fault with some aspect of the layout, it could be suitably modified without unreasonable expense and the criticism that sometimes generates. Gorbachev may not have been aware of the sensitive implications of this issue or its possible ramifications, or he may have been unable to withstand certain pressures; but whatever the reason, this project was something completely new.

I was dismayed by the news from Kruchina, as I sensed that the rumors about the general secretary's passion for building villas and dachas would be greatly boosted by this latest development.

Choosing my words carefully, I asked Kruchina about the chances of finding some less conspicuous place, not in full view of the population of Moscow and the tourists who are driven around the Lenin Hills on their way to the observation platform. With a sigh of regret he replied that he had made some proposals, but to no avail, and that Gorbachev had obviously made up his mind. From my knowledge of Moscow I suspected he was right, but I suggested some places where such a house would not stand out quite so starkly. Then I added: "What about Shchuseva Street? Those are nice apartments."

"They're already living there, but there's something about the place they don't like," Kruchina replied. "I suggested to Gorbachev that he move into one of the state-owned houses in the Lenin Hills, where Khrushchev and a number of other senior party and government people once lived; or that he might wish to build a new house well inside that same area, as all the utilities have already been set up. But he wouldn't hear of it."

Without attempting to hide my indignation, I told Kruchina exactly what I thought: the chosen site should be out of the question, as the resulting rumors would bring bad publicity that would be hard for Gorbachev to counter. With a sigh, Kruchina pointed out that there absolutely had to be a view of the general secretary's alma mater, Moscow State University.

I was unable to offer any helpful suggestions, nor could Kruchina persuade Gorbachev to change his mind. In addition to the choice of the site, he was also bothered by the cost of the project, which could be conservatively estimated at several million rubles.

"We've found an architect and some designers, but we need builders and especially stonemasons, skilled woodworkers, and other specialized workers. Not to mention the hardware that will be required—and that's not so easy to find these days." He drank some tea, constantly wiping away beads of sweat that testified to his inner turmoil and the ultimately fatal strain that his job inflicted on him.

I remember driving past Gorbachev's house in the Lenin Hills once, while I was still not sure of its exact location, and seeing a grim, dirty-gray concrete structure with narrow asymmetrical windows, with no evidence of architectural flair at all. It looked like a hospital, the first floor being nonresidential and occupied by the security personnel. The layout of the living quarters was depressing. The general secretary, together with his daughter's family, occupied the whole of the upper floor. Kruchina and his deputies often traveled abroad to select kitchen furniture and equipment, as well as wallpaper, curtains, tiles, lamp brackets, chandeliers, lamps, and much more. He was particularly proud of a kitchen he had bought in Germany, which incorporated the most advanced design features. He was most impressed by the automatic washing machines and dryers, the large refrigerators and freezers, the various automatic cookers and ovens based on new physical principles, the food processors, as well as many other appliances about whose purpose he could only speculate. The six-room apartment, with two bedrooms, two bathrooms, large amounts of auxiliary space, and floors inlaid with exotic woods, was intended to accommodate two people.

The furniture for the apartment constituted a whole chapter in the work of the Department of the Administration of Affairs. Sets of furniture made of exotic woods were ordered from the Lyuks furniture factory. The apartment was constantly being renovated, altered, and touched up.

Before the finishing touches could be put to it, however, a nationwide antiprivilege campaign had started. The house in the Lenin Hills began to attract more and more attention from the public and from the deputies. Guides on sightseeing buses on their way to the observation platform near Moscow University would remind tourists that they were passing the home of General Secretary Gorbachev. Everyone would look out the windows to gaze upon a piece of architecture strongly reminiscent of a prefabricated school from the early 1960s. The antiprivilege campaign had not yet reached the general secretary, but for safety's sake he had already decided that it would be more prudent for him to move quietly out of the six-room apartment and into a vacant three-room apartment, on the same floor, intended for the security personnel.

Then began a new saga—this time involving the renovation of yet another apartment. I do not know how much hard currency was spent on acquiring imported equipment and fixtures, but the amounts disbursed by the party's budget for the construction of this presidential nest were enormous.

The Secretariat or the Politburo had to approve all Central Committee construction projects. But I never saw the corresponding document about the house in the Lenin Hills or the estimate of its construction costs. The paperwork might conceivably have been completed while Lukyanov was still in charge of the General Department. When fulfilling the general secretary's instructions, Kruchina invariably found himself in difficulties. In later years, however, when delegates to the Twenty-eighth Party Congress were demanding full budgetary disclosure, his woes became particularly stressful. Indeed, he was stretched to his physical and moral limits. The prospect of abuse from the general secretary hung over him perpetually, like a sword of Damocles.

As for Gorbachev himself, one wonders how a simple peasant boy who lived for many years in exceedingly modest circumstances demonstrated such a remarkable flair and talent for the construction of luxury homes, dachas, and apartments for himself and his family, decorating them with beautiful furniture, the finest of fixtures and appliances, and imported materials. Gorbachev's obsession with building lasted until his final days in office.

While Ryzhkov was still chairman of the Council of Ministers, Gorbachev did his utmost to evict the prime minister and all his deputies from the government building in the Kremlin. It was no easy task. Ryzhkov was apparently telling his associates that he was not going to be the first prime minister to be evicted from the Kremlin, the traditional seat of government. It is hard to say whether this played some part in his resignation; but the first thing Gorbachev did after the appointment of Valentin Pavlov as prime minister and the approval of his cabinet was to move the government to a building on Pushkin Street. This meant that the second-floor office where Stalin once worked was now vacant. Gorbachev was free to move to new accommodations.

Toward the end of 1990 Gorbachev invited Plekhanov, Kruchina, and me into his office and told us, at first in a roundabout way, that the second-floor suite had to be renovated in a manner compatible with the status of the president of the USSR. He gave us a detailed description of how he envisioned his office and the adjoining rooms after renovation. His current office on the third floor and the Politburo conference room were to be converted into a reception room for foreign guests, a television studio, and a small office, while the rest of the space would be occupied by his personal living quarters. The apartment was to include a kitchen, a dining room, a lounge, halls, two bedrooms, an office, and various other rooms.

Kruchina and I discussed this new assignment at length. Both of us were upset at the thought of yet another apartment in the Kremlin. The preservation of Lenin's apartment, as a memorial, made sense. In those days many high-ranking party and government officials lived in the Kremlin, as none of them had apartments in town and few even had dachas. At first we could see no reason why the general secretary and president needed an apartment inside the Kremlin walls. It later occurred to us that he had come to this decision because he had begun to fear for his life. He now traveled in an armor-plated ZIL limousine and had ordered an increase in the number of his bodyguards. Plekhanov had also taken other security measures. We felt that a good case could be made for an apartment safely tucked away inside the Kremlin, where a special regiment was stationed. There was another possible explanation, of course: Gorbachev may have fancied that his apartment would also become a memorial, in honor of the man who reformed the Soviet Union.

Security questions were doubtless important, but then so was the trouble that rebuilding a unique structure within the Kremlin, designed by the eminent Kazakov, was certain to cause. The Society for the Protection of Cultural Monuments, as well as the general public, could be counted on to protest.

Kruchina and I assumed from the start that halting the project was out of the question. The best we could hope for was some plausible excuse for delaying it. There were plenty of good reasons for wanting the whole thing canceled. Apart from anything else, the fabric of this venerable building had deteriorated so badly that its structural integrity could not be guaranteed.

But Gorbachev was in a hurry: he wanted those plans right away. Some six weeks later the plans drawn up by Plekhanov and his staff were presented to him. It was always hard to tell whether a proposal had met with his approval, but this one clearly did. He even made a few comments of his own. A revised version was adopted practically unchanged, and to the best of my knowledge the security and administrative people made a start on the actual construction. The events of August 1991 obviously upset these plans. I understand that the intended renovation of the general secretary's office in the Central Committee building was also halted. As I learned from Kruchina, all current occupants of the fifth floor were to have been evicted, so that it could be turned into a residence for the general secretary as well as a reception room for foreign guests and a television studio.

Among all the actions of the general secretary and president, this remodeling and reshuffling of floor space was perhaps the most fruitful. Had circumstances not taken such a sad turn, who knows what new ventures might have engaged the attention of Mikhail Gorbachev, the master builder?

STILL MORE PERKS

Privileges went beyond food, apartments, dachas, and a whole range of modestly priced imported luxury goods, some of which found their way onto the black market. They also included chauffeur-driven limousines and other cars, and medical treatment. Special aircraft were made available free of charge, and large amounts of hard currency were allotted under the heading of "representation expenses" for foreign travel. When Gorbachev traveled abroad, his wife was also paid a daily allowance, despite the fact that both the Soviet security services and the host country made every provision for the general secretary's needs during such visits.

Of course, not all high party and government officials were guilty of excesses. Many of them displayed the most commendable modesty in their lifestyles. Nonetheless, criticism of the privileges of the nomenklatura made the leadership nervous. Gorbachev was opposed to the elimination of privileges for lower-level officials, and wavered for a long time before closing the restaurant on Granovski Street, though he allowed its clients to continue placing special orders for food from their place of work. The question of who was to use the dachas of the KGB's Ninth Directorate was resolved in a matter of minutes. Members of the Politburo were invited to move to government dachas. Central Committee secretaries were sent to the Central Committee's dacha compounds, officials of the Council of Ministers went to their own dachas, and Shevardnadze was offered the dacha of the Foreign Ministry, which apparently had not been renovated since before the war. The state-owned villas that became vacant were distributed almost at random, in the midst of great confusion. The new occupants included the Fourth Directorate of the Council of Ministers, the Supreme Soviet of the Union, and the workers at a number of factories. When Plekhanov went to inspect the dachas eighteen months after they had been transferred to their new occupants, he found that imported bathroom fixtures, wallpaper, and parquet floors had been ripped out.

Only one family in this era enjoyed privileges on the same scale as in Brezhnev's time. That was the family of the general secretary and president.

This was also true of the distribution of imported goods. Under the guise of a cleanup, Gorbachev originally limited the purchases his associates were allowed to make to a certain fixed amount, before denying them this option altogether. That left him as the sole beneficiary of this privilege. He and his family eventually began making their purchases from catalogs, which was much more convenient.

There was much rumor and speculation in the press about Gorbachev's suits, which were allegedly being made to measure by famous designers. I do not know the whole story and am not much of a judge of clothes, but I know that the suits he wore were made by two congenial and talented tailors on Kutuzovski Prospekt. With outstanding taste and finesse, and using imported material, they promptly executed his orders, dressing him in a manner compatible with his status on the world stage. I remember comparing his suits with those worn by Reagan, and later Bush, and concluded that either the United States lacked high-quality tailoring of the sort I have described or no one there could afford it. As for Raisa'a wardrobe, its provenance must continue to be her little secret.

As I have said before, I remain convinced of the need for the president to live in dignified circumstances. The president of a great country cannot wear the frayed suits of past years or go around in patched-up shoes. On a miserly salary of four thousand rubles he clearly could not afford to buy decent clothes for himself and his wife, let alone help his mother, his children, and so on. But these things should have been done legally and in the open.

Just as the dust was beginning to settle after the whirlwind transfer of so many villas, houses, and state sanatoriums and vacation homes, Gorbachev decided to allot the dacha at Pitsunda to the Fourth Directorate of the Ministry of Health. Shevardnadze, who was surprised and shocked that the Politburo had not been involved in decisions about the dachas, pointed out that it was wrong to apportion property belonging to another republic, especially if it was located in a pine forest that had been turned into a nature reserve. The rumor mill had been active back in the 1950s, when Khrushchev started to build the dacha; so what point was there in stirring things up again? These remarks stopped Gorbachev cold. He realized that he had been single-handedly disposing of state property, and that he could eventually be held strictly accountable for his actions. Ever the consummate striptease artist, though, he would still instruct Plekhanov to transfer a particular dacha to the Foreign Ministry, while keeping what he liked for himself. In this way Zavidovo remained under its previous jurisdiction, though it cost the state dearly.

The leadership had hundreds of servants at its beck and call. Each dacha, as we have seen, had its own large array of servants. These people, most of whom were military personnel, did their utmost to make life comfortable for their wards. In return, however, they endured tyrannical behavior, being treated like house serfs. In some households conditions were so bad that the staff would literally run away, warning fellow servants to avoid working for the clan in question.

THE PARTY LEADER AT
WORK AND PLAY

At first Gorbachev's election as general secretary did little to change his pattern of work and recreation. He still got up at 7:00, went for a walk and a swim, and then studied the newspapers. His limousine and its escort vehicles would arrive at his house at 8:30, and by 9:00 he was at work. As general secretary, the nature of his work changed and its volume grew. He had a much fuller schedule. In the morning he met Lukyanov, the head of the General Department, and discussed the latest documents received by the Central Committee. Their total volume was quite large, but Gorbachev carefully examined everything submitted to him, which covered a vast amount of varied information pertaining to the work of the Politburo and the Central Committee Secretariat. All telegrams were also placed on his desk each morning.

Once he had looked through the mail, he would receive two or three *obkom* and *kraikom* secretaries or, less frequently, Central Committee secretaries. Then he started work on questions that held out some promise of change. The need for economic reform made it essential to focus on problems of a global nature. In 1985 preparations were under way for a meeting on the acceleration of scientific and technological progress and reforms in a number of industrial sectors. At that time there was still no strategy for change. Gorbachev himself took a piecemeal view of perestroika, understanding it to mean the acceleration of economic development and changes in certain economic structures, leaving production methods and the relationship between consumers and producers unchanged. This was when he made a number of hasty and ill-considered moves, such as the decree against alcoholism, restrictions on entrepreneurial activity, and an attempt to speed up development while failing to make fundamental changes.

Personnel questions were often taken up before lunch. Gorbachev would spend some time alone with Ligachev, trying to figure out who should be assigned where. Later on, Razumovski and his deputy Yevgeni Razumov also took part in these discussions. The new party leadership had a tragic flaw: Gorbachev, Ligachev, and Razumovski knew very little about the cadres, either in the center or in the localities. They tended to pick people much more on the basis of their résumés, someone else's recommendation, personal impressions, or likes and dislikes than for their actual ability. Personal loyalty to the new leadership was naturally a crucial factor in career advancement.

Between 1:00 and 2:00, Gorbachev usually had lunch, often gulping his food down in five to seven minutes; he would say "just wait a minute" and disappear into the lounge for a snack.

Lunch occasionally lasted longer than that; sometimes Gorbachev would rest or see his doctors, who sometimes gave him a massage. Five or six times during the afternoon he spoke to Raisa, who was always well informed about his plans and activities.

He spent the evening absorbing more information and reading documents. He was so fond of perusing foreign reactions to his initiatives that he often read out loud passages that I had read to him several times before. He would put such material to one side and take it home with him. Unless there was some urgent business, the general secretary left work after supper, between 8:00 and 9:00. Virtually his first act on arriving home was to take a walk with Raisa, lasting an hour and a half or two hours. Then he would return to his desk and prepare for the next day's schedule. Between 11:00 and midnight, sometimes later, he would call to instruct me to do something before he reached the office the next morning and plan certain other items for the morning schedule. At the same time he would call several other Politburo members. Few of his associates dared call him at the dacha, as he had made it abundantly clear he did not want to be disturbed.

At first Gorbachev used to arrive at work earlier than usual on days when the Politburo was scheduled to meet. He would study the documents and other information relevant to the agenda. Until 11:00 in the morning he received those whose new appointments were to be confirmed at the meeting. They were usually *obkom* and *kraikom* secretaries, the secretaries of the republican parties, ministers, and members of the military high command. The Politburo meetings started at 11:00, and could last until 9:00 or 10:00 in the evening, with a small break for dinner or no break at all.

During the early part of his tenure, Gorbachev used to invite a few close associates in after the meeting to discuss their impressions of the speeches made by Politburo members; they would comment on the language used and either endorse or denounce the speaker. As time went by, however, the general secretary stopped coming early. He neglected to prepare for the agenda items under discussion, evidently relying on what he already knew. It was frequently not enough. Then, having revealed his ignorance, he tended to latch on to some idea from the speech of a Politburo member and enlarge on it. This not-so-subtle technique left his audience feeling helpless and resentful. He was, as I could see, increasingly weary of meetings.

Unless meetings and talks with foreigners were scheduled, Gorbachev began to arrive at work later and leave earlier. At home, however, he still stayed up late and slept less, and less soundly, than he would have liked.

The general secretary spent his vacations in the Crimea, in later years in his newly built villa at Foros. Officially he was entitled to forty-five days of leave in the summer, but he was usually away for only a month. During his first few years in office, he took a winter vacation, too, at Pitsunda. The situation in the country, which in any case was not conducive to relaxation, eventually prevented him from doing so. Other members of the Politburo followed his lead.

While on summer vacation, Gorbachev often worked, receiving all urgent information and documents. Sometimes he would have Chernyayev write articles and books—among them *The New Thinking*—for him. He sent a draft of the book to aides and Politburo members to whom he habitually entrusted sensitive matters. With the help of some twenty people, the book was finalized and published in the West, where it made a substantial profit.

Gorbachev had no particular pastimes, such as hunting or fishing, although he handled a hunting rifle quite well, as I saw while he was on a trip to Belovezhskaya Pushcha. As first secretary in Stavropol, he often met visiting Moscow dignitaries, organizing recreation and entertainment for them, including hunting. Whether he liked it or not, therefore, he had to learn how to shoot.

For him, game playing meant politics, at which he was a grand master. The gregarious Brezhnev was fond of inviting friends, some of them from the Socialist countries, to his seaside vacation home in the Crimea. By comparison, Gorbachev was a hermit while on vacation.

After Gorbachev distributed the state dachas in the south to different organizations, senior officials in both party and government began to find that arranging their vacations could be quite stressful. Tensions arose over the choice of locations and dates. Their habits were so ingrained that none of them was prepared to go to an ordinary sanatorium. The dacha situation around Moscow was also tight, with only government dachas available.

That was all well and good. On the other hand, it meant that the Central Committee secretaries, Politburo members, and deputy chairmen of the Council of Ministers had lost their aura of majesty and mystery and were now seen by the public to be ordinary mortals. It was a shocking revelation. In our particular country, as in central Asia, godlike status had always been an attribute of leadership; no ruler who failed to understand that could ever hope to stay in power for long. The more despotic and aloof our rulers were, the longer they stayed on their thrones.

The machinery of government that had taken decades to develop continued to work smoothly. Decisions were still being adopted, but the party and government apparatus no longer felt sure they were the right ones.

At Politburo meetings government ministers would suddenly flare up, referring in strong and often sarcastic language to the draft decisions before them, the state of the country, and the laxity with which plans were being carried out. Worse still was a disdainful silence, or an unwillingness to express any views at all. Criticism from the Politburo now aroused skepticism and mirth rather than fear. I remember seeing one minister, after the adjournment of a Politburo meeting, mimic the general secretary's voice, accent, and gestures as he proposed a mock plan of action, prompting sad laughter among those standing around.

Those who worked in the party and government apparatus were naturally more sensitive to the country's woes than their superiors, as they were better placed to understand in fine detail what had gone wrong.

I began to take part less often in the preparation of reports and speeches. Sensing my antipathy to his phrase mongering, Gorbachev doubtless recruited new people who were less weary of the tainted and increasingly foreign vocabulary that he favored. I made no secret of my feelings about the general secretary's passion for writing and talking, having raised the matter with him repeatedly. Back in 1987 I had had a number of conversations with him during the evening hours, when he was more relaxed and it was possible to raise a variety of topics. I told him then that I was afraid words were becoming devalued. Too much had been said in too short a time. Books of his speeches, which once sold briskly, were now gathering dust in the warehouses. Words had to be used sparingly, and not at all unless they conveyed some new idea. I discussed this matter with Yakovlev, who also felt that Gorbachev's only hope of avoiding ridicule was parsimony in the use of words, coupled with an impressive array of deeds.

I had many friends in Volynskoye, and on occasional visits there I could tell that they were worried and uncertain. The teams of Central Committee consultants and staff on loan from various institutes, whose job it was to prepare speeches or reports for Gorbachev, were no longer full of enthusiasm for the ideas contained in the presidential text. The ideas themselves were increasingly flimsy. Sensing their confusion, I would sit down with them to discuss various issues, or simply to talk about the difficulties facing the party and society as a whole. Some of them were reluctant to speak their minds, doubtless fearing that I might misconstrue their remarks. That was not the first time I had found that my status and the nature of my job tended to inhibit frank discussions. Only people I had known for many years would confide in me their innermost thoughts about current events and their alarm over the state of the country. It was harder for me to discuss many issues on which I was familiar with the underlying politics, the infighting in the Politburo, the character of the general secretary, and the influences to which members of his immediate entourage, and others who were further removed, subjected him.

Gorbachev's team of speechwriters included a variety of people. All of them were erudite, accomplished party workers and academics; but some of them gradually withdrew, probably because they regarded all their late-night endeavors as a repetitious waste of time. Any progress made was on paper alone, while in practical terms nothing changed.

7

THE TWILIGHT
OF PERESTROIKA

When did I first sense the approach of the twilight of perestroika? It came gradually, though its onset coincided with the first signs of uncertainty in Gorbachev's statements and actions, when he began to cast around for new methods of government, blaming his failures on others and fearing to acknowledge his mistakes. He kept on talking and making hasty decisions that led nowhere. Perhaps the twilight of perestroika began slightly earlier, when the Politburo, Central Committee, and government ceased to act in concert. I clearly saw what was happening when Gorbachev, though well aware of the true situation, began to voice insincere and unwarranted optimism. He was obviously expecting a miracle to extricate him from the quicksand.

The more alarming the state of both party and country, the more varied were his confidential meetings with the representatives of different groups. When meeting with democrats, he assured them that he would uphold freedom, glasnost, and radical democratic change, yet when talking to the proponents of more gradual reform, he would state that only the Communist party could put perestroika into effect. Gorbachev must have been aware of the failure of reform, the grave state of the economy, and his responsibility for what had happened. It is therefore conceivable that he felt compelled to switch to the left flank of the perestroika forces so that he would be standing beneath the banners of his recent critics while delivering the coup de grâce to the Soviet Union. In the meantime, however, he repeatedly ran from one side of the sinking ship to the other, confusing everybody and hiding his true intentions. Fear may have clouded his awareness of his own instinctive attempts to survive, but his frantic political maneuvering was clearly visible to a bystander.

Another possibility is that the insincerity and impracticality of many of his proposals became obvious within the party, and this may have led to discord in the Central Committee and other party committees and organizations. At the plenum of the Central Committee in January 1987, when outlining his plans for the democratization of society, Gorbachev said that the elected representatives of the people and the party were being led by the apparatchiks, and not by the members of the Central Committee, the party's executive committees, and the soviets. The system had to be changed. Of course, he forgot to say that the entire government, the Presidium of the Supreme Soviet, the labor unions, and other nongovernmental organizations were in fact being led single-handedly by the Politburo—in other words, by the general secretary. If any perestroika was needed, he should apply it to himself first.

Nonetheless, it was certainly correct to raise the issue of the democratization of society. There was a clear need to reduce the apparatus of government and give it new functions. Having described the inadequacies of that apparatus, the general secretary then proceeded to take concrete action and was able to implement such decisions successfully. For all practical purposes, the economy was managed until recently by the Politburo and the Central Committee Secretariat. The Council of Ministers merely rubber-stamped many decisions of the party organs, or performed specific tasks contained in the approved plan of action. This fact explains a great deal. Over the past few decades the Central Committee had established a large staff of experts to handle the preparation of the complex documentation needed for the adoption of its decisions. It contained not just departments dealing with party committees and organizations and work in the ideological sector but also sections that were fully qualified to deal with machine building, construction, chemicals, agriculture, the economy, science, and education. Within the apparatus there were also large and highly skilled departments dealing with the defense industry, the administrative organs, international affairs, and others.

In the Soviet Union there could be no discussion or decision on any even remotely substantive matters without the approval of the Central Committee's departments. On many issues, they or the Secretariat would themselves forward draft decisions to the Politburo, which were then adopted as decisions of the Politburo and the Council of Ministers.

After the Central Committee plenum on cadre policy, Gorbachev ordered Ligachev and the Secretariat to come up with proposals for sharp reductions in the size of the apparatus. Before the resulting draft went to the Politburo, Gorbachev studied it carefully, striking out many departments altogether, or merging them, cutting the size of staff. These reductions applied not only to the departments supervising the economic organs but also to those engaged in purely party or ideological work. When considering draft decisions and preparing reports, the general secretary often brought in staff specializing in those issues, as well as his own aides. Reading the documents out loud, he would remark on infelicitous wording and, with the help of those present, suggest replacements. He would ask: "Why do we need a department on the chemical industry, or a section dealing with siliceous organic compounds, to name just a few? Out they go!"

He was right, of course, but that was the setup he had inherited. The trouble was not with the machine-building or construction departments. The entire system of government still reflected the demands of the wartime economy and the postwar reconstruction effort, when tight discipline, control, and accountability were essential. Everything had to be changed, but it had to be done in such a way as to avoid destroying the economy and setting the country back several decades.

At that time, however, Gorbachev was cutting the number and size of departments for a single purpose: to enhance the autonomy, prestige, and accountability of elected organs. Such a move was a vital way of averting criticism, in the light of the forthcoming elections of people's deputies to the Supreme Soviet, first of the whole USSR and then of the individual republics. As the party went to the elections, its slogan was "Greater autonomy for the deputies and delegates, greater freedom of action for the representatives of the elected organs."

The process of democratization started with the decision to hold competitive elections for the people's deputies. Several candidates were to contend for the same seat. This democratic principle is sound but dangerous, as Gorbachev realized earlier than most. With the country in turmoil he felt that many party and government figures would be unable to compete. He therefore devised an arrangement whereby deputies would be elected not only by local constituencies but also by organizations. He argued that the public mood would be more amply expressed in the Supreme Soviets if it were given an occupational as well as a territorial basis; therefore labor unions, the Komsomol, the party, and the

various unions and organizations of writers, journalists, artists, and so
on, should all be represented there.

The idea seemed fine. The party, as well as the unions and other organizations, welcomed it. On his instructions, a set of rules governing representation were prepared: parties, labor unions, and other large organizations were each to have one hundred representatives. It was, as I have
said, a clever scheme, but it also ran into some practical difficulties, as
these "hundreds" were also supposed to be elected on a competitive
basis. That would have invalidated the whole purpose. Here again a
negotiated settlement was reached, whereby each organization was free
to choose as it wished. When discussing the matter with his aides, Gorbachev said, "We are surely not going to have respected people compet-
ing like that in the plenum."

He had by then begun to worry about his declining popularity. He
was afraid to run for election in a constituency, in case he lost to the
competition, but was also unhappy about the prospect of a secret ballot
in the plenum of one such "hundred." His argument was: "The whole
thing could be sabotaged by a huge number of 'no' votes. Any candidate
who demands results and makes others accountable is obviously going to
be unpopular somewhere or other. So we can't have competitive balloting in the party for the hundred seats."

His concern was understandable. He had not been feeling well, and
had lost plenty of sleep. As his close associates could see, he seemed to
have aged rapidly. He was no longer the same man. Irritation lurked just
beneath the surface, in his words and the tone of his voice. He made
unexpected decisions, often changing his mind. Before the elections, for
example, he was unsure where he should run for office. He would often
turn to his entourage and speculate: "If I get elected in a constituency,
Communists are going to say that I was unwilling to seek election in
behalf of the party. And if I run for office at a Central Committee
plenum, the people are going to think I don't trust them."

He had a point. My feeling was that he should run for election in
some large constituency where the electorate consisted of both Communists and non-Communists. I told him that he was, after all, running for
a seat as a people's deputy, not as a delegate to a party congress. He
appeared to agree; but doubtless after talking it over with the Politburo,
he decided to seek election within the party.

Much later I realized why Gorbachev decided to run for election at a
party plenum. He had decided against running in Moscow, as he might

lose on account of the strong opposition there. Choosing some other constituency would be an indignity, especially if he had to campaign against rival candidates. He was afraid of losing to his increasingly powerful adversary Boris Yeltsin.

Razumovski and the staff of the party's Organizational Department then began work on the list of the "hundred." They included many members of the Politburo and the Central Committee, as well as *kraikom, obkom,* and republican secretaries. Gorbachev was not pleased. Well aware of the complexity of his participation in the "hundred," he sat with Razumovski for two whole days at the long conference table, crossing out the names of potential candidates. It was very important for him to be in the right company. What was supposed to be a list of party representatives began to look as if it had been prepared by some organization of writers or artists. It now contained the names of famous writers, and artists, as well as those of industrial and collective farm workers; some party officials were struck off the list, while others were added. Gorbachev's main task now was to secure the names of some well-known representatives of groups or organizations of intellectuals, such as writers, journalists, or academics. Coffee, tea, and sandwiches were served while work proceeded, hour after hour. The list simply had to be ready by the time the plenum convened, in a matter of days. Moreover, it should not give rise to misgivings, as that could lead to changes and fresh nominations, with unforeseeable results.

When the plenum eventually convened, participants naturally had questions, the most common of which was why their name was not on the list. Many members were privately—and justifiably—afraid of electoral constituencies, with competitive balloting. Gorbachev took the floor and explained why that particular list was necessary. He spoke at length, though many of his listeners already understood his logic, which was that a good main course always requires certain trimmings. For the sake of a number of candidates who absolutely had to be on the list, it was proposed to include some famous artists and writers, as well as some workers and peasants. That would make it impossible for anyone to argue that it was a "hundred" of party officials, so as to avoid offending well-known figures from outside the party. In actual fact this clever scheme was not an entire success, as the epithets "Red Hundred" or "Black Hundred" became attached to the deputies thus elected.[*]

---

[*]The Black Hundreds were anti-Semitic nationalist extremists in the nineteenth century.

Party discipline was still in operation, so there was no lengthy debate, and the elections went off relatively smoothly. Some ballots had names crossed out, but that was fairly normal. Had the election been competitive, however, many candidates might have lost any hope of serving as deputies. This kind of election was simpler, as success was guaranteed, with no need to harangue the public or be held accountable for one's performance as a deputy. Here there was only one hurdle: confirmation by the Central Electoral Commission, and that was essentially a formality.

Meanwhile, in the country as a whole, an unprecedented electoral campaign, in which several candidates ran for each seat, was in full swing. Passions mounted as a variety of organizations and pressure groups fielded vast forces. Ferocious verbal exchanges between rival candidates were commonplace. The surest way to succeed was to outdo everyone else in lambasting and denouncing the government and the party. All candidates used this technique, each in his or her own way. A second method was to promise prosperity. People believed such claims.

All these critical remarks found a sympathetic audience among the general public. People had expected a great deal from perestroika and Gorbachev's innovations, but four years later, in the midst of mounting confusion and hardship, their faith had worn thin. The people could see that ethnic conflicts were becoming exacerbated, crime was on the rise, and shortages were rampant. With chaos looming, people sought salvation by repudiating those under whose rule life had become harder. They were capable of idolizing those who had brought well-being and glory to their country, but would not forgive a worsening of their living conditions.

Political agitation seemed to be concentrated in a number of big cities, while the situation in many regions was quite calm. Despite the competitive nature of the elections, the people voted for candidates known for their abilities, integrity, and fairness. They could tell which were the most meritorious candidates, and did not allow those with no valid claim on their loyalty to get elected to the Soviets.

But candidates running for election as deputies, not to be outdone, promised everything under the sun, from a cleaner environment to better-stocked shelves in the stores and a new apartment within five years. The most pathetic and tragic side of all this was that the electorate was ready to believe them. Even doubters were swayed, because everyone wanted to hear words of hope; under the circumstances, they could not fail to leave a favorable impression.

How many factories in the chemical and pharmaceutical industries had been closed because of poor waste control systems? How many grim and horrifying articles were published in newspapers and magazines in those days? Yet later on, when the political situation changed, the flood of protest from the public and the media stopped abruptly. Waste management is a definite necessity, as it protects the lives and the health of the public. On the other hand, its cost is exorbitant. The Soviet Union, in any case, lacked the technology needed for pollution control. That, however, is beside the point. Ecological issues were exploited at the time as a political battering ram, in order to sway public opinion. People readily succumbed to demands for the closing of factories as a way of striking back at the authorities, who in their opinion were poisoning them.

But one should not be too quick to judge the events of this initial phase of democratic reform. The party leadership was itself to blame for the public's frustration over the endless wait for a chance to express its will freely in normal elections. After this phase, the electorate became more discerning. Both the nomination and election of candidates proceeded with greater caution, so that only those who took their duties seriously actually served as deputies. In those days, however, things were quite different. Passions, turmoil, and economic confusion drove the leaders of the various movements far apart, into battles over sovereignty and the clash of irreconcilable opinions. Our country thus strayed from the path now being taken by Europe and, indeed, by the rest of the world. How much farther will we continue to stray? Is the process already irreversible?

The peoples' deputies were now in place, after the elections to the Supreme Soviet of the Union. Next came the Congress of People's Deputies itself and the formation of its governing bodies. It was still unclear whether two and a half thousand deputies would attend each session, or whether they would elect a smaller number to serve on the Supreme Soviet. Gorbachev felt that this question needed further thought. He was uncertain about the future course of events and about the real mood of the deputies. Many surprises still lay in store. Meanwhile, however, he was preparing to assume the post of chairman of the Supreme Soviet of the USSR, an objective he had been pursuing for some time.

He now realized that it had become increasingly inappropriate for him, in his capacity as general secretary, to travel abroad and hold talks with foreign leaders.

His Western partners thought so too. Therefore, breaking his pledge not to hold two posts, he began the theoretical and practical groundwork for his election as head of state, discussing the matter first with close associates and then with the members of the Central Committee. Everyone, apparently, had been expecting such a decision. They talked themselves into agreeing that the reason perestroika was tumbling out of control was that the leader of the party was not the head of the Supreme Soviet. Then, having secured agreement, or at least having aroused no objections, he moved on to the next preelection phase, in which he campaigned among members of the Central Committee. He invited in a large group of secretaries from the Central Committee of the republics and those from the *kraikom* and *obkom* levels and suggested to them that under conditions of democracy, party leaders should head the Soviets, at all levels.

"In civilized countries the ruling party appoints its leader as president or head of the government," he argued. "It would be wrong for us to depart from democratic traditions. We ought to follow the example of the West in both central and local governments. I invite you to comment on this issue. With a tough political fight on our hands, we must not lose control of the levers of state power."

When told to nominate their own candidates for election to the Soviets, the secretaries reacted with silent bewilderment. They saw no reason why Gorbachev should not take such a step himself, but failed to see why they should follow suit. One of them eventually took the floor, warning against undue haste. Clearly, the secretaries were not ready to assume power in the soviets. Some saw it as an extra burden, while others were apprehensive about the prospect of not being elected. Support for the idea was scant.

Gorbachev's consummate mastery of the art of persuasion then came into play. Skillfully marshaling his arguments, his eyes and voice imbued with sincere conviction, he captivated his audience to the point where the secretaries began to waver. I sensed that they were mentally comparing their current duties with those of the heads of the soviets, and realized that their resistance was broken. Even those who did not want to hold two posts themselves gladly gave their consent to Gorbachev's becoming chairman of the Supreme Soviet, provided they were left alone. The rest now simply believed it was necessary for both the general secretary and them to head two organs.

This operation, which lasted three hours and, in Gorbachev's own words, was a nerve-wracking experience, ended in outright triumph. Another hurdle lay ahead, but he would have help in surmounting it from the first secretaries of the committees and the deputations from the republics, *krais*, and *obkoms*. Everything would go the way he wanted. The general secretary already had more than enough experience in assuming new posts.

The Congress of People's Deputies opened on 25 May 1989. It was a fine, warm day: the grass was bright green and the trees were covered with emerald foliage. The deputies were a mixed bunch. Some were industrial workers noted for their high output but not for their oratorical skills. Others were party workers engaged in running the economy. These were no Ciceros either, having long ago lost the ability to make convincing, impassioned speeches. A new group of deputies, no strangers to public speaking, had a mastery of language and oratory, as well as a good theoretical background. It had become fashionable to denounce Soviet rule for everything under the sun; but one area where it was immune to criticism was secondary and higher education, especially science. Its opponents, among whom were many university graduates, scientists, writers, journalists, and lawyers, could hardly complain of being poorly educated. Admittedly, they had not worked in industry or agriculture or been involved in the practical side of the economy, but that did not matter. These were educated people with a talent for expressing their views.

The hall was packed with deputies, guests, and the press. As I surveyed the newly elected deputies I felt that dull, sleepy meetings would soon be a thing of the past. The deputies were already forming caucuses to refine strategy and deploy their forces, while the deputations were also busy. The Baltic republics had opted for open rebellion. The first secretaries complained about the unruly behavior of some of those present, who had been silent back home but were noisily pushing their own agenda at the congress. The hall swarmed with activity, like an anthill. In the front rows, where the deputies from Moscow and Leningrad were seated, there were a large number of deputies from every *oblast* in the country. They were working out their debating tactics, though their positions had been agreed upon in advance.

The party group of deputies held a meeting, chaired by Gorbachev, the day before the opening of the congress. It did not go smoothly. The Communists were also divided and could not agree on a unified approach to the election of the presidium and the other governing bodies of the congress. The Central Committee's Organizational Department had previously helped with such tasks, whereas now its staff members were reluctant to get involved, fearing that they might be accused of putting pressure on the deputies. Intimidated by Gorbachev's remarks at the plenum about the commanding functions of the apparatus, they now either preferred to do nothing or met with the deputies on their own ground.

The result was an interesting situation. The Politburo and the Central Committee Secretariat, which for many decades had regarded the party apparatus as a means of control over local party organs, was now accusing it of exceeding its authority. Gorbachev himself had repeatedly urged the staff of the various departments to keep a grip on the work of the party committees and to do much more cross-country traveling in order to make sure the party line was being followed. The apparatus even had a special post of "instructor," whose duties included offering the party organizations and committees advice on how to operate. Those same staff members were now being slighted and criticized, and forbidden to perform what had once been one of their duties. When they saw how easily the Politburo's faults had been blamed on the "little guys" of the nomenklatura, they shrugged their shoulders in bewilderment.

The congress began with organizational and procedural issues. The atmosphere became heated from the very first minute. V. Tolpezhnikov, head of medical emergency services in Riga, demanded that the person or persons who had ordered the beating of peaceful demonstrators in Tbilisi on 9 April 1989 be publicly identified. He also proposed that the congress honor the memory of those who lost their lives. It was like a spark, igniting air that was laden with combustible fumes. The congress exploded in a cacophony of shouting, applause, and commotion. The doctor knew exactly what he was doing. Many deputies became emotional and agitated. Lines formed at the microphones. They all wanted to state their views and be seen on television defending a worthy cause, so that their constituents would feel they had chosen wisely. The Muscovites were particularly active, though they also came under fire. Many people resented the fact that Moscow was so well fed, well maintained, and well supplied with foodstuffs, by comparison with other cities. An interregional group was formed to lead the opposition factions. The air was thick with offensive adjectives as a full-scale battle raged, with deputies at times almost coming to blows. The party, its apparatus, the army, and the KGB were hit with a barrage of criticism. The privileges of the nomenklatura were a favorite target. There were grounds for criticism, of course, but much of what was said was distorted and untrue. Moreover, there was no one to answer back. The Communist deputies tried to shove their way through to the microphones, but were forced to wait. Those who did speak, for the most part, sounded feeble and unsure of themselves. The only sincere and compelling rebuttals of the blatant lies that had been uttered came from a few indignant women, who were none too choosy about their language.

Aside from the party, the army was another major target for critics. Tolpezhnikov's opening remark had set off a stream of accusations against the soldiers, officers, and generals deemed responsible for dispersing the demonstrators, with loss of life among the civilian population of Tbilisi. The military high command and the Georgian leadership were asked for an explanation. After all, those present did stand in memory of those killed in various regions of the country. As I watched the proceedings, I began to wonder why the military was being singled out. Why were people who had carried out orders being humiliated in this way? Were not soldiers the children of the people? Was it their fault they had been sent to Afghanistan? Had they just taken it into their heads to disperse the demonstrators in Tbilisi? I may have been mistaken, but I had my own views on the subject and conveyed them to Gorbachev.

THE TBILISI UPRISING AND ITS AFTERMATH

At the time of the events in Tbilisi, when military personnel were involved in dispersing demonstrators and in the deaths of innocent people, the Soviet people should have been given an honest account of what happened. Gorbachev knew much, if not everything, about the events of those days, as he was promptly informed of events anywhere in the country, regardless of his whereabouts.

He was certainly informed of the situation in Tbilisi in April 1989. Those memorable days were full of important events. On 2 April Gorbachev flew to Cuba, keeping his promise to visit the Island of Freedom, as we called it for many years. He had scheduled that visit on the way back from New York in December 1988, but the catastrophic earthquake that struck Armenia cancelled his plan. This time he arrived as planned and met Fidel Castro and the Cubans. It was quite a successful trip, despite some slight friction over perestroika, whose outer limits were not fully understood, either in the Soviet Union or in Cuba. On his way back home, Gorbachev spent a few days, densely packed with meetings, in Great Britain.

It was around this time that I became firmly convinced that the general secretary had completely abandoned the modesty and the comradely attitude to his entourage that should be expected of a Communist. Instead, he behaved much more like an emperor, with dozens of people, including the members of his delegation, in attendance both inside and around his residence. A succession of adjutants, security guards, and maids went up to his private quarters on the first floor of the embassy. One day the general secretary was delayed for some reason. Kruchina and I strolled around the block a few times, but he had still not come down. Perhaps he had been taken ill, we thought. In fact, it turned out to be nothing more than a change of schedule, which meant he had to change clothes, with all the resulting fuss that I could never fathom.

While Gorbachev was in London, matters were coming to a head in Tbilisi. As far as I know, the general secretary was briefed by Plekhanov, who was in constant touch with Moscow. F. Bobkov, the first deputy chairman of the KGB, had managed to reach me on the special line to tell me of the latest alarming developments; I then told Gorbachev that things seemed to be slipping out of control. I imagine he phoned Moscow right away, but in any case he was briefed exhaustively on his return. The Politburo members who met him at the airport had agreed, among other things, that Shevardnadze should go to Tbilisi on a peace-making mission. However, the foreign minister, no doubt after consulting with Gorbachev, did not make the trip.

I later learned some more details of the events in Tbilisi from Dzhumber Patiashvili, formerly first secretary of the Georgian Communist party, who had flown to Moscow and was trying to get an appointment with Gorbachev. The two men had once been on friendly terms. After sitting doggedly in the reception area near Gorbachev's office for two days, he was told to wait in his hotel until he was called. I knew Gorbachev well enough to realize that he was doing his utmost to delay their meeting. Eventually, contrary to logic, he asked me to meet Patiashvili myself, and to find out what he wanted. When bad news or troublesome visits loomed, Gorbachev tended to pass them on to someone else. He treated documents in the same way, instructing someone else to receive them and prepare a response. In the case of Tbilisi he was again true to form, letting Ligachev, Razumovski, and the military bail him out.

Patiashvili looked crushed when he heard of the general secretary's refusal to meet him. In a halting voice, with tears in his eyes, he explained that Shevardnadze's trip had not gone ahead as scheduled because the conflict had already become irreversible, and that all decisions had been agreed on, though he did not say with whom. Patiashvili was in a tight spot. He could not tell the whole truth to anyone but Gorbachev, but he did not want to take the blame himself. His poor relations with Shevardnadze, which dated back to their Komsomol days, complicated matters further. By the time the first Congress of People's Deputies opened, however, Patiashvili had somewhat changed his tune. The increasing tendency to blame the Tbilisi events on the military was meeting with unexpectedly broad support. Soldiers, officers, and generals had been made into scapegoats. I was not only astonished but shocked by the ease with which the political leadership was shifting the blame onto the men in uniform. None of the politicians had the courage to defend their subordinates, the ones who actually did their bidding.

The military merely executed the wishes of others. I continue to believe that Gorbachev should have taken a stand on the principles involved, when the matter came up for discussion at the congress. I fully realized how difficult this was and how much courage was needed for someone to shoulder blame in this way. The deputies and the entire country seemed to be expecting such an acknowledgment. But it never came. I once raised the matter with Gorbachev.

"I think you should take responsibility for what happened yourself," I told him. "It's wrong for you to just look on, like a bystander. Even assuming that you knew nothing about what was happening, you're still responsible as general secretary, commander-in-chief of the armed forces, and chairman of the Defense Council. Your subordinates might have misled you. Whether they're good or bad, mediocre or talented, you appointed these commanders, and you've got to have the guts to accept responsibility for any error of judgment you may have made. Then you should find out who exactly was to blame and punish the guilty parties, if any, yourself. But you should not allow them to be exposed to angry denunciations from all quarters. If you do the courageous, honorable, and noble thing, people will believe you and forgive you. That way you deflect the criticism from innocent soldiers and uphold the honor of the army."

Gorbachev said nothing. I knew I had touched a raw nerve, and I'm sure he resented it.

I still believe that the spectacle of the general secretary and the commander-in-chief of the armed forces just sitting there without saying a word did not enhance his authority, and that in the eyes of many people, especially the military, he lost all credibility at that point. This in turn became one of the reasons for the widening gulf between the president of the USSR and the officer corps—indeed, the entire army.

Day after day the advocates of different political viewpoints fought for influence over the deputies and society. It was an exhausting and, for most of those present, tedious process. Gorbachev presided over the meetings, maneuvering this way and that, placating, calming, or encouraging the various factions as the need arose. His patience, however, was wearing thin. He tended to raise his voice and lose his temper. When he switched off the microphone while Andrei Sakharov was speaking, the hall erupted in a raucous chorus of both approval and indignation. Everyone was dissatisfied with the presidium, claiming that the wrong people were being called on to speak, discipline was lax, the rules of procedure were being ignored, and chaos prevailed. During intermissions Gorbachev would retire to the presidium lounge in a state of utter exhaustion. This room was really intended for the presidium; the Politburo had previously assembled in there during party congresses and solemn ceremonial meetings. This time, however, the leaders of the party were not elected to the presidium. They sat in the amphitheater or with their delegations, though they often gathered in their old room where they used to relax over a cup of tea. The other members of the presidium went to a plainer room one floor down.

Upstairs, meanwhile, the members of the Politburo, who now found themselves, for the first time, incapable of controlling or altering the situation, were conferring anxiously in an attempt to find solutions. What was going through their minds? Most of them realized that a door had just been opened, and that a motley crowd had burst through it. They were frightened by the kind of sentiments the crowd was voicing in front of the entire nation. Moreover, those sentiments were disturbing to millions of citizens who were staring in disbelief at the Tower of Babel displayed on their television screens.

THE CONGRESS OF PEOPLE'S
DEPUTIES AND THE SUPREME SOVIET

While national party congresses and congresses of people's deputies were in session, Gorbachev usually arrived at the Kremlin Palace between thirty and forty minutes before the beginning of the meeting but occasionally just as the meeting was being called to order. The security agents, who kept track of his movements, would often tell me, for example, that he had just passed through the Triumphal Arch, was approaching the Kremlin, or had just driven through the Kremlin gate. The chief of security usually met the general secretary as he entered the palace through a special entrance. Aides helped him off with his coat and escorted him to an elevator that took him to the third floor, where he had a small study and could avail himself of the services of medical personnel, a masseur, and a hairdresser. Gorbachev started his day with a shampoo. The hairdresser, who was waiting as he entered the corridor, smoothed out his hair, shaved the back of his neck and his sideburns ever so slightly, and then combed and dried his hair. For several years he used the same hairdresser as Brezhnev, but for some reason, he was dismissed. His replacement was a young woman. While his hair was being done, the general secretary occasionally called me in with the documents of the day; then, after I had finished briefing him, he decided who should be sent a memorandum, either for action or for information. By the time he appeared in the Kremlin Palace of Congresses he had already conferred with Kryuchkov, Vlasov or Pugo, Yazov, Shevardnadze, the prime minister, or various Central Committee secretaries, so as to be up to date on events at home and abroad.

After freshening up and allowing the hairdresser to work her customary wizardry, Gorbachev took the elevator down to the presidium room, where the Politburo used to meet. After an exchange of greetings he would sometimes sit down for a cup of coffee, though he usually went with the others straight to the presidium, where the agenda and the choice of chairman for the meeting were discussed. During the meetings Gorbachev often left the hall and went to the presidium room for a cup of coffee, a phone call to Raisa, or a meeting with Politburo members, aides, or republican leaders. During the early days of the first Congress of People's Deputies, Gorbachev left the hall frequently. He would hold talks with members of the national or republican leadership and leaders of the opposition wing.

After a few days it became obvious that the Communist deputies were very much on the defensive. Gorbachev also understood what was happening. He waited a long time, however, before assembling the *obkom* and *kraikom* secretaries in the Secretariat conference room, where he tried to stiffen their resolve. While discussing the course of the debate in the congress, Gorbachev heard a number of reproaches. The leadership of the delegations and the party organs of the Central Committee were accused of failing the deputies, and he was told that the party's effort was poorly organized and had neglected the individual approach. The general secretary had no program of his own with which to counter these complaints. For want of a better solution, he suggested that they make more of an effort to get to the microphones. That was the technique used by the opposition, whose representatives conferred unceasingly, elaborating measures that would guarantee success. Relentless hammering away at the party, the privileges of the nomenklatura, and the state of affairs in the country was the method of choice. One heard speakers lashing out at the military, using the same old vitriolic language, all of which was acclaimed in certain segments of society. The public was still only partially aroused, but one had the impression that it found such criticism appealing.

The members of the Politburo were now meeting more often. I had never seen them looking so alarmed. They discussed the proceedings in the congress and tried to devise countermeasures, so as to stabilize the situation. Their one conclusion was that addressing the assembled deputies was pointless, and that the deputies, particularly the waverers most susceptible to extremist slogans, had to be approached individually. The democrats, however, had been doing just that, and doing it cleverly and relentlessly. Speakers at the congress were saying that attempts were being made in the hotels to persuade, bribe, and even terrorize deputies. Telephone threats were being made at night to people's hotel rooms. Many deputies were frantic and scared.

The longer the congress lasted, the more obvious it became that in such an atmosphere of agitation and discord there could be no question of making constructive decisions. A proposal to elect a standing Supreme Soviet from among the members of the congress was adopted. Yet vigorous campaigning for personal candidacies continued. Many of those who were most fiercely outspoken at the congress, occasionally committing breaches of decorum, were not elected to the Supreme Soviet.

The mechanism of majority voting excluded unworthy candidates, thereby enraging the democrats. They then devised the notion of the "aggressively submissive" majority, meaning the mindlessly unanimous voting patterns of the central Asian deputies. Another source of division was the stance taken by the Baltic deputies, many of whom were ready to walk out. More arm twisting and maneuvering then followed.

One should remember that this congress was the first of its kind, and that it was attended by deputies still ablaze with the excitement of the electoral campaign and still hurling barbed and occasionally thoughtless accusations at one another. Everyone was anxious to make his mark and get his name on the speaker's list at soon as possible, so as to pound away at the power structure. Their speeches were part of that same surge of passion that was to continue sweeping the country, finding support among deputies and even among many party staff members. When the congress set about electing the Supreme Soviet of the Union, with its chairman and deputy chairmen, the different factions and splinter groups did battle once more. The nomination and election of Gorbachev was no easy matter. Many speakers, among them some of his supporters, made suggestions that were certain to displease him, calling upon him to quit as general secretary, turn his attention to matters of state, and explain about the construction of his dacha at Foros. Sakharov pointed out that his personal support for Gorbachev in the elections was contingent on the further course of the debate on basic political issues, and that if the elections became a mere formality he would refuse to take part in them.

L. Sukhov, a truck driver from Kharkov, recalled a question he had put to Gorbachev at the Nineteenth Party Conference: "As I listened to your fiery speeches, even those that you started by rudely interrupting other speakers, I compared you not with Lenin and Stalin but with the great Napoleon, who led his people to victory fearing neither bullets nor death. Unfortunately, sycophants and his wife caused him to turn the republic into an empire. I am mortally afraid that the same could happen here, and if it does, our revolutionary cause would be doomed. As I see it, you are also incapable of escaping the vindictiveness and influence of your wife. I shall vote for you, but remember what I'm saying, so that the people will really believe that we are moving toward the goal of the Communist movement."

The polemical debate on Gorbachev's nomination, which then followed, was unprecedented. Boris Yeltsin was also nominated, though he chose not to compete with the general secretary's supporters. The results showed that out of 2,221 deputies, 2,123 had voted for Gorbachev.

Lukyanov was elected chairman of the presidium of the Supreme Soviet. Gorbachev had fulfilled one of his ambitions.

By the time it was over, the congress had swept through the country like a hurricane, leaving extreme agitation in its wake. It was also a shock to the world community, which looked on apprehensively as the Russian bear came lumbering out of its den, on its way to the civilized world. No one could be sure it would not wreak havoc when it reached the company of respectable bourgeois democrats. But the bear was now on the move around the republic. The spirit of change was contagious. Besides stirring emotions in the union republics and the autonomous regions, it also ignited smoldering passions that had often flared up in the past in eastern Europe.

Further congresses of people's deputies of the USSR were held and the struggle continued, but the balance of power had shifted in favor of the Supreme Soviet of the Union. Lukyanov was its chairman and Gorbachev became the first president of the USSR. Unlimited power was now concentrated in the hands of the general secretary/president, who, being endowed with emergency powers, could have carried out any reforms, completed perestroika, and achieved the same results as those achieved, in a very short time, in China, without destroying the country or hacking it to bits like a side of beef being prepared for the supermarket.

The congress had shown what everyone had long suspected and what the analysts already knew. The party could not fight in the new circumstances. It no longer controlled the processes taking place in the USSR or at the congress. One further reason for this state of affairs was that, as the debates in the congress had shown, large segments of the public had already withheld their support from the party during the elections. The party largely ignored this fact. Moreover, the congress had widened the gap between the party and the public, while inspiring people who had never been interested in political battles.

The first congress showed that the Central Committee and its apparatus were also unprepared for the new format of political debate and contention. Communists therefore began to doubt the leadership's ability to uphold their principles and ideals. Lastly, the congress had confirmed a bitter truth: the lack of authority on the part of the Politburo and general secretary, and their inability to mobilize the party's forces in their hour of need. One wonders, of course, whether the problem was really just their inability.

The Congress of People's Deputies and the entire democratic process took place in circumstances unfavorable to the party. Perestroika was faltering, the socioeconomic situation was deteriorating, and the party nomenklatura and apparatus were both being blasted for their past and present mistakes. Moreover, the central information media had wrested themselves free from the party's traditional control. The picture that emerged from the Twenty-seventh Party Congress and the Nineteenth Party Conference showed that the party was in even worse shape than had previously been thought.

I am inclined to believe that Gorbachev felt the matter was not worth considering. The newly elected president so relished the fulfillment of his dreams that the turmoil at the congress and even the difficulties involved in his own election failed to alert him as they should have. If anything, he grew even cockier and ever more convinced of his own invulnerability. He would ruthlessly force his ideas on others, and could be impolite, or even offensive, when talking to his comrades, high officials from the republics, provinces, and party organizations, and members of the Central Committee and the government. They doubtless wondered how such a charming, intelligent, and considerate man could suddenly become so curt and tactless. Many people must have noticed that he unceremoniously used the familiar form even when addressing older women. When he lost his temper he would start shouting and using questionable language. He still retained, however, his ability to charm people.

"Alex," he would say affectionately to Yakovlev, who was still smarting after the general secretary had forced him out of the Presidential Council, "how are things? Why don't you work over this speech a bit, and then we'll take a look at it together."

COLLISION: GORBACHEV AND YELTSIN

On 28 June 1988 the Nineteenth Party Conference, the first since the war, opened in Moscow. It was needed in order to adopt a number of resolutions and other party documents and to try to resolve the question of electing new members to bring the Central Committee up to full strength. This latter objective was hampered by the fact that the Twenty-seventh Party Congress had overlooked the need for a written record that could have helped the party conferences proceed with such elections. But the mere fact of its being held and adopting resolutions made it a major event in the life of the party. Its agenda included the democratization of Soviet society, political reform, efforts to combat bureaucratic rigidity, interethnic relations, glasnost, and legal reform.

By mid-1988 both the party and the country were seething with ferment, being divided between those who found the ongoing reforms too revolutionary and alien and others who took them for granted. Factions formed along new fault lines. Glasnost had given everyone the urge to speak. The truth, half-truths, and outright lies were being purveyed by press and television, while some implausible-sounding stories about the party apparatus were also making the rounds. Individual Communists could not fail to be affected by the high tension all around them.

The manner in which delegates to the conference were elected had been radically changed. Caught up in the prevailing mood, the Communists tended to prefer impassioned orators capable of finding fault with the party. As a result the participants in the conference included not only sensible, democratically minded people but also blatant populists whose main goal was to be seen on television.

It was a highly exceptional conference, replete with criticism of the leadership and sensational speeches. First among the delegates was Vitali Korotich, editor of *Ogonyok*, who declared that, according to his information, some high-ranking delegates who had taken bribes were present in the hall. His words caused a stir. The representative of Altai promptly asked that they be named. It was decided that a commission should be established to verify these allegations. In making such a statement, Korotich had relied on material from an investigation being conducted by Telman Gdlyan and V. Ivanov from the procurator general's office. As it later turned out, they had given him documents suggesting that a number of *obkom* secretaries from Uzbekistan had been taking bribes. And that was what he produced at the conference.

There can be no doubt that some highly placed officials indeed accepted bribes and gifts in the most varied forms; it was impossible not to notice the nouveaux riches who used their positions for private gain. But it is wrong to lump them together with the many other officials of similar rank, or to implicate an entire nation. Some very clever people were using the Uzbek affair as a means of seizing the moral and political high ground. The fight against corruption is a sacred cause that cannot be advanced by individuals who are themselves tainted, nor by clandestine methods.

Realizing that wrongful accusations against the people could prove costly, the critics then aimed their fire at other levels of the establishment. They not only suspected but actually made unproven accusations against men who for various reasons could not have been involved—among them Yakovlev, Medvedev, and Gorbachev. But their main target was Ligachev.

Gorbachev was deeply upset by the torrent of accusations, some of which were aimed at him. What upset him most, however, was the insinuations about wrongdoing by factory workers in the Stavropol *krai* and his own involvement in their schemes. Stung by these charges, he ordered the procurator general and the KGB to stop the slander and report to him on all details of the case. The Uzbek affair was discussed at closed meetings of the Politburo; instructions were issued and, to some extent with Gorbachev's consent, several Central Committee members were arrested and tried. They were later released for lack of evidence and because of irregularities in the way they had been questioned.

When questions related to the so-called Uzbek affair surfaced at the Nineteenth Party Conference, they began to overshadow all constructive discussion of the current problems facing the party and the nation. They did not surface accidentally. Someone was determined to prove that the party leadership was corrupt and criminal, and that the party itself was inherently antipopulist and bloodthirsty. If actual proof could not be supplied, then they sought at least to discredit the party and all it had accomplished. All kinds of documents and information were dredged up for the purpose. With each new disclosure of privileges enjoyed by the party apparatus, the hall erupted with indignation. The delegates demanded to know where their money had gone and how the party "fat cats" had acquired their wealth.

Another significant reason for the feverish mood among the delegates was the impact made on the young generation by revelations about the crimes committed by Stalin from the 1930s through the early 1950s. Older party members knew about them already, either from firsthand experience or from the proceedings of the Twentieth and Twenty-first Party Congresses (in February 1956 and January and February 1959, respectively) and from letters sent by the Central Committee to the party organizations. After the Twentieth Party Congress, the presidium sent a closed letter describing all the horrors perpetrated by the leadership under Stalin in those days. Those facts had now reappeared in the press, on Gorbachev's initiative.

Ligachev's address to the conference made the discussion even more

dramatic. He had long been a favorite target of the media and representatives of various democratic segments of public opinion, and here again
he came under fire from different directions at the same time. He was
accused, among other things, of a preference for administrative command methods of running the party and the country, of imposing strict
press controls, of allowing the Communist ideology to collapse, and of
being unable to uphold the principles of party work. In fact, he became
the whipping boy, instead of Gorbachev himself. For a number of reasons, however, no one dared dismiss him.

Under the circumstances he decided to address the conference and
rebut his critics, explaining his true position. During an intermission he
told Gorbachev of his intentions. The general secretary advised him
against taking the floor at the conference. "Why does he need to speak?"
Gorbachev later said to me. "It's only going to make things worse. You
can see the situation we're in."

He was right, of course: tensions were running high. But Ligachev
went right on preparing his speech. His aides brought him typewritten
pages, which he then corrected and sent back to be retyped. I guessed
that he would keep his speech in readiness, but would deliver it only if
absolutely necessary. I was wrong. He had made up his mind and was
soon called on to address the conference.

He fully explained his position, responding to criticism and explaining
his relations with Yeltsin, which were another sore point with the delegates. His speech, which was frank and at times harsh, was widely commented on, not only in the hall but among the general public, mainly, I
suppose, because of the tense state of his relations with Yeltsin. The
quarrel between the two men had started long before. I do not know
precisely what caused it, though I suppose a clash between two such
stern temperaments was inevitable, despite their long-standing friendship. By his own admission, Ligachev had been a kind of godfather to
Yeltsin, having helped him climb through the ranks of both the party and
the state hierarchy. Their falling out might perhaps date from the time
when Yeltsin was working in Sverdlovsk. From what I was told, their
misunderstandings may have occurred as follows.

Agriculture had long been in serious trouble in many parts of the
Soviet Union. This was also true of the Ural region, including the
Sverdlovsk *oblast*, where for many years the leadership had been drawn
from people in industry and construction. Though well acquainted with

those sectors, they tended to neglect agriculture. Letters complaining of food shortages poured in. Senior local officials said that they were overloaded with industrial and defense-related sectors and were unable to improve the state of the rural areas, which people were leaving to find jobs in the city.

The Central Committee's Agricultural Department, which was then keeping a close watch on the situation in various regions, decided to study the agricultural sector in the Sverdlovsk *oblast*, invite the local leadership to a meeting of the Secretariat, and figure out ways of making improvements. A team of experts from the Central Committee and various government departments went to the *oblast* and prepared a memorandum criticizing the failings of the party *obkom* and presenting some substantial conclusions and proposals. The Central Committee considered the findings of the group but then, in response to objections from the *oblast* itself and not wishing to offend its hard-working leadership, referred the memorandum back to the *obkom*. The deputy head of the Central Committee's Agricultural Department went to Sverdlovsk specially for this purpose. However, the Central Committee document was criticized by speakers at the plenum of the *obkom*, including its highest-ranking officials.

When the Central Committee discovered how Sverdlovsk had reacted to its decision, it summoned Yeltsin to Moscow for a serious talk on the matter. I am not familiar with all the details, but I do know that Ligachev, who was then head of the Party Organizational Department, was somehow involved. Yeltsin discussed the issues, candidly and in the proper party spirit, with the Central Committee. Ligachev liked him, and it was soon decided that it would be better for him to be invited to Moscow and placed in charge of the Central Committee's Construction Industry Department. Yeltsin promptly immersed himself in his new task. When Gorbachev became general secretary and Ligachev was given greater latitude in personnel matters, Yeltsin was offered the post of first secretary of the Moscow *gorkom*. The career of his predecessor, Viktor Grishin, who had become resigned to the people he had to deal with and to the city's shortages, was coming to an end. Moscow had problems with social issues, food supplies, and housing and needed a new man.

Yeltsin was the right man for the job. The fact that he had no connections to corrupt city officials was greatly in his favor. There were misgivings about the wisdom of choosing someone from Sverdlovsk, since there must have been qualified local candidates. But these objections were overruled, and Yeltsin was elected first secretary of the Moscow *gorkom* and a candidate member of the Central Committee.

His arrival was marked by numerous innovations. Personnel changes were made. These were necessary because the apparatus at all levels of government was not only old but had developed a business-as-usual mentality. As he struggled to cope with the deterioration of the city's food supply and its mounting social problems, Yeltsin began to feel cornered. Meanwhile Ligachev, as head of the Central Committee, was demanding strict accountability. He may at times have exceeded his authority, but for whatever reason, Yeltsin rarely attended Central Committee meetings and their relations grew tense.

There was another reason for their estrangement. Instead of producing results, a second round of personnel changes had simply provoked moans of discontent from the public and grave concern among the party's top echelons, where the wisdom of appointing Yeltsin was now being called into question. As tension mounted, Yeltsin felt isolated, as if surrounded by a vacuum. His performance suffered as a result. He often remained silent at Politburo meetings, evidently failing to understand the endless chatter that went on there, sometimes for eight or ten hours at a time, often without a break.

In the summer of 1987 Yeltsin wrote to Gorbachev about the state of perestroika, saying that the work of the Central Committee Secretariat was unfocused and that he could no longer work in the Politburo. I believed then, and still believe now, that he wrote that letter out of sheer desperation. Gorbachev, for whom maneuvering had become a habit, was really taking two steps forward, three to the side, and one backward, and everyone found such conduct disconcerting. He would tell Marxist hardliners that he was fighting for the "bright future" of communism and would never swerve from that path, while assuring free-marketers that the only possible way to proceed was through the expansion of market relations, democracy, and freedom in accordance with the Austrian or Swedish models. The general secretary's pluralism of opinions was so advanced that he had everybody confused. Yeltsin could not have failed to be aware that Gorbachev's duplicity was arousing doubts throughout the entire political spectrum.

Gorbachev mentioned the letter, but without disclosing its contents. In response to Yeltsin's question he suggested that they meet later, preferably after the October Revolution holiday, on account of the special celebrations that were to be held for this, its seventieth anniversary.

The Central Committee held a plenum in October to consider the main substantive issues to be raised in the general secretary's jubilee report. It was a perfectly ordinary, practically routine meeting. When Gorbachev had finished speaking, Ligachev, who was presiding, inquired whether there were any more speakers. No one asked for the floor. The resolution was about to be read out when Ligachev glanced around the room and announced that if there were no more speakers, they would move on to the next agenda item.

Chance then took a hand in the proceedings, dictating, as it often does, the entire subsequent course of events. Looking over the front row, where candidate members of the Politburo and Central Committee secretaries were seated, Gorbachev interrupted Ligachev: "I believe Boris Nikolayevich Yeltsin wishes to speak."

I do not know for sure whether Yeltsin really had anything to add, as only the members of the presidium had a clear view of whether his hand was raised. In any case, he got up and went to the podium. In a brief statement he broadly endorsed the thinking behind Gorbachev's report, but then turned to the matter of perestroika. The published record of his remarks, as amended by him, is an accurate rendering of what he said. He made a number of points: perestroika was bogged down and was being applied inconsistently; the Central Committee Secretariat was not doing its job properly, and at times was even hampering progress; the Moscow party organization was of little help, and its decisions were stale and out of touch with current realities; and so on. Somewhere in his statement he used a phrase that could be taken as a reference to the resurgence of the cult of personality. What had been a fairly humdrum, sleepy meeting suddenly came to life. Tensions mounted as various speakers took the floor in response.

His face purple with rage, Gorbachev suspended the meeting. I could see that he was struggling to contain his anger, but the suggestion that he aspired to greatness had hit a raw nerve. Had it not been for that, he would probably not have felt compelled to send all the king's men to the podium in his defense. The entire Politburo and all the members of the plenum girded themselves for combat. Gorbachev, meanwhile, was trying on the mask of the peacemaker. He doubtless did not want to have a hand in widening the conflict, but the machine had already been set in motion. The Central Committee members hastily jotted down the main points they intended to make, and I could see that Gorbachev was deciding the order in which the Politburo would address the assembly.

The bell sounded, and everyone returned to their seats. I suddenly noticed the Central Committee members had changed. Though they had always had misgivings about Yeltsin in the past, now it was as if a dam had burst, loosing upon the hall an outpouring of disjointed, rabid expressions of hostility. Gorbachev no longer tried to preserve decorum. Rank-and-file members of the Central Committee, including some from Moscow, as well as members and candidate members of the Politburo, all joined in the feeding frenzy. They not only endorsed Yeltsin's own suggestion that he should resign from the Politburo; they demanded his resignation. When it was all over, however, Gorbachev turned to Yeltsin and asked: "Tell me, Boris Nikolayevich, can you go on working the way you did previously?"

By then it was late, and emotions were running high. Yeltsin insisted on resigning from the Politburo as currently constituted, while assuming, of course, that he would remain first secretary of the Moscow *gorkom*. He later sent Gorbachev a letter to that effect, but much of what had happened was irreversible. As a result of the extreme emotional strain, Yeltsin suffered a nervous breakdown and had to be hospitalized.

When the doctors reported an improvement in his condition, a plenum of the Moscow *gorkom* was scheduled and he promised to attend. Gorbachev, Razumovski, and, to the best of my recollection, Ligachev were also present.

This meeting followed a similar kind of scenario, as Yeltsin's critics vociferously savaged their prey, now that he was visibly weakened and staggering from the previous onslaught. I had seen it happen before: in a sudden spurt of courage, inveterate sycophants and toadies who had failed to say a word in defense of the hapless victim would gleefully trample all over him.

The appointment of the inexperienced and irresolute Lev Zaikov to replace Yeltsin on the Moscow *gorkom* did not restore calm in the city. Yeltsin was soon being widely remembered as a decisive man of action. But by then he had already been made head of the Committee on Construction and Architecture, a ministerial position.

The battles waged by Gorbachev, Ligachev, and the majority of the Central Committee members against Yeltsin now proceeded in full public view. He had many sympathizers, who somehow stayed in touch. The greater Yeltsin's authority, the more profound the alarm felt by Gorbachev, who now viewed the new minister as a political adversary to be reckoned with. He made some attempts at reconciliation, in the hope of restoring Yeltsin's former subordinate role, but to no avail.

The battle then entered a new phase: the quest for ways of discrediting Yeltsin using some modern technology. One such effort was the publication in *Pravda* of an article taken from an Italian newspaper about Yeltsin's trip to the United States, and the showing on television of part of a speech he made during that trip.

Ligachev's speech at the conference, where he attacked Yeltsin's policies, roiled the atmosphere even further. As the conference drew to a close, Yakovlev, finding his efforts foiled by Gorbachev, went straight to the podium and just stood there, waiting. The audience insisted he be allowed to speak. Gorbachev called me over and said: "Have him come into the presidium room, and tell him I'll give him the floor; only he should sit down, not stand in front of the podium like that."

I walked over to where Yakovlev was standing and invited him into the presidium room. He was very agitated. I did my best to calm him down, by telling him that Gorbachev had promised to give him the floor but that he wanted him to sit somewhere in the front rows. He then went to the front row, and Gorbachev soon gave him the floor.

Yakovlev's speech was a critical, conceptual response to the remarks of Ligachev and many other questions. It really amounted to a broad survey of perestroika as he understood it, and a listing of the areas where action was needed. He ranged over the shortcomings of perestroika, the slow pace of change in the party, and the possible emergence of a new personality cult, as well as the inadequacy of the aid made available to Moscow. Yakovlev proposed that whenever a new general secretary took office, virtually the entire Politburo should be dismissed and the apparatus replaced, and that the party's budget should be published.

In conclusion, he demanded the repeal of the decision made in the 1987 plenum describing his speech as "politically erroneous." The only mistake he acknowledged was his own failure to speak out earlier, before the seventieth anniversary of the revolution.

Feelings ran high as the meeting turned into a replay of the October plenum, with members opposing Yakovlev's request. For the party and the general public, accustomed to moderation in speeches and decisions alike, it came as a bombshell, wrecking the monolithic unity of the party.

The irreversible changes that had been set in motion within the party from the very first day of the conference—the first of its kind in fifty years—shook the Soviet Union and the whole world. People realized that without proper order the country's achievements could be wiped out, together with its very statehood. Not everyone understood the intentions of the leadership. I certainly did not. On a number of occasions I raised the matter with Gorbachev, but he brushed me off with the following remark: "Just wait and see what I can do."

The Politburo, the members of the Presidential Council, and later the Security Council and the government were all unaware of the schemes he was hatching. Even his closest associates were confused about his true intentions. Did he have a grand strategy for the dismantling of the party and the collapse of the Soviet Union? I am inclined to doubt he did, but he did have some ultimate objective, which could not be achieved without the destruction of the existing system. Most people thought perestroika was meant to enhance their country, making it more powerful and prosperous. As events showed, however, that was not part of the general secretary's purpose. As the country slid toward disaster, with official state policy looking more and more like a slalom course, people began to wonder what he really did want.

THE PEDESTALS ARE SHAKEN

After the Nineteenth Party Conference there were still plenty of people in the Central Committee and among the leadership of the local party committees who remembered the plenum at which Gorbachev was elected general secretary. They had not forgotten his first timid steps, his lack of confidence, and his need for advice and help. Though their help had been valuable to him in 1985, those same people now proved to be a nuisance. Such was the tragic fate of those in the entourage of leaders: they became unnecessary because they knew too much and were not sufficiently servile. Now it was preferable to bring in young men who looked up to their idol.

By 1990 Gorbachev was a changed man. To carry out his plans he now needed different working methods and different people in the party leadership, the Central Committee, and the government. Even after a drastic overhaul of the ranks of *obkom* and *kraikom* first secretaries, he was still furious. During the intermission at one plenum, roiled by criticism from the floor, he said: "How can I work with people like that? We need new blood in here, and the sooner the better."

The Twenty-eighth Party Congress gave him such an opportunity, and he prepared for it vigorously. He wanted it to be as resonant, open, and democratic as the Congress of People's Deputies. The principle of competitive elections was therefore used. Everything proceeded along the same lines as in the Supreme Soviet, with the same kind of lively campaigning. Some of the delegates elected in the party organizations, where criticism of the failings of the leadership was particularly intense, were capable of delivering the most virulent speeches, regardless of their audience.

The party's Organizational Department no longer provided its former control and assistance. Its members, whose numbers were now much reduced, were afraid of interfering in the affairs of party committees and organizations, and especially in the election of delegates. In fact, they could not have done so even if they had wished. Some offices in the department were now down to four or five individuals, who were supposed to supervise regions stretching from Kursk to the Trans-Caucasus. This meant the Central Committee secretaries were denied vast amounts of information about what was happening around the country, while the party's republican, *obkom*, and *kraikom* committees knew little about the actions of the central government. Travel to the regions, even long-distance phone calls, had been curtailed. Normally, such loss of control would not have been serious, but with the highly centralized system that had been in force for the previous several years, local initiative was not particularly welcome.

Perplexity reigned in the party committees. Worse still, the general secretary, after his election as chairman of the Supreme Soviet and then as president of the USSR, had lost interest in the discussion of party matters at meetings of the Secretariat and Politburo. They now tended to occur on an ad hoc basis. The few documents that did reach the regions gave incomplete information about events in the country and the party and in the tasks confronting party organizations.

In most parts of the country competitive elections were the rule for party delegates. As a result, extraneous factors sometimes came into play, leading to the rejection of candidates who had unfairly been found wanting. That, of course, was not what determined the positions taken by delegates to the congresses. Had the situation in the country and the party been more stable and had everyone been more convinced of the wisdom of the chosen course, those same people would have acted accordingly. The blame lay not with competitive elections but with the party and national leadership.

Yet the leadership, or at least the general secretary, did learn something from the Party Conference and the Congress of People's Deputies. In the days leading up to the congress, Gorbachev thought carefully about his future status in the party. While he clearly relished his roles as chairman of the Supreme Soviet and, even more, as president of the Soviet Union, Gorbachev now regarded party matters as dreary and burdensome. It seemed he would have to quit as party leader and concentrate on matters of state. This option had been raised by people's deputies, by many Communists around the country, and, later, by members of the Central Committee. Two factors militated against such a decision, however. First, resignation from the post of general secretary would severely weaken Gorbachev's position, exposing him to criticism from left and right. The advent of a new party leader would effectively dethrone the chief agent of perestroika. Second, Gorbachev himself had tempted all the *obkom* and *kraikom* secretaries to occupy key posts in the party committees and soviets. If, having secured his position as head of state, he then withdrew as party leader, he would be supplying his critics with extra ammunition. Gorbachev held brainstorming sessions on this question with members of his entourage. He would ask: "Even if I quit as general secretary, why can't I stay on as leader of the party? After all, Lenin was the leader of the party, while at the same time heading the government."

He sat waiting for his aides to respond. Some found the idea impractical, while others saw it as a brilliant solution. I felt tempted to say that the idea was both brilliant and feasible, but he should first have to have at least some of Lenin's qualities. So far—and this is hardly a reproach—they had not been much in evidence. I said nothing, though.

"What about introducing the post of leader of the party?" he suggested, after listening to a few comments.

That was quite a bold idea. A year or two previously it might have worked, whereas now both the party and the general public were, to put it mildly, less enthusiastic about Gorbachev. If the idea failed, it would mean his political death. A simpler solution had to be found.

Increasingly fanciful suggestions were made, complete with historical analogies. Unfortunately, the leaders whose names were mentioned had all manifested dictatorial tendencies that would be unacceptable in a democratic context. For that reason the decision made was quite a modest one: the general secretary should be elected by the whole congress, as would his deputy, who would focus on party work and the conduct of Central Committee Secretariat meetings.

Gorbachev then began to look for that second man. Having mentally parted company with Ligachev after his critical comments in the press and at the Congress of People's Deputies, Gorbachev did not consider him a contender for the post. A new person was needed. But he would have to be more than untainted. In order to pass the party's rigorous selection process, certain positive qualities were required. He would have to be the leader of a major party organization, have a reputation as a liberal, and have practical work experience in the party or government, or in the management of the economy. And that was not all. Those who imagined that the No. 2 man in the party would have to be an intellectual powerhouse, with great firmness of character and outstanding oratorical gifts, were gravely mistaken. Such a candidate would, instead, be expected to "know his place" and avoid overshadowing the top man, and to have an aptitude for passing off his own ideas as those of the general secretary, or at least for not claiming them as his own. But where could such candidates be found? There were plenty of people with those shortcomings in the party: the difficulty lay in finding those with the required merits.

It was a real problem. There was a solution, but it was risky. Gorbachev could promote some other reliable member of the Politburo, and let the members fight it out among themselves. As previous experience had shown, that would keep the second-ranking man busy for a long time and make him dependent on the general secretary for support. It would preclude any scheming, though of course it was risky, as there was always a chance they would all come to terms among themselves.

Consideration of potential candidates then began, with Gorbachev very much in charge and intent on keeping his choices a closely guarded secret. Equally secret was his list of Politburo members who should be made to quit and those who would replace them. Selection was based on a well-tried principle: he needed his own people, but not the kind who would ever contradict him.

Such backstage intrigue may well have been the only way to form a team, but it seemed underhanded, and left a bad taste in people's mouths. Were not normal elections a possibility? Everyone knew which members had shown qualities of leadership, so why could they not simply be elected? Such reasoning, of course, would occur only to those who have never been at the top.

It was now spring, and the congress was fast approaching. Gorbachev was worried about its outcome. He often dropped in at Volynskoye, or later Novo-Ogaryovo, which was closer to his residence, to visit his speechwriters, who were now hard at work. They were rarely sent to Zavidovo, as it was too far and had the wrong kind of atmosphere. I could tell that the speechwriters were also tired and dispirited; they felt that they were preparing mere words, rather than accomplishments, for the history books. The last five years had been largely a void, a time of failed hopes, shattered illusions, and declining living standards. Society was seething with anger. As the president's mail suggested, Communists were being victimized, even those who toiled at open-hearth furnaces or tilled the fields.

On 2 July 1990 the congress opened. Gorbachev announced from the presidium that 4,683 delegates had been elected and that all were in attendance, except for 26 Communists. Controversy flared up as soon as the meeting proceeded to elect its governing organs. A miner from Magadan proposed that all power in the party should be transferred to the congress, that the Central Committee and the Politburo should resign, and that none of their members should be elected to the governing organs of the congress, as they had failed to carry out the decisions of the Twenty-seventh Congress. He also called for a personal assessment of each secretary and Politburo member.

Maneuvering adroitly in order to take the heat out of the debate, Gorbachev promised to come back to this question later. He never did, but calm was restored. A strictly functional presidium, with unusually few members, was elected, and other governing organs were also approved. The meeting would then have started on its agenda had it not been for the numerous provocative questions raised by speakers from the floor. Gorbachev did not take the floor to deliver his report until two and a half hours later, when passions had cooled.

In his report Gorbachev still managed to sound optimistic and hopeful, emphasizing the wisdom of the path chosen and the impossibility of following any other. The more he talked, however, the more tense the hall became. Familiar phrases like "the Socialist choice," the "Communist perspective," and the "expression of the interests of the working class, the peasants, and the intelligentsia" floated down from the podium. He also enumerated other principles the party was supposed to espouse. Did the general secretary himself believe what he was saying? Or were his subsequent actions—or inaction—a response to changed circumstances? Those who knew him well could never be quite sure where his sincerity began or ended.

At the Twenty-seventh Congress Gorbachev had declared that it was a mistake for the party even to countenance the notion of private property, but at the Twenty-eighth Congress he spoke of the need for various forms of property as an economic incentive. The word *market*, which he had previously used only with great caution, now became a panacea. The issue here, of course, was not his change of position but the need for him to explain his reasoning to the party and the nation. Many people were still mouthing Gorbachev's old slogans, long after they had been discarded and replaced. People began to wonder whether the general secretary and the Politburo were really in control, or whether they were reeling this way and that under the impact of criticism. I remember a conversation I once had with a *raikom* secretary I had met while working at *Pravda*. He had this to say: "Why can't you people at the top make up your minds? You change your theories so fast we can't keep up. I often go to factories and farms to explain the situation to the people who work there; I tell them that Socialist principles are unshakable. But the next thing I know, you have a new set of ideals. Out I go again, and they remind me that I said something else three months earlier. They want to know whether I have an opinion of my own. Well, I certainly do. And it is that the people we have elected leaders are like weathervanes. Why don't you get your story straight the first time, and then tell everybody about it? You shouldn't think that out there in the heartland there are a bunch of idiots who can't see what's going on. We can see everything, but so far we've kept quiet."

The congress insisted on hearing reports from the party leadership, and Gorbachev had to agree. The first speaker was Ryzhkov, followed by Medvedev, who had long been blamed for destroying Communist ideology, whereas he claimed that it had already collapsed when he took over. Then came Yakovlev, Shevardnadze, Zaikov, Ligachev, and other members of the Politburo. Speakers from the floor voiced their dissatisfaction with what they heard, and demanded that the leadership repent and acknowledge its mistakes. It sounded much like the Congress of People's Deputies, with the same categorical assertions and the same wrangling over access to the microphone. Could it be that such conduct was in style and that the representatives of Western democracies expressed their views in the same way? Another possibility was that delegates were shouting to relieve the pain induced by endless waffling and practical impotence.

And so it went on, day after day. Sensing that for most of them it would be their last congress, the Politburo members were irritated and apathetic. In the room where they assembled, one could see the full spectrum of emotions: anger, hopelessness, militancy, and disbelief. An increasingly worried Gorbachev now went out into the hall more often, giving interviews under the glare of the television lights and engaging delegates in conversation, as he had done during the Congress of People's Deputies. People crowded around, so as to appear on television. Gorbachev also tried to make similar forays among the delegates to the Central Committee plenums, but no crowds formed around him. People did not leap from their seats, and few even bothered to approach him. He often returned from the hall acutely depressed.

As his confidence and energy ebbed, it sometimes seemed that he had tired of the whole process and regretted taking on such a heavy burden. He and the Central Committee were constantly being accused of failure to act. Occasionally, his usually strong nerves would crack when the criticism hit on an especially sore point, as when he was invited to spend more time on domestic issues and less on foreign travel. That really hit home. No longer able to restrain himself, he lashed out at the speaker who had made the proposal, using the most insulting language. His indignation on this question smoldered for a long time after that, but the secretary of the Altai *raikom* who had drawn attention to that shortcoming was not deterred, and restated his position.

The congress then entered its concluding phase, the elections of the general secretary and his deputy. The following were some of the divided opinions that were expressed from the very start: the general secretary should be entrusted with the completion of perestroika; it was impossible and improper to hold two posts; the general secretary was not concerned with the party's affairs; and problems would arise if the Supreme Soviet prohibited the simultaneous holding of two posts. But Gorbachev was determined. T. Avaliani, first secretary of the Kiselev *gorkom*, in Kemerov *oblast*, was the sole surviving candidate, after the numerous other nominees had withdrawn. He had come up the hard way and did not flinch from competition with Gorbachev. The fact that he got only slightly more than 500 votes was not in itself surprising. What was surprising was that 1,116 of the 4,538 delegates voted against Gorbachev. That was a far cry from the handful of wayward members whose imprudent votes, according to some sources, prompted Stalin to kill off virtually all the delegates to the Seventeenth Congress. In 1990 such a result sent a very grave message. It was a major moral defeat, a vote of no confidence by one-quarter of the congress. Gorbachev was inwardly shaken. He had not expected an easy ride, but such a political knockdown at that stage in the proceedings was a shock.

One more trial lay ahead: the election of the deputy general secretary. Besides Ivashko, the planned candidate, Ligachev was also nominated. Both had passed fairly smoothly through the confirmation hearings, though it seemed that Ligachev had been grilled more intensely and could expect further difficulties. The outcome, not surprisingly, was the election of Ivashko as deputy general secretary. Ligachev got only 776 votes in favor and 3,642 against.

I happened to have witnessed the final scene between Gorbachev and Ligachev. On his way back from the chamber after the vote, Gorbachev unexpectedly bumped into Ligachev in the narrow passageway between St. George's Hall in the Kremlin and the Palace of Congresses. After a moment's confusion, he made a surprising remark: "I voted against you, Yegor." To which Ligachev replied: "And I, Mikhail Sergeyevich, voted for you to be general secretary."

The two men then parted, forever. I well remember how much Ligachev had helped Gorbachev while he was running for election to the post of general secretary in the spring of 1985. Those were the days when he had the party cadres in his pocket: he sought the support of dozens of Central Committee members and *obkom* and *kraikom* secretaries for Gorbachev's election at the extraordinary plenum of 1985. Five years later, their thinking, character and principles had grown far apart. Gorbachev had a knack for discarding old connections and comrades at work. I do not think he ever had any friends, certainly not in Moscow. One wonders whether he even had any comrades. The members of the Politburo and the Central Committee secretaries, who were better qualified to answer these questions, used to wonder why Gorbachev avoided everyone's company. Perhaps he espoused the philosophy of the British statesman who once said that England has no permanent friends or enemies, only permanent interests.

When a suitable occasion presented itself, I once mentioned this matter on the phone to Raisa, who was always interested to know what ordinary, and not so ordinary, people thought of her family. I told her it was a pity that the leader of the party did not get together with his associates in a normal domestic setting and discuss with them matters of everyday concern. She was not pleased to hear what I had to say, quickly brought the conversation to a close, and hung up. Five minutes later she called back: "Don't you know that the Politburo members and the Central Committee secretaries get together around New Year's Day with their wives?"

Yes, I did know that. First of all, though, such gatherings were held only once a year, and, second, as I learned from the Central Committee secretaries, the gatherings in question were stiff, formal affairs, rather like Politburo meetings, only with wives and champagne glasses. Many members found the atmosphere oppressive and did their best to stay away.

My remarks must have touched a chord, however, as the next day Gorbachev asked me to prepare a list of his aides and advisers, and their wives. He may have intended to organize some kind of get-together, but probably decided against it when he realized how many people would have to be invited. What mattered was not the holding of social gatherings, still less of elaborate dinner parties. Human warmth and mutual respect were lacking in the general secretary's relations with his colleagues. In such stressful times, when his staff was working so hard on his behalf, a little warmth and encouragement, perhaps even solicitude, were sorely needed. I have always believed that money alone, especially such miserly salaries as ours, is never enough to induce people to share such vast burdens, but that they are prepared to assume heavy responsibilities only because they believe in certain ideas. It was therefore all the more galling for Gorbachev's aides to see him treat them like servants. Several members of the Politburo and certain aides were unable to meet for months at a time to report on the state of affairs, so they chose to write letters instead. Gorbachev often found it unnecessary to answer questions put to him by his associates.

Is the struggle for political power above normal human feelings? Could there be some people who are so intent on achieving power that nothing else counts—or even exists—for them?

The arduous process of electing Central Committee members at the Twenty-eighth Congress was followed by a plenum, at which members of the Politburo and the Secretariat were elected. Gorbachev was also running for election to the Politburo, as the organizers of the congress had forgotten that the general secretary had to be elected not only to the Central Committee but also to the Politburo. Ryzhkov, Ligachev, Medvedev, Yakovlev, Zaikov, and Slyunkov and many other former senior officials were now missing from the highest organs of the party, having been replaced by newcomers with certain other qualities and shortcomings to which I have already referred. The Politburo now included all the first secretaries of the republican parties. The Central Committee also looked quite different, having retained only some 20 percent of its former members.

During the congress I once went into the room where Gorbachev had gone to work alone and found him busy preparing a list of Central Committee members. He would no longer entrust this task to anyone else. He was also unable to consult with the current members of the Politburo, since he knew that virtually all of them were about to leave the political scene. Nor could he consult Razumovski, who had tendered his resignation some time before, on grounds of ill health; in any case, he did not like him. And talking to Ligachev was clearly out of the question.

Gorbachev was sitting alone and forlorn in this small room, drawing up a list of members of the plenum, an organ whose power had for many decades been unparalleled in the Soviet Union. I looked at the pages of scribbling on the table and sensed that I was a witness to a tragedy of a magnitude no one could yet imagine. As the intransigent attitudes and bitter hostility of those members were soon to show, this was no longer the monolithic plenum of times past but a gathering of representatives of various platforms within a once mighty party.

8

DISMANTLING THE UNION: "I CANNOT BE A PARTY TO THE DISINTEGRATION OF THE COUNTRY"

On the morning of 15 March 1990, crowds of people's deputies steadily made their way from the Rossiya and Moskva hotels to the Kremlin. At 10:00, in the Kremlin Palace of Congresses, a meeting was to take place during which the results of the previous evening's vote for the post of president of the USSR were to be announced. The huge hall was full. The audience included not only the deputies but numerous guests as well: ministers, staff members from various government departments, and diplomats from dozens of countries, surrounded by television crews, radio correspondents, journalists, and photographers.

The hall was abuzz with excitement and commotion. The vote-counting commission had been unable to keep its work secret, and the results were quietly spreading among the delegates. From their own experience, however, everyone knew better than to reach conclusions before the official announcement was made.

Bells sounded in the lobby, summoning the delegates to their seats. I took my seat among the representatives of Northern Ossetia. A few minutes before, I had walked around the Palace of Congresses and been in the room where the presidium assembled. The members of the Politburo, who had gathered in their room, already knew the results of the voting. Gorbachev looked as if he had been told at daybreak. Though tired after a sleepless night, he was clearly pleased with the outcome. Smiling broadly, he casually acknowledged the congratulations of well-wishers and summoned his aides to one side before asking them to prepare the text of an oath of office. This was a new procedure, for both him and the country. But his aides were familiar with United States practice and anticipated no difficulties. In any case they had a draft with them already. The language of the oath would not pose a problem.

The members of the presidium took their seats. When the chairman of the vote-counting commission was given the floor, a deathly silence fell over the hall, so that the only sound was the humming of the ventilation system. He then announced that Mikhail Sergeyevich Gorbachev had been elected as the first president of the Soviet Union, with 1,834 votes in favor, out of a total of 2,486. The new head of state was given a standing ovation. The oath of office came later, on 28 May, when, his hand on the Constitution of the USSR, he swore to uphold its letter and its spirit.

That was how the Soviet Union got its first president. Just eighteen months later it had more than a dozen presidents.

THE PRESIDENTIAL APPARATUS

The next day Gorbachev sent for me, to consider a single issue. The president was going to need a suitable governing apparatus. We had discussed this matter earlier, when he was merely contemplating a run for the presidency, but we had talked in general terms. This time we were examining several concrete proposals. No one had any idea of what kind of apparatus he needed, especially as he still had a fully fledged governing structure in his capacity as general secretary. In my presence he contacted his aides, and then Kryuchkov and Lukyanov, and asked them to prepare some proposals for the formation of his presidential apparatus. "You put down your ideas, too," he told me. "Remember, the apparatus must be small but efficient."

That was easy to say; but before considering the structure and size of the apparatus, one would first have to knew whether the Council of Ministers was to remain in existence. Gorbachev had previously hinted that he did not need a government with so many ministries or so many employees. When I raised the question again, I realized that the president would not find it so easy to answer. "You think about it," he said, "and we'll talk about it later."

Kryuchkov, Lukyanov, and Shakhnazarov had each produced some ideas of their own for a possible governing structure. After a while, Gorbachev sent for me and handed me these documents. He had already looked at them and found them divergent in several ways and unlikely to result in a small apparatus. Gorbachev had been developing some proposals of his own about the form of the government. He walked up and down the office, reasoning as follows: "We need five or six ministries, or in any case not more than eight: energy, defense, transportation, economy, finance, and a few more—we'll have to work that out. All other tasks will be handled regionally, in the republics. But even the remaining central ministries would be cut back and overhauled. We don't need the Council of Ministers, the way it was. The president is at the head of everything, and a Cabinet of Ministers headed by a premier would take care of the day-to-day running of the economy. There would be fewer deputy heads, and the president and premier would share the same governing apparatus and technical services."

Gorbachev continued to speculate about the governing structure, naming a few potential senior government officials, though I felt his thinking on the subject was still tentative. It would be very difficult to alter the structure of government from above without making changes at the local and regional levels. What would he do about the nuclear industry and nuclear power stations, for example? He would need a ministry of foreign affairs and another one for foreign trade. Who would be in charge of the banks? When I proposed that the new government or its top officials should elaborate an integrated structure for the management of the economy, Gorbachev agreed. "The presidential structures would also have to include units servicing the Cabinet of Ministers," he concluded.

A week and a half later I submitted an outline for the presidential apparatus. The exact nature of the government was still unknown, as proposals were not yet ready. All the units of the apparatus, together with their relative status and their relationship to one another, were set forth in a chart on a large sheet of paper. Gorbachev examined it, read the explanatory memorandum, and asked us to leave it with him for a while. A few days later he returned the chart and other documents. He also proposed to merge certain services, while making others autonomous, and added a new unit connected with his duties as chairman of the Defense Council. He introduced the post of first deputy chairman of the Council and its apparatus, overseeing the armed forces and the defense industry, the MVD, and the KGB. He later appointed Baklanov to this post.

Once I had amended the chart I called Gorbachev, who summoned me to the Great Kremlin Palace. An animated campaign was then in progress for the post of chairman of the Supreme Soviet of the RSFSR, the main candidate being Boris Yeltsin. The old animosities and biases had surfaced again, dividing the deputies into two camps. The party had decided to back Vlasov, chairman of the Council of Ministers of the RSFSR. As no successful candidate had emerged after two ballots, the party decided to switch its allegiance to a new contender, Ivan Polozkov, leader of the newly founded Russian Communist party.

Gorbachev then made an unprecedented move: he went to the Congress of People's Deputies of the RSFSR, where he made a speech obliquely supporting the party's candidate, and then stayed in the hall until the voting was completed. As president of the USSR, he never went to the Congresses of People's Deputies of the RSFSR, either before or after Yeltsin's election. He went there only after the events of August 1991, when he was present in quite a different capacity and did not have to be too particular about where he sat.

In 1990, however, during the elections for chairman of the Supreme Soviet of the RSFSR, seating was a principal issue. It proved necessary to convene a meeting, to which Lukyanov was invited in his capacity as an expert, to discuss the matter. It was decided that Gorbachev could hardly sit in the front row. Someone suggested he might sit with the presidium, only three or four rows higher than the deputies who were conducting the meeting. This idea was ruled out because Gorbachev had made up his mind to attend with the president's flag of the Union.

The flag and other presidential symbols were first introduced by Gorbachev. He may have seen that the president of the United States always had the national flag close by when he moved about, or perhaps his aides suggested the idea to him; but whatever the reason, he ordered that the Soviet flag be placed next to him and that the symbol of the Union be painted on presidential aircraft. The security service headed by Plekhanov carried out his wishes. Thereafter the red flag, placed in a special holder, appeared in the president's office, conference rooms, and other premises where he was present.

On that particular day, when a decision was to be made on where he should sit at the Congress of People's Deputies of the RSFSR, the flag proved to be crucial. As the hall and the presidium had been discarded as possible sites, it was proposed that he be seated on the balcony, where both the president and the flag would be visible. He would have been slightly to one side, but above the deputies. The whole idea was that his presence should inspire the supporters of the party candidate for the post of chairman of the Supreme Soviet of the RSFSR. It could be that either the flag or the president were insufficiently prominent. But whatever the reason, his foray into the congress failed to yield the desired result, as Polozkov was not elected.

Some progress was made, however. One day Gorbachev invited me to join him on the balcony of the Great Kremlin Palace. He took the chart showing the structural outline of the apparatus and, while the discussion continued, studied it carefully, erasing liberally as he did so. He eliminated some more units, added others, altered the hierarchical status of certain units, making them directly subordinate to himself, and approved the size of the apparatus and the recruiting arrangements. All department heads and his own entourage were appointed directly by the president and were subordinate to him. He asked me to make proposals and to be in charge of the apparatus.

We had to form departments serving all the highest levels of the leadership: the president and vice president of the USSR, the Security Council, the Defense Council, and the corps of aides and advisers to Gorbachev and Yanayev. By previous standards, the number of staff involved was enormous. Toward the end, the office of the president alone included Medvedev, Revenko, Akhromeyev, Zagladin, Yegorov, Karasev, Ignatenko, Ozherelyev, Chernyayev, and Shakhnazarov, as well as Pryakhin, Gusenkov, and a number of assistants. As in the United States, the staff of presidential aides included its own services, such as assistants, consultants, secretaries, and typists/stenographers. The president could also directly appoint a large number of temporary advisers, among them Abalkin, Sitaryan, Osipyan, and a number of other distinguished academics, economists, and political scholars.

The structure of the presidential apparatus, as designed by Gorbachev, inevitably underwent changes in response to practical necessity. As we have seen, at first the Cabinet of Ministers was to have been fully subordinate to the president and to have consisted of five or six ministries, the absolute maximum being eight. But intentions and actual performance soon parted company. To my amazement I found that an autonomous, full-scale organ of government practically the same size as the former Council of Ministers was taking shape. Just as the simplest living organisms grow to form a whole organism, here too a powerful governing structure was being regenerated. At the suggestion of Premier Pavlov and the whole Cabinet of Ministers, Gorbachev made the proposals, and the Supreme Soviet of the Union endorsed the formation of a whole series of new ministries, which were practically indistinguishable from the old ones.

That effectively demolished the idea of setting up a small but efficient governing apparatus and related services. The apparatus of the Cabinet of Ministers was more than two thousand strong and, together with the ministries, could draw on the services of some 16,000 managerial and technical personnel. By August 1991 the apparatus of the president of the USSR consisted of fewer than 400 people, including the technical staff. The merging, and consequently the reduction, of these structures was therefore out of the question. Instructions, signed by Gorbachev, for the establishment of a joint apparatus were ignored. He was aware of this, and asked me: "Look, you sort it out with Pavlov. Why do I have to do everything? Can't you decide anything on your own?"

What could I decide? If the decrees of the president of the USSR on vitally important matters of state were never put into effect, how was it possible to "sort out" the problem of reducing and merging the apparatus? Gorbachev saw that the Cabinet of Ministers was ignoring the problem, but he said nothing. Whether it was fatigue or something else, Gorbachev was occasionally unable to stand firm, or to deny requests, especially if they came from influential people. This trait was clearly illustrated by the matter of the further use of the building of the Council for Mutual Economic Assistance (CMEA).

Ivan Silayev, the chairman of the Council of Ministers of the RSFSR, requested the president's permission to take over the building, on the grounds that he needed space for the ministries and service of the Russian Federation, and the CMEA building was situated near the Russian White House. Gorbachev instructed Pavlov to accede to the prime minister's request. Not long afterward, a memorandum arrived from Lukyanov, claiming that the people's deputies were short of work space and requesting the transfer of the old CMEA building to the Supreme Soviet of the Union. The president responded by instructing Pavlov to consider Lukyanov's request with all due attention. Next came a request from Gavrili Popov, mayor of Moscow, followed by an equally positive decision requesting the transfer of the building to the Moscow City Council. In response to the last application, from Yeltsin, Gorbachev again issued similar instructions. Such was his approach to many other matters, including those of real substance.

* * *

The transformation of the party's general secretary into the president of the USSR was not a smooth process. His management style, and many of the methods and habits he had acquired over many years as party secretary in Stavropol and Moscow, followed him into the office of the chief executive. He needed some kind of structure similar to the Politburo, in which he could make statements, issue orders, and consider issues requiring his attention, particularly legislation on national problems. Apparently Yakovlev suggested this idea, which, falling like a seed on fertile soil, did not take long to germinate, resulting in the creation of the Presidential Council. The new body included government representatives and prominent citizens—Chingiz Aitmatov, Nikolai Ryzhkov, V. Yarin, Aleksandr Yakovlev, Valentin Rasputin, Stanislav Shatalin, V. Medvedev, and several others, including me.

The council was a good idea, but there was a slightly amateurish air about it. The Soviet Constitution made no provision for such a body, its size and composition being determined by the president. It had no well-defined functions. It met five or seven times, considering various current issues, including problems posed by the conversion of military industries and economic affairs. Neither the qualifications nor the status of its members were commensurate with the gravity of the problems at hand. In any case, it was by now futile to offer Gorbachev advice of any sort, as he did not need it. The council's meetings were therefore irregular and ill organized. The president found that convening the council's meetings was a chore that soon turned into a nuisance. This was especially true of the meeting at which he invited members to comment on the situation in the country. For the first time, they felt needed and able to offer their own assessments and propose their own solutions.

Gorbachev was quite taken aback by what he heard. Yarin, Rasputin, and various others found that the people had grown tired of experiments, vacillation, and idle chatter. In most of them the word perestroika produced a nauseous allergic reaction, as they felt a worthy cause had been spoiled and reduced to nonsense. When I saw Gorbachev's complexion turning livid, I knew there was trouble in the offing. Without giving the floor to all the remaining speakers, he adjourned the meeting, and was in no hurry to reconvene it.

Pacing nervously up and down his office, Gorbachev said, "What a load of rubbish! And these are people I trusted; I plucked them out of nowhere. And Yarin, of all people! Though I hardly expected anything else from Valentin Rasputin."

The fate of the Presidential Council was sealed. In November 1990, eight months after its creation, it was disbanded. Various explanations are possible. Gorbachev may have realized its futility, or may have been unhappy with its composition; alternatively, he may have been influenced by criticism from the national Supreme Soviet, whose deputies viewed it as a fount of inanity and inertia. The final decision was made so abruptly that the council's members had no advance warning of their dismissal. I knew that many of them found such high-handedness deeply offensive.

The dissolution of the council was a bitter blow to Yakovlev. "Didn't you know that we were out?" he asked me. I shook my head slowly, finding the whole thing just as disconcerting as he did. "Ah well, the Lord moves in mysterious ways."

Yakovlev soon had a conversation with Gorbachev, who tried to assuage his resentment by assuring him that his benefits and allowances would remain the same and by promising to make him head of the newly constituted corps of presidential advisers. He was unable, however, to keep that promise. Medvedev, who, like Yakovlev, had previously been a member of the Politburo and the Presidential Council, also became an adviser. It was plainly out of the question for him to be subordinate to Yakovlev; so both men had to be made senior advisers. Gorbachev also did not want to keep the former transportation arrangements, as I learned from Plekhanov. The same happened with salaries, as the other presidential advisers would have been unable to understand why some were being paid more than others. Such differences could have been a source of additional conflict.

People were mortified to learn that the president of the USSR was not a man of his word. Yakovlev took his onerous duties very seriously; yet, seeing that Gorbachev no longer trusted him and did nothing to defend him from criticism in party and other newspapers, he finally made up his mind to quit his position as senior adviser. In the spring of 1991 he went to Gorbachev and tendered his resignation.

Gorbachev later told me: "Aleksandr came by and handed me his letter of resignation and detailed note explaining his reasons. I urged him not to rush into it, to think it over. Take his letter, but don't act on it."

In early June, while on vacation in Valdai, Yakovlev sent Gorbachev another letter of resignation. This time Gorbachev returned it with his signature.

I found this turn of events troubling, but not surprising. Since Shevardnadze's unexpected resignation, nothing would have surprised me. Unfortunately, Gorbachev was a poor judge of character and had, no doubt inadvertently, appointed obsequious, incompetent, and even dishonest people, while frequently complaining about their shortcomings. He was to blame for the unhealthy, insincere atmosphere that had long plagued his inner circle. He was jealous of the actions and successes of others and never seemed to trust anyone. These traits were not always perceptible, however, so people were initially attracted to him.

DISTRUST

In the early years of his tenure as general secretary, Gorbachev had been much admired by academics, writers, journalists and politicians. Some were attracted by his relative youth and his university education, and others by his experience of party work and his rapid rise to the top. In any case, he moved easily among that segment of the intelligentsia that sought not only change but also a leader capable of uniting all the progressive forces in society. In a sincere, altruistic spirit, people tried to help Gorbachev by suggesting new ideas and submitting projects they had spent years elaborating; they did their utmost to add impetus to perestroika and ensure its success.

In those days most people believed things could get better under Gorbachev, and that a free, creative atmosphere could prevail throughout society. Even at that early stage, however, a disconcerting stiffness was evident in Gorbachev's attitude toward those who had come to help him. They felt he questioned their sincerity and trustworthiness, as he never spoke frankly. The resulting alienation and inertia, coupled with the general secretary's tactlessness, served as a barrier, inducing many people to find pretexts for leaving his service.

I had always assumed that his relationship with Lukyanov, which dated back to their student days together at Moscow State University, gave Gorbachev confidence in his advice and assistance. But that was not the case. He often spoke contemptuously of Lukyanov's professorial tone and condescending recommendations. "He's just trying to intimidate me with all that talk of negative mail and public opinion polls," he would say, indignantly. "The Soviet people are behind me, and he has no business talking down to me like that."

While I could not have known the details of their past and present relationship, I could sense Gorbachev's hostility toward Lukyanov. Gorbachev returned many of Lukyanov's memorandums, dealing mainly with the Supreme Soviet deputies, without even looking at them. Some of his remarks showed that he resented Lukyanov's popularity in the Supreme Soviet and the fact that he was more widely read and better educated. Gorbachev was often unable to restrain his animosity. Lukyanov was not entirely above reproach, as he was ambitious, touchy, and suspicious. Yet he did his duty honorably, fulfilling all the instructions he received from the general secretary. Unfortunately, that was not enough. At the Sixth Congress of People's Deputies, in 1991, Gorbachev virtually accused him of involvement in the events of August of that year, and asked the Procurator to investigate. Both the deputies present in the hall, and all those watching that sickening scene on television, certainly got that impression.

As I have noted previously, I recommended Chernyayev, a cultivated and capable man, as an assistant on international affairs. Yakovlev endorsed my judgment, and Gorbachev agreed to appoint him. It was a wise choice, as his performance later proved. He involved Chernyayev in the consideration of all international issues, including negotiations, stating that he was the only one whose writing was in the same style and spirit as his own. When vacation time came, he would take Chernyayev with him to Foros, where he put him to work preparing books, articles, and political documents. Throughout the entire time he spent with Gorbachev, I was never in any doubt about his professional or other qualities. For that reason I was astonished when Gorbachev once remarked that Chernyayev was not to be trusted, as he could be the source of information leaks, and asked me to limit the range of secret information reaching him.

I was even more shocked to learn from Gorbachev that his aide Ignatenko had been accepting bribes from various foreign media representatives. This was hard to believe. Ignatenko had worked for many years in the Central Committee apparatus and had helped write several books, including Brezhnev's *Small Earth* and *Resurrection*. Various journalists had told me that while working at *Komsomolskaya Pravda*, Ignatenko had displayed a picture of himself, as a child, being held by Brezhnev, who was then fighting in the Caucasus. He had been awarded the Lenin Prize for his televised serial about the foundation and development of the Socialist state. Yakovlev also knew him well and recommended him to Gorbachev.

"Why would anyone be paying him money?" I asked.

"For an interview with me he collects tens of thousands of dollars from the journalists," said Gorbachev, in a tone that suggested neither surprise nor complaint.

I was startled less by the bribe taking than by the calm, matter-of-fact way in which it had been announced. My only response was to ask whether anyone had confirmed this information. He replied: "It's been going on for some time. In fact, I once asked him why the people who were going to be interviewing him were practically all from the same country. I trust he realized that I knew quite a lot about him. But I'll tell you something: the people in whom I am most confident are the ones who have some material incentive for the work they do." As I left the president's office, I was horrified and puzzled by the sudden realization that the leader of the party and state believed bribe takers and saw nothing wrong with their behavior.

Kryuchkov later showed me a KGB memorandum on Ignatenko's kickbacks and other questionable dealings. Gorbachev had written up an order for an investigation, only to delete it at the last minute. The president had Kryuchkov continue his investigation. In any case, he forbade me to send any documents to Ignatenko, doubtless fearing that he would sell them. After August 1991 he was swiftly removed from his position as press secretary and appointed director general of TASS.

Nor did Gorbachev trust Shakhnazarov. He frequently complained that decisions on the conflict in Nagorno-Karabakh were being leaked to the Armenian diaspora, though he did nothing about it. It was only when highly confidential information from foreign sources was leaked to the parties involved from a meeting of the Security Council that he ordered Kryuchkov to investigate. At the same time he issued orders excluding his aides and advisers from future Security Council meetings. The range of confidential issues to be discussed at the council was also sharply curtailed.

The large size of the president's personal staff, and the fact that he did not fully trust all of them, made the atmosphere extremely tense. Each individual fought to enhance his own influence and special privileges, and many of them wrote memos complaining that their merits were not appreciated. Worse still, the president's distrust began to extend to high government officials as well. Gorbachev was unhappy about some actions taken by Shevardnadze, whom he suspected of working on his own account and being concerned primarily with boosting his own authority. He no longer trusted Yakovlev either, whom he also found to be "playing his own game." He increasingly tended to dispatch him to dachas on the outskirts of Moscow to prepare documents.

As soon as Gorbachev felt that some high-ranking government official, such as the prime minister, the foreign minister, or a senior military officer, was gaining in popularity, he would start making disparaging comments about him. Criticism of any politician in the press or the Supreme Soviet automatically meant that the president was about to feed that individual, bound hand and foot, to the deputies and the press. I can safely say that he suspected most of his associates of disloyalty, greed, and a desire to unseat him. Some episodes of an anecdotal nature were particularly intriguing. Gorbachev did not like to be called at his suburban residence, making an exception only for Kryuchkov, Yazov, Pugo, and Ivashko. He, on the other hand, used to call up so often that he seemed occasionally to have forgotten that he had discussed the same subject with me only fifteen minutes earlier. Sometimes he phoned for no reason whatever. "Where are you now?" he would ask and, having heard my reply, would say: "O.K., I'll call you later."

As he made similar calls to other people, I tended to believe that his habit of checking up on us reflected the paranoia of a man who trusted hardly anyone. My thoughts on this were soon confirmed.

Toward the end of the summer of 1990, while on vacation in the Crimea, Gorbachev unexpectedly called me around eleven o'clock one morning. I could tell from his tone and the kind of things he was saying that he was extremely agitated and upset over something. "Do you know where Yakovlev is at this moment?" he asked me nervously. I answered that I had no idea; as it was a Saturday, I thought he could be at his dacha. "No, no!" he shot back. "I called there, and he's not in. What about Bakatin, at least, do you know where he is?" My astonishment mounted, as I tried to figure out what exactly he wanted from me. It seemed to me that on a summer weekend people would be either at their dachas or perhaps somewhere in the woods; or perhaps they had gone for a swim in the river. "As usual, you know nothing," he snapped back at me. "Moiseyev, the chief of the general staff, is also not where he's supposed to be," said Gorbachev with a tragic note in his voice. "They told me that all of them had gone off hunting. As soon as you find anything out, let me know." Then he hung up.

This conversation left me feeling uneasy and annoyed, deep down inside. Why should he feel alarmed to learn that someone had gone for a stroll in the woods, or gone fishing? And how could he be up on every-one's whereabouts while he was at the seaside? Someone had obviously been keeping a close watch on certain people's movements and reporting back to him.

Some forty minutes later the phone rang again. It was Gorbachev, saying that he had managed to contact the cars, which were in the woods, apparently somewhere in the Ryazan *oblast*, but there was no one there apart from the drivers; everyone else had gone off. The drivers had gone to fetch them. "How come they're all together like that? What are they up to?" he inquired nervously. I cautiously suggested that they might have gone picking mushrooms. "What do you mean? They've got a few generals with them as well; they're obviously up to something."

My peace of mind was destroyed. I figured he would keep on phon-ing, and that I would be stuck next to the phone for a long time to come. Yet the next call did not come until late that night, when he told me, in a calmer voice, that he had talked to Mikhail Moiseyev (general of the army), who had explained that he had gone to the hunting reserve and had quite by chance met Yakovlev and Bakatin (minister of Internal Affairs) there. "I never did get through to Aleksandr; I was told he was off in the woods somewhere. I'm sure that's not all there is to it. I didn't expect that from him," he concluded.

He did not particularly trust Vadim Bakatin, and grew quite alarmed when he began scoring points with his speeches in the Supreme Soviet and the Congresses of People's Deputies. He encouraged him as best he could to run for the post of president of Russia. "He won't get past Ryzhkov," he said. "But he could be useful; he might siphon off some votes. And we'll help Ryzhkov all we can."

This kind of checking up was frequent. And the more relations between him and Yakovlev, Bakatin, and Shevardnadze deteriorated, the closer he monitored their actions. He would often say: "Aleksandr seems determined to get to the top; what more does he want?"

As tension mounted between them, Yakovlev leaned more and more toward quitting his job. A veritable epidemic swept through the presi-dential entourage, which lost two academicians, Petrakov and Shatalin, as well as Shevardnadze. Ryzhkov and Ligachev had already gone; the number of Central Committee members among his entourage was much reduced, and Marshal Akhromeyev, another assistant, also quit.

That honest and deeply patriotic soldier found himself in a tragic position that eventually led him to make a fateful decision. He had fought in the Second World War and achieved the highest military positions and honors in recognition of his service to the people and to the defense of his country, securing military parity and ensuring peace at home during the coldest years of co-existence. Then after all that, he was criticized for acquiring a state-owned refrigerator, or some other appliance, for his dacha. It was sickening to read in the press, or hear from the people's deputies, about the "abuses" committed by the marshal, and to contemplate the pettiness of those who did not have the courage to defend Akhromeyev. None of them spoke up, and said: "We are all deeply indebted to this man; he fought for us in the front line. How can we treat him like this? If anything, the deputies should insist on awarding him a fully equipped dacha, after all his tireless efforts on our behalf, in both peace and war."

Gorbachev was the supreme commander of the Soviet armed forces, chairman of the Defense Council, and president of the USSR; yet he disowned his assistant and, by his indifference, exposed to ridicule a marshal who was renowned all over the world. When I was with Marshal Akhromeyev on his visit to the United States, I could see that the American military and Ronald Reagan treated him with the same respect and deference they showed Gorbachev himself. He was treated with equal respect even before he had become chief of the general staff. And now he was being tossed to the mob. Such treachery on the part of the president could not fail to inflict a severe wound on this venerable and distinguished soldier. The criminal abuse that was heaped on him after his death was also no doubt prompted by the disdainful attitude of the Soviet leadership, whose members were unwilling to bid farewell to a man who had done so much to bolster their country's defenses and later, when the need arose, to help it disarm.

Two months before the events of August 1991 Marshal Akhromeyev tendered his resignation to the president. He complained frankly of the disrespect shown toward him, the public dishonor being heaped upon the military, and disarmament measures that he considered hasty, ill considered, and above all unilateral. For all those reasons, he said he no longer felt entitled to occupy his post at the president's side, and refused to be a party to the demolition of the armed forces and of the Soviet Union itself. Gorbachev was taken aback and asked the marshal to postpone his decision. He had originally brought Akhromeyev on board in the hope of using his name to camouflage the concessions, some of them unwarranted, that were made to the United States at the time. He made no secret of his motivation. "You understand why I need him, don't you?" Gorbachev said candidly; "as long as he's with me, disarmament problems are going to be easier to handle. Our military and the people in the defense industry trust him, and he's respected in the West."

Marshal of the USSR Sergei Akhromeyev left this world without betraying his principles, or the oath he had taken as a soldier, or his comrades in arms, with whom he had fought his way over thousands of miles. He had strengthened the army and instilled in his soldiers and officers a sense of loyalty to their homeland.

Any spirit of creativity among the members of Gorbachev's entourage had long vanished, and tensions were now running high. Whereas the formal, bureaucratic nature of my work had once been merely irksome, it eventually became downright oppressive. No doubt for a variety of reasons, Gorbachev was increasingly tired and irritable during the last two years of his tenure, losing his temper often. I became aware that the years were slipping by, my health was deteriorating, and the strain of fourteen-hour days with no holidays or vacation time was becoming excessive. Reforms had been bogged down for some time. At the top, sordid infighting was in progress. I was seriously considering moving back into journalism. Even while working on the president's staff, I had managed to devote some time to books, restoring rare editions and organizing the bookbinding department. I was waiting for the right moment to submit my resignation, though I knew it would meet with a frosty reception. Something had to be done, however. The only person I could consult was Leonid Ilichev, an academician and deputy foreign minister who was held in high esteem by Gromyko, Shevardnadze, and many senior party officials. Fate had thrown us together in the early 1960s, when he was a Central Committee secretary and I was working at *Pravda*, doing something I really enjoyed. Suddenly I was told I was being reassigned, whether I liked it or not, to a post as assistant to Ilichev in the Central Committee. I worked with him for several years, before returning to *Pravda*. When I went to see him this time, he sympathized with me and told me how he had also once been obliged to quit journalism, his preferred line of work, for a political post; but he advised me to keep up with my writing and not to be depressed.

Ilich may have been right, but even so I felt increasingly alienated from my surroundings. Virtually none of the people with whom Gorbachev had embarked on radical reforms in 1985 was still on board.

Some he had ousted, while others had left of their own accord, leaving me stranded in a milieu that meant less and less to me.

Actually there were two men whom Gorbachev, by his own admission, trusted implicitly: Yazov and Kryuchkov. He would call them several times a day and often meet with them. They kept him constantly informed about the situation in the country and the armed forces, political trends, and actions they had taken or proposed to take. Gorbachev knew everything there was to know and every day would glance through or carefully study hundreds of pages of assorted information. He told me to stay in constant touch with Kryuchkov and Yazov, to consult with them and help them out where possible. While frequently in touch with them himself, the president would often arrange for someone else to send them a request for the preparation of some document or other. At first I thought nothing of it, but later I realized that, trust or no trust, Gorbachev was simply hedging his bets by resolving certain sensitive issues through third parties.

Kryuchkov, Yazov, and probably also Pugo, the minister of internal affairs, were Gorbachev's main support, until it became clear to them that the nation, the armed forces, and society as a whole were headed toward a disaster that could tear apart the Soviet Union, leading to ethnic conflicts, massive flows of refugees, and economic collapse. Our counterintelligence people had intercepted certain information in the possession of Western intelligence agencies concerning plans for the collapse of the USSR and steps necessary to complete the destruction of our country as a great power.

The defunct Presidential Council was replaced at a session of the Supreme Soviet by the Security Council. This organ, for which there was a constitutional basis, consisted of Bakatin, Bessmertnykh, Kryuchkov, Pavlov, Pugo, Primakov, Yazov, and Yanayev. To the best of my knowledge, all of these people were committed to reform and to the strengthening of the Soviet Union. They helped Gorbachev grapple with difficulties until it seemed that the collapse of the state, economic chaos, and bloodshed were imminent. From then on their paths were bound to diverge.

Bakatin and Primakov had no precise functions but carried out individual instructions, while the other members had high-ranking positions and important duties. The Security Council had no formal mandate, and no one knew what it was supposed to do—least of all Gorbachev; after convening it a few times, he concluded that it was just an added burden and a waste of time. He had for some time been making all decisions on his own, sometimes entrusting their implementation directly to third parties, and needed advice from no one. The democratic principles he professed in public had actually become an impediment. The president had virtually stopped briefing the members of the Security Council and senior government officials on the majority of domestic and international issues, and no longer circulated memos on his talks with foreign statesmen or public figures. When he convened the council on 1 August 1991, Gorbachev said only a few words about George Bush's visit to Moscow. It was as if the president of the United States had come to tour the Kremlin and stroll with Gorbachev in Red Square. His account of the visit was so terse that members came to see me or phoned later to find out if I knew anything more. The outcome of the visit was kept secret from the members of the Security Council and, even more so, from senior party officials.

It was, in fact, an unusual visit. Gorbachev had confined all negotiations with George Bush to a tight circle of trusted associates, spending most of the time in one-on-one dialogue, after which he would leave at the first opportunity. At lunch one day, while the waiters were still serving coffee, Gorbachev rose from the table and said, "George, come over here with me for a minute."

They walked away from the table and went downstairs, accompanied only by an interpreter, and out the back door into the Kremlin's Ivanovskaya Ploshchad. From there they proceeded to Red Square. They had long before established a trusting relationship and were now engaged in a frank conversation that had started in Washington, when Bush escorted the general secretary on his movements around town. Gorbachev realized then that Reagan's tenure was coming to an end and that he would have to be on good terms with his successor. Bush, then vice president, stood a good chance of being elected, as he frequently remarked to the members of his entourage. Gorbachev was aware of all this.

While Bush was driving with Gorbachev from the embassy to the White House, the two men had had a confidential talk devoted, as Gorbachev said, to an outline of the future phases of perestroika. He did not say what that outline involved, but I noticed several times that he asked his personal envoys in Washington to tell Bush that "the agreements we reached in the car are still good," and that he would make sure they were fully implemented. During that trip Gorbachev had obviously assumed certain obligations, and kept Bush regularly informed about their practical implementation.

Gorbachev's close personal relationship with Bush built up his confidence in the success of the policy he began to pursue after his trip to Washington. Government and business leaders in the United States, however, were more pragmatic. They preferred to confer cash prizes and other personal awards on the Soviet leader, while with few exceptions the promised credits never reached our country. Those credits were frozen, thus denying us a chance to relieve our economic distress, which was becoming more acute with each passing month. I am sure Gorbachev understood this and also realized that friendly relations are one thing, but that financial dealings are quite another. The West would not, indeed could not, underwrite a shaky, vacillating policy line.

The real results of Gorbachev's negotiations and the resulting obligations were never fully explained to the leadership and the Supreme Soviet. As we have seen, the Security Council was never taken very seriously. Its meetings, usually devoted to minor, if not incidental, issues, were not held regularly. What were those issues? For a meeting held in April 1991, its members were briefed on the activities of the Council of the Federation, and discussed the fulfillment by the republics of their financial obligations to the federal budget. The republican leaders, suspecting that other regions of the country were looting their wealth, were following separatist paths. References were made to their poor grasp of economics and the impropriety of certain remarks made at the meeting of the Council of the Federation. Possible ways of improving the situation were also discussed. On 30 April the Security Council took up the question of the earthquake in Georgia and of assistance to the republic. It also considered the possibility of a presidential decree imposing emergency regulations in various sectors of the economy in response to strikes and work stoppages.

On 8 May 1991 it discussed the possible admission of the USSR to the International Monetary Fund and the World Bank; on 1 July, with Yanayev in the chair, it discussed the situation in Nagorno-Karabakh. The last meeting was held in August, and dealt with the visit of President Bush and progress in the negotiations on a new Union Treaty that were being held at the suburban residence of Novo-Ogaryovo. The Security Council also took up the question of the agro-industrial complex and conditions at the start of the huge harvest campaign, but made no decisions on them. The meetings were purely for purposes of relaying information. On agriculture, in fact, not even the Cabinet of Ministers was able to make a meaningful decision, as the levers of control were already in the hands of the republics. The matter was therefore referred to the Council of the Federation.

Although the Security Council came into being as a constitutional organ, it was incapable of resolving practical issues in any field. Its failure merely served to underscore the magnitude of the crisis and the government's inability to restore order. For all practical purposes, the decisions of the Cabinet of Ministers, as well as presidential decrees, were also blocked. The heads of state of the countries formerly composing the USSR met increasingly often without Gorbachev, against his wishes. Actions taken by the republican leadership effectively removed the president of the USSR from the decision-making process.

To the very end, however, Gorbachev failed to realize this. He was convinced that by concentrating in his hands the power of both party and state, and by securing emergency powers, he would wield unconditional control over a great country. In fact, all he held in his hands were the reins: his teams of horses had bolted long ago and were now pulling someone else's wagon in a different direction. Unfortunately, the refined political sensory organs that would have been needed to grasp these facts suddenly deserted the president as he reached his sixtieth birthday, on 2 March 1991.

GORBACHEV TURNS SIXTY

For most men in the Soviet Union—at least for those working in industry, agriculture, business, or institutes—reaching sixty is a time to apply for a pension. Politicians, including Gorbachev, regard the age of sixty as the onset of maturity. Pensions were not for him, though his strength was clearly flagging. He tended to repeat himself more and more, lose track of the discussion, and forget who said what to whom. And his old ailments, such as intense headaches and exceedingly high blood pressure, had resurfaced. This latter problem worried him more than anything: he was afraid he had a hereditary disposition to strokes or similar trouble.

Back in the spring of 1983 he had astonished me with a most unexpected remark: "You know something? I'm going to die soon." He stared sadly into the distance, engrossed in his gloomy thoughts. I asked him what had made him suddenly turn to mysticism, and inquired whether his doctor had given him bad news. "My father died at my age, and I have exactly the same symptoms," he replied.

I was well aware that he was then healthy and still robust; as for blood pressure and arteriosclerosis, and other vascular diseases, practically everyone suffers from those, especially sedentary people who are fond of good food. He was a terrible hypochondriac. As a young man he used to go for health treatments to Zheleznovodsk, where he would constantly urge the doctors to find things wrong with him. He had a good appetite, and if he refrained from eating it was only to avoid putting on weight. Twice a week he would try to have "slimming days," when he ate only cottage cheese. A special cottage cheese with sour cream was prepared for him, and he had to last twenty-four hours on it. He often did not: he would order coffee, which was served with cookies, pastries, small open-faced sandwiches, candy, whipped-cream fruit mousse, and fruit candy. Quickly dispatching his own serving, he would get up and walk slowly around the big conference table, stopping behind one guest or another. Engrossed in the conversation and perhaps not even aware of what he was doing, he would collect leftovers from first one, then another. He left me with the impression that his elaborate dietary game plan merely led to binges and more weight.

During long Politburo meetings, unless the general secretary was on a slimming diet, he and other members of the party leadership were served a hefty dinner. He preferred plain food, and was particularly fond of buckwheat groats, with chunks of lamb or beef. He had hot cereal at breakfast and even sometimes for supper. It came, of course, with plenty of other things. He loved pork fat with large cloves of garlic.

The general secretary's sixtieth birthday was a noteworthy event. Under Khrushchev and Brezhnev, lavish and tumultuous hospitality would have been the rule. The entire leadership used to assemble, with all their friends and comrades, relatives, and acquaintances. Glasses were raised to the good health of the great, wise man, and to his further success in the building of a new society. The awarding of high honors was duly washed down in accordance with the best bibulous traditions. Gorbachev's birthday was more modest. Not even the most virtuoso sycophant would have proposed a toast to him as a great, wise man, or still less to his success in the building of a new society. And the general secretary's friends and comrades were few and far between, as he tended to keep everyone at arm's length.

Very few high honors were conferred on Gorbachev on this occasion, and there were even fewer flights of rhetoric. He had my full support in that. I did not believe that pomp and circumstance were needed. But there was a small reception. The secretaries of the Central Committee and the party's Moscow *obkom* and *gorkom* assembled in the Secretariat room to offer their best wishes to Gorbachev. They sat around the table for a few minutes, listening to Gorbachev speak with heartfelt sincerity of the role of the party in his life and in perestroika. He was so adept at weaving an elaborate fabric, designed to lull his audience's vigilance, that several times I found myself actually believing what he said, though his intentions ran contrary to what he said. Perhaps he believed what he said, just as he believed he was doing the right thing.

The reception ended with champagne and photographs, all in an unfestive mood. Gorbachev left immediately for the Kremlin, where he was to receive birthday wishes from the Security Council, and then from senior officials of the government and the Supreme Soviet at another reception. Kruchina went to make sure that wine was served to the party staff members, who had been left all alone, doubtless hurt by the stiff formality of their half-hour meeting with their leader.

At the same time in the Kremlin a second round of congratulations was beginning. Lukyanov made a moving speech and gave the general secretary a gift. Then came best wishes from Yazov, who offered a saber with an inlaid sheath and a hilt of yellow metal. Pugo gave him a case with a Makarov pistol with an inscription on it, and a clip with cartridges. That was Gorbachev's second Makarov pistol; the first one, with gold inlay, had been given earlier by Chebrikov. The president of the USSR was well armed and dangerous. He kept one pistol in a safe at work.

Bakatin gave him a marble bust of some poet or other, which Gorbachev soon returned. Kryuchkov and some others sent their gifts straight to the general secretary's dacha. Gifts were also received from heads of state, embassies, and a number of our government departments. These were all individual gifts, whereas the Central Committee and the Security Council collectively chose an exquisite handpainted box of the Palekh school with a picture of the Kremlin on the top, as Gorbachev had requested.

Then came the turn of the president's aides and advisers, who couched their best wishes in eloquent terms. Gorbachev found the words of Chernyayev and Shakhnazarov particularly original and cordial, and said so at a meeting of the Security Council.

After the speeches and the traditional embraces, often accompanied by kissing, each group of well-wishers moved into the next room, where food had been laid on a large table and drinks were brought round in glasses of varying shapes and sizes. The alcohol stimulated a new surge of conviviality among some, though many merely sipped their drinks briefly before leaving to get on with the pressing and difficult business at hand. The official celebrations thus came to a close. Gorbachev went home to his dacha, without inviting any of his associates to join him there. In fact, I doubt that anyone in the party or goverment leadership had ever been to his dacha. A number of his subordinates, somewhat surprised at the stiffness and formality of the birthday party they had just attended, gathered in the Kremlin for another round of drinks, this time in a warmer atmosphere, and began talking about hard times, in the best tradition of the intelligentsia of Russia.

DEAD END AT NOVO-OGARYOVO

The Novo-Ogaryovo "brainstorming sessions," as the press aptly dubbed them, and the process of regulating relations among the former union and autonomous republics that began in that suburban residence, will leave their mark in a context wider than the history of our country. They cannot fail to become a symbol of the capitulation of the central government, the collapse of the statehood of a great power, and blazing ethnic conflicts, and will be recorded as such in the annals of world history, thus immortalizing the name of their designer: Mikhail Sergeyevich Gorbachev.

These sessions were to trigger many subsequent phenomena in our society, with consequences that are still unpredictable. The legal basis for these changes was to have been the new Union Treaty. The need for such an instrument was motivated by the increasing noncompliance with decisions of the central government and presidential decrees on the part of regional and local authorities around the country. A long-standing dispute over whose laws and whose constitution should have priority had reached the point where the republics were implementing the decisions of the central government as they saw fit; they had also begun withholding full payment of their taxes to Gosbank, imposing restrictions on military units stationed on their territory, and limiting the movement of scarce foodstuffs.

At the same time there was no pressing political need for a new Union Treaty. It was much more a consequence of economic collapse and of an atavistic desire on the part of individual regions to withdraw into isolation during turbulent times, so as to protect themselves from predatory neighbors. This latter motive played a crucial role in fomenting nationalist sentiment and bloody ethnic conflicts, which in turn accelerated the centrifugal forces at work in the country. For that reason the new Union Treaty was needed as a result of the collapse of the economy, an ineffective domestic policy, and the central government's inability to put its announced reforms into effect or consolidate the various forces in society.

Most sensible people had always known that self-isolation within the boundaries of each ethnic region could only aggravate the socioeconomic plight of the national groups that made up the USSR. Going it alone, as we were often warned, was no way to survive; it would merely complete the destruction of the economy. But it was difficult to make people see reason at a time when ambitious political leaders were flexing their muscles and nationalist feelings were being stirred up. Constant retreat was then the only option. The successes of some separatist forces merely whetted the appetites of others; then, as in a test tube, the chemical reaction went out of control and proceeded until a new substance had been formed. In addition to separate armies and defense industries, demands then arose for separate currencies, secure borders, customs posts, and emblems of statehood.

As the central government was unable to lead the nation, it became necessary to distribute authority among the various powerful regional leaders. Many people felt that this option would at least stave off disaster. All the president of the USSR could do was reserve for himself and the central government certain powers capable of sustaining the office of the presidency and the symbols associated with it. While bargaining to extract those minor conditions for itself, the central government had to fight very hard and was not always too choosy about its methods. The site chosen for this showdown was Novo-Ogaryovo, a prerevolutionary estate about twenty-one miles from Moscow.

Part of the property, consisting of several handsome buildings located in a pine grove high on the bank of the Moscow River, had once belonged to a Russian industrialist. Deep inside the estate was a stone mansion built in the Gothic style, in which party and government leaders had lived after the revolution, among them, according to our security people, Voroshilov, Khrushchev, and Chernenko. Gorbachev later used it for what he called "personal meetings at home" with Ronald Reagan and other Western politicians.

Closer to the highway there was a two-story reception house, having only one office and bedroom but a number of large dining rooms. On the covered and heated verandas there were also huge tables capable of seating between seventy and eighty guests. It was decided that the meetings of the Council of the Federation devoted to the drafting of the new Union Treaty would be held in the second-floor room of this reception house.

The organizers felt that Novo-Ogaryovo should go down in history as the result of the New Thinking, of a democratic approach to the formation of another society on the rubble of the former empire. The treaty was expected to bring to mind the Camp David Accords, which are still widely remembered and talked about.

Early in 1991 a small group of specialists was formed to begin work on the draft of the new Union Treaty. It was headed by Academician V. Kudryavtsev, vice chairman of the Soviet Academy of Sciences, and two representatives of the president, T. Revenko and G. Shakhnazarov. It was a long and painstaking job, involving economists, jurists, and experts in political science from the various republics. The initial draft needed further consideration at a higher political level, and also had to be discussed with the leaders of the union and autonomous republics. Gorbachev decided to assemble them all at the estate.

At the time, I could not think of a more important issue than the preservation of our Union. Toward the end of 1990 I had a frank talk with Gorbachev about the fate of the USSR. Opportunites for such encounters were increasingly rare. He did not like talking about unpleasant topics and did his best to avoid such "awkward" conversations. This, however, was the most important topic of all. I had often raised it before, but perhaps less emphatically, though deep fissures had appeared in the national fabric since 1988, together with breakaway tendencies in some republics. A faint chill of alienation was already discernible in the words of many writers, academics, and other intellectuals and, when the subject of national unity was discussed, in those of politicians. Some old Ukrainian friends of mine told me that one should not worry too much about agitation among representatives of the Trans-Caucasus region, Mol-davia, or the Baltic republics. But real trouble could start as soon as Ukrainian nationalism reared its head. That would mean the end of the USSR. Such a notion was unthinkable to me. How could our Ukrainian brothers, bound to our homeland by many centuries of friendship and years spent struggling for our common cause, betray our Union?

At the time, any thought of a split between Russia and the Ukraine seemed to me the wildest heresy. I was unaware, however, of the secret declarations of certain factions that were propelling the country toward disintegration. The Baltic republics were quite another matter. They had always felt more a part of the West, particularly after the Soviet state had, through collective efforts, built up their industries and infrastruc-ture, mainly in the form of roads designed for use as runways.

So I was sitting in the president's office, waiting to hear his views on the future of our Union. This was for me a fundamental issue, on which my cooperation with the president depended. I had gone to work for him not seeking honors, of which there were none, and not for the salary. I always wanted only one thing: to help my country out of its dif-ficulties and turn my homeland into a powerful state worthy of the peo-ples who lived in it. Gorbachev knew of my conviction and for that rea-son, it seemed to me, gave a forthright answer: "The Soviet Union will remain in existence. You mentioned the damaging consequences for the economy. That's true, but you don't see the political and social disaster that would occur if the state falls apart. Ownership of factories is only one side of it: What about whole territories, and the revision of borders? We have tens of millions of Russians, Ukrainians, and Belorussians living outside the borders of their particular nationality. Have you thought about them? You can't permit a massive migration of ethnic groups. And what about Lithuania, where Klaipeda belongs to us, and a number of areas once belonged to the Poles?"

The president then listed the territories in the Caucasus and central Asia that could trigger disputes among the republics, *krais*, and *oblasts*. He wound up his monologue on an optimistic note: "As long as I am president of the USSR, I shall not allow the destruction of the Union. That's why the constitution contains mechanisms to ensure against rash decisions. And then there's the economy. What are they going to do without oil, gas, or fuel resources in general? Once you cut the umbilical cord and reduce subsidies, they won't last six months. When I was in Estonia I already talked about the trade balance, and showed who is sitting on whose neck. And you can see this in everyday life. Another thing: Estonia is not the only territory that has attached itself for sustenance to the powerful body of Russia. So relax; don't worry about it."

"I'm not opposed to sovereignties," I responded, "but I'm alarmed about the situation because I can see the damage that interethnic hostility can bring. That's why I cannot be a party to the disintegration of the country. I can't be your assistant on that. I also doubt the feasibility of a 'civilized divorce.'"

"What are you talking about? I just told you: the Soviet Union will continue to exist. I'm standing firm on that."

The conversation ended on a sour note. The president came very close to losing his temper. He often flared up and started accusing the people he was talking to of everything under the sun: chauvinism, imperial designs, or worse.

It was hard to tell whether Gorbachev had spoken sincerely or whether he was merely trying to camouflage his true intentions. He must have realized that everyone could see him retreating from one position after another, thus bringing the eventual collapse of the Union ever closer. Notwithstanding all his promises, without a referendum, and in violation of the Soviet Constitution, the Baltic republics broke loose from the Union, thereby opening a breach in its economy and its defensive posture. More important still was the fact that hundreds of thousands of Russians, Ukrainians, and Belorussians, whom the democratically minded Baltics did not regard as people at all, were abandoned.

One more event lay between that conversation and the collapse of the Soviet Union: Vilnius. I cannot be sure of the extent to which the president was involved in that operation, though it is obvious that he was kept abreast of events as they unfolded. It was at this time that he instructed a number of members of the Security Council to draft measures for the introduction of a state of emergency in individual territories as well as throughout the country. Whether this was designed to preserve the Union or to avert the collapse of the central government is anyone's guess; though, in the light of subsequent events, the latter hypothesis seems more plausible.

Preparations were under way for a meeting of the Council of the Federation, on 24 May 1991, which was to determine the fate of the country. Vans carrying council members from the union and autonomous republics had already arrived, and the representatives of the republics were strolling around the grounds of the estate in the warm sun, awaiting the arrival of the top leadership. The representatives of Russia, Ukraine, and Kazakhstan had arranged their own transportation and were already there. Then the president of the USSR arrived. Everyone went upstairs to the small conference room on the second floor. Crystal chandeliers, fine furniture and carpets, and elegant wall paneling made an impressive setting in which to work, though from a strictly practical point of view it was not ideal. There was ample room for fifty people around a large table, but the acoustics were poor, the ceilings were too low, and the light too diffuse. Everyone took a seat. Gorbachev sat at the small table reserved for the chairman at the end of the conference table, with Lukyanov to his right and Pavlov to his left, then Yeltsin, Nikolai Dementei, Nursultan Nazarbayev, and thereafter in the order in which the republics are listed in the Union constitution. Leaders of the former autonomous republics sat at the end of the table.

The meeting was called to order. The president proposed that they discuss the questions posed by the title of the new Union Treaty, the status of the signatories, the principles for the formation of a new Union, the structure of its highest organs, as well as taxes and property. These, the main issues in the draft treaty, had been the subject of endless wrangling at all meetings of the Council of the Federation.

The title "On the Union of Sovereign Socialist Republics" was proposed in the text of the draft treaty, thus preserving the abbreviation USSR. The federal structure was to be retained, with the necessary central organs for the management of the major sectors of the economy. Gorbachev opened the discussion by stating that comments had been received on a number of substantive issues, and that ways had to be found to resolve those issues and move ahead. The position taken by Russia in the discussion was crucial, so everyone listened attentively to what Yeltsin had to say. His view was that the draft needed a thorough discussion, but that the title should be "Union of Sovereign States." The central government should be as the republics wanted it to be, with whatever resources they felt they could transfer to the president of the USSR for purposes of government. Maximum powers should be delegated to regional and local government. It would be possible to sign the treaty, having first settled property and tax issues. Each sovereign state would collect taxes within its jurisdiction and then would itself transfer the necessary amount to the central government. Such a treaty should be signed from the start by the republics that constituted the federation.

Ukraine took a tough position similar to that of Russia.

The assembled representatives realized that signing the Union Treaty was not going to be easy. The leaders of many former autonomous republics agreed to sign the treaty as sovereign states. M. Shaimev, chairman of the Supreme Soviet of the Tatar Autonomous Republic, expressed its view when he insisted that the document could be accepted only if the republic signed as an independent entity. "I like the way Russia is defending its sovereignty," he said. "But similar processes are under way in Tatarstan, and we shall not renounce our sovereignty. If we fail to uphold this principle, the people will not understand and will be indignant. There are also economic issues. Why do the chemical and defense complexes have to be transferred to Russian jurisdiction? There are some sectors that ought to be directly subordinate to the central government."

From the very first meeting, statements like this exacerbated an already volatile situation. The debates became increasingly acrimonious. The president of the USSR proposed that they continue work on the draft, in order to narrow their differences, and that the discussion be continued at the next meeting.

Everyone then proceeded to the banqueting hall, where the members of the Council of the Federation and all those in attendance were invited to dinner. The tables had been laid on the glassed-in verandas. The waiters served wholesome and abundant dishes, with few frills. Vodka and brandy were served. Gorbachev sat in the middle of the table, with the leaders of Russia, Ukraine, Belorussia, the Union government, and the Supreme Soviet of the USSR. A good meal and a glass of liquor usually softened the sharp edges of controversy. Implacable foes grew more conciliatory, or appeared to agree, on matters on which they had been far apart in the conference room. Conversation tended to move to more general topics, with good humor and toasts. Whenever passions were running high, Gorbachev often used such recesses as a means of assembling the parties around the dinner table. However, he was deluding himself if he thought that the Union Treaty could be finalized in this way, because as soon as the meeting reconvened everything fell back into place.

The Council of the Federation met again on 3 June 1991. Work proceeded with attempts to persuade various republican representatives to soften their positions. But it was not easy. Objections were raised when Gorbachev proposed that they move through the articles of the draft treaty, find language agreeable to all, and then sign each page as they went. The Russian Federation insisted on discussing matters of substance; so back they went to the title, sovereignty for the republics, and property issues. On page one of the draft treaty only paragraphs two and four were agreed. Some forty republican leaders were present at the meeting, each with his own views, his own approach, and his own demands. Virtually no solutions had been found on the issues brought up by each member in the text of the draft; bitter wrangling was commonplace. On matters of substance, no one was prepared to back down. The meeting ended after midnight, having made no progress.

On 17 June at 3:00 in the afternoon, all the members of the Council of the Federation met again at Novo-Ogaryovo. An attempt to conduct a paragraph-by-paragraph review of the text was quickly aborted. The leaders of the former autonomous republics objected to any restriction of their rights. They considered themselves to be sovereign republics and demanded to be treated as such during the drafting of the treaty. As the representative of Northern Ossetia put it: "Otherwise let the nine union republics sign the treaty, and we may as well go home."

A recess was then announced, in order to calm passions. Thereafter the debate was more tranquil, though no substantive concessions were made. The Soviet Union was headed toward a situation in which its fifteen constituent republics would be replaced by thirty sovereign states, including all the republics within the Russian Federation. The Russian leadership, feeling much like a farmer watching his grain leak from a tattered sack, found this prospect disturbing. More squabbling ensued, before someone proposed that the discussion be suspended until the next meeting.

On 23 July at 2:00 in the afternoon the council met again. The president was in a grim mood. Things were getting worse by the day, and political passions were at an all-time high. Gorbachev was coming under increasingly heavy attack in the press; criticism was now coming not only from the right but also from the left—from both opponents and associates. The newspaper *Sovietskaya Rossiya* published a document entitled "To the Peoples of Russia," signed by a group of prominent politicians and citizens opposed to Gorbachev's policies. Many such statements had appeared previously in the press, but this one was signed by Yuri Bondarev, Oleg Baklanov (who was the president's deputy on the Defense Council), and many more.

The chairman's nervousness spread among the participants. The question of membership in the Union was debated for two and a half hours, but to no avail. The main issue, which had to be resolved that very day, was financial payments to the central government. Yeltsin insisted on fixed payments, to be channeled through each republican government, while Gorbachev argued that the taxes due from each individual enterprise should be both assessed and collected by the central government. "Unless this provision is written into the treaty, I may as well go home," Gorbachev said, as he began gathering his files and preparing to leave. He had planned this move carefully in advance, as a means of putting pressure on the participants; but Yeltsin, who was not intimidated, replied: "Don't force us to decide the matter without you."

In his embarrassment, Gorbachev did not know which way to turn. Walking out would have been ridiculous; while coming back in would be difficult if not impossible and could be politically fatal. Such a childish gesture, coming from a man of his rank, would not be taken seriously. He had obviously not done his homework, or had perhaps failed to allow for his changed position. The seconds ticked by, as the members of the council held their breath. It was even too late for him to react with indignation to the remarks of the Russian leader. Finally Gorbachev could think of nothing better than declaring a recess, vesting all his hopes in the evening meal.

At supper it was agreed that Yeltsin, Lukyanov, Pavlov, and Dementei would try to find wording for the article in question.

Many other contentious issues still lay ahead, as confusion mounted over the fate of the Union, its economy, and its armed forces. What would be left for the central government? Would it be able to unite what had once been the Soviet Union? Several republics had already pulled out of the debate on the draft treaty and were refusing to sign it. In addition to the Baltic republics, Moldavia and Georgia, Ukraine was now also unwilling to sign. The former autonomous republics within Russia were now talking ever more frequently and insistently about independence: Tatarstan had been joined by Bashkiria and Yakutia, while similar questions were being raised with ever greater emphasis by the representatives of Karelia, Chuvashia, and Chechen-Ingushetia. These issues were also being discussed in Buryatia, Tuva, and the Gorno-Altai autonomous *oblast.* Those who advocated a single Union found much that was baffling in the draft treaty. It made no reference to a federation, or even a confederation, but simply to some amorphous, truncated entity. Russia and Ukraine did not want enterprises within their territories to pay funds directly into the Union budget; instead they intended to send the money directly themselves, once the central government had explained what it planned to do with it. That in turn would require full disclosure of the budgets of the armed forces, the KGB, and other government departments. Most industrial and agricultural facilities, including those related to defense, as well as the land and subsoil, would be under the jurisdiction of the republics.

By mid-August only eight of the fifteen former constituent republics of the USSR were ready to sign the treaty. The remainder either refused outright or preferred to withhold their signatures until better times. Some of the former autonomous republics of the RSFSR were also unable to sign the treaty.

Feelings were running high in the Cabinet of Ministers. At one of its meetings some members challenged the wisdom of signing the document, as it would lead to the disintegration of the Union and the dismantling of the state. Similar sentiments were voiced in the Supreme Soviet. Lukyanov objected to the idea, as he always had. He saw in it not only the demolition of the central government but the disbanding of the people's deputies and the elimination of all parliamentary structures. Many professional organizations as well as ministries and government agencies also voiced their concern over the prospect of such a treaty.

Experts regarded the treaty as a grave threat to the whole of the former Union, since even a partial signing, by just a few republics, would negate its legal status by creating a new political entity. Those who did not sign could already consider themselves outside the Union, as the former entity would have ceased to exist.

Such developments were disturbing to those factions that opposed the collapse of the Soviet Union. They were convinced that such an outcome would cause economic and financial bankruptcy, and wreck the armed forces and all other economic and political structures, while decimating our common culture and aggravating ethnic tensions. A determination to avert such a scenario was, to the best of my knowledge, the sole purpose of those who sought to halt the country's collapse in August 1991 and save society from its possible consequences, including the loss of innocent lives. Today bloody conficts are raging in various parts of the former Union, and they show no signs of abating.

9

THE DISINTEGRATION
OF THE PARTY

Today is Saturday, when I am allowed to bathe. The little window opens and the warden announces in a stern, loud voice: "Wash time! Get ready!" Everyone has been ready for some time. The bed linen has been collected, and the soap is ready; now we have to wait for someone to come and get us. Ten minutes later, we hear the order: "Okay, let's go!" The people who escort us downstairs to the baths are a mixed bunch, some quite human and others chillingly indifferent. The bath is actually a shower, consisting of four nozzles that produce spurts of water, varying from hot to cold, when anything comes out at all. The warden announces that we have twenty minutes. As clouds of steam swirl about us, we hurry to wash both ourselves and our underwear. The showers and the changing room are dirty and messy, but the main thing for us is to get some hot water, so as to warm up a bit. Twenty or thirty minutes later, we are escorted back, half wet and half washed. I have difficulty climbing the steep stairs. Supper is at seven, and soon I'll be getting ready for bed. I dread the nights, when you're left alone with your thoughts and start to explore your own past.

My memory dredges up many details from its secret recesses, arranging them in logical chains of conclusions.

From time to time, when he was in a good mood, Gorbachev would recite poetry in a quiet voice. His favorite poet was Vladimir Mayakovsky. He once admitted that he used to declaim his poems from the stage during special events at school, and he knew many of them by heart. In the company of his associates, however, he usually quoted the same lines from the poem "Vladimir Ilich Lenin," with significant glances toward those listening: "The party alone will not betray me."

And the party was faithful to him. It was betrayed and abandoned by its own leader.

I have yet to come to grips with the fact that the party, which was preparing to celebrate its hundredth anniversary, has ceased to exist. Little time was required in which to discredit and demoralize it and to destroy it as an organization. A month before it happened, I imagine no one could have predicted such a swift demise for the Communist party of the Soviet Union—the largest party in the world, which had to its credit seven decades of leadership of an enormous country and numerous successes, and which had previously enjoyed the respect of the people.

Clearly frightened by the events of August 1991, Gorbachev quickly shed his powers as general secretary and distanced himself from the party, which was eventually disbanded and eliminated with his blessing and in his presence. Had he shown greater courage and self-control, this may not have happened. Despite all the upheavals in the party, millions of Communists remained loyal to their general secretary to the very end. Even if the general secretary's actions—or rather lack of action—had prompted doubts, open indignation, or just bewilderment in their ranks, the party organizations and committees for the most part supported him. The sense of alienation, however, was palpable, and Gorbachev could not have failed to notice it.

Toward the end he began to dread Central Committee plenums and frank meetings and encounters with the heads of party organizations. When they met with the Central Committee secretaries and members of its apparatus, the members of the Central Committee and secretaries of *obkoms* and *kraikoms* vented their confusion: "What's going on? Why has the apparatus stopped functioning? We've lost touch with the center. Gorbachev has been avoiding us and refusing to answer questions about the party's future. Above all, he has been doing nothing about the problems facing the country."

The influence of the general secretary was, of course, crucial to the party's work and authority. In all fairness, however, it should be pointed out that even he would hardly have been able to wreck the party so thoroughly and so quickly if the party itself had not been willing to elect such a leader and if it had not been in such grave, indeed critical, trouble.

The more I analyze the performance of the various party structures, particularly at the highest levels, the more I conclude that many of the party's woes were inescapable. Among the various reasons for this state of affairs, two stand out: the decline in the intellectual powers of the party's leaders and the absence of any competition whatsoever among different ideas and practical programs for the socioeconomic and political development of society.

The trouble started with the loss of authority at the highest level of leadership. Lenin, a highly cultivated man and impassioned polemicist, who brought outstanding talents as a theorist, strategist, and tactician to the political struggle, was succeeded by a less impressive and less well educated political leader. Yet even Stalin, though clearly lacking in oratorical skills, was undoubtedly well grounded in theory, well read, and a most able organizer. However, he came to symbolize the excesses of a system not based on the rule of law, thereby inflicting on the party deep scars that never healed. For all his natural gifts, his successor, Khrushchev, was an uncultivated man with only a mediocre theoretical and ideological background. His command of written Russian was so bad that he made numerous mistakes in the texts of resolutions and even in the spelling of his associates' names.

I have seen letters, articles, and decisions written in Stalin's own hand. The precise amendments he made to the texts of numerous documents were clearly the work of a sophisticated politician with an excellent command of the language. The many notes he wrote in books in his library showed he had read widely and was familiar not only with the works of scholars with a Marxist background but also with those of philosophers, economists, and historians who held opposing views. Resolutions in Khrushchev's hand, some of which I have seen, unfortunately convey the impression that they were written by a poorly educated individual more accustomed to quite a different type of work. The material he dictated to stenographers was certainly interesting, with a rich and earthy vocabulary. Much of it, however, was not suitable for publication. I remember editing the verbatim records of his remarks for publication in the press and finding it very taxing indeed.

The advent of Brezhnev did not significantly enhance the intellectual image of the party and state leadership. Any scholar who scours the archives searching for the originals of his autobiographical works *Small Earth* and *Resurrection* will, I am afraid, be wasting his time. His pen never went near paper, and not only in documentary or fictional works. His associates, the party, and, I imagine, the general public were well aware of this. He was forgiven a great deal because of his mild, generous disposition and his doubtless sincere desire to bring the people relief from experimentation, while allowing the bureaucracy to collect the tribute to which he felt they were entitled.

Andropov flashed briefly through the gloomy firmament, like a ray of sunshine. He was unquestionably talented, highly educated, and culti-vated, but his tenure was so short that it is difficult to say anything spe-cific about it. He was followed by Chernenko, who also failed to demon-strate any positive qualities that might have enhanced the party's intellectual standing. Last came the educated and capable Gorbachev, the apex of whose accomplishments as a theorist is represented by the book *New Thinking*, and perhaps by material as yet unpublished. Schol-ars will eventually focus on his reports, articles, interviews, and other utterances, which are certainly absorbing; though it should be borne in mind that they often passed through the hands of collective editors who were capable of expunging certain important ideas from the text. Apart from the purely intellectual decline of the successive general secretaries, there was a tendency toward a more gray and faceless leadership. That is why the last general secretaries, particularly Gorbachev, were chosen as the best contenders in a mediocre field. One should not generalize, of course. Among the members of the Politburo and other senior party officials, there were undoubtedly some brilliant people, but they wielded little influence.

Fate had decreed that intellectual mediocrity was not to be the party's only ailment. Throughout its entire existence, the party had known the clash of different opinions. It had fought with opportunists, deviants, and splinter groups, as well as with Mensheviks, Trotskyites, and other real and imaginary opponents of the party line. But it had never had to fight corruption and greed in high places. Those were pages of the tragi-comic history of the party. The virus of dishonesty gravely impaired the party's immune system and wrecked its stability. A number of secretaries of *obkoms* and *kraikoms*, as well as members of the Central Committee, were implicated in all kinds of illicit schemes. There was nothing wrong, according to the prevailing ethos, with giving expensive gifts to high officials, including a number of general secretaries. On the eve of national holidays the field liaison officers were run off their feet deliver-ing boxes from the southern regions to the Central Committee's secre-taries and members. Andropov clamped down on this practice, which had been rampant in Brezhnev's time, but echoes of it persisted long afterward.

In order to prevent the question of expensive gifts for the general secretary, including those given by foreign sources, from being raised at party congresses, the delegates were also given a "little something for themselves." Under Brezhnev it was television sets or watches, while less expensive items were given during Gorbachev's tenure. Recipients felt little compulsion to surrender their gifts to the party and the state. To the best of my knowledge, Andropov's behavior in this regard was above reproach.

Gorbachev and Raisa were a somewhat different matter. At first some of the gifts received by Raisa were returned to Gokhran. The press commented briefly, and then said no more about it. The general secretary began to receive large amounts of prize money from various foundations, and his bank account was constantly replenished by hard-currency royalties for his book *New Thinking* and other works. The awards were so numerous that special emissaries were sent to receive them. I never could understand why all such funds were not automatically deposited in the budget of the state that was paying Gorbachev's bills. Besides hard currency, he also received large medals of gold, silver, or platinum, as well as collectors' coins made of precious metals, none of which, according to Kruchina, were surrendered to Gokhran.

An episode involving a hundred thousand dollars was utterly beyond my comprehension. After returning from Japan, and a meeting on one of the islands of South Korea with Ro De U, Gorbachev called me into his office and took from his briefcase an envelope that, in his own words, contained one hundred thousand dollars. "Ro De U gave it to me," he said, with no further explanation. "Figure out how we can spend it."

I still find it incredible that the leader of South Korea, with which the Soviet Union had only just established relations, could give Gorbachev, the president of a superpower, one hundred thousand dollars—and at their very first encounter. However, the way the South Koreans habitually do business is their concern. But how could Gorbachev have accepted the money? In return for what? Having taken it, why did he not promptly forward it to Gosbank? And why, when my assistant and I had drawn up papers transferring the money to a children's hospital in Bryansk, did he do nothing with them for six months? Was he waiting until scandal erupted around him?

Such behavior had disturbing implications. Assumptions aside, however, an increasing number of people were aware that many questions pertaining to gift giving had not been answered. Letters were coming in, demanding to know who was paying for the president's dachas, what happened to the gifts Gorbachev and Raisa received, and what gifts the Soviet Union was giving in return. Doubts about Gorbachev's hard-currency income, his foreign and domestic bank accounts, his dachas, apartments, and fees were widely aired and could not have enhanced his authority or that of his subordinates and the party as a whole. The mail we received tended, intentionally or otherwise, to link all delicate issues with our international relations. Why, the writers wanted to know, did the Soviet Union disarm so fast and in such a lopsided fashion? Why did it withdraw its troops from the countries of the former Warsaw Pact with so little concern for our property and our other interests?

Corruption was not the party's only ailment. The sense of purpose that had brought it to power and sustained it during industrialization and the heroic defense against Hitler's armies began to lapse in more peaceful times. Members were joining for the wrong reasons; the leadership was now dominated by old men, and the party began to lose touch with the people. A key player in this process was Ivan Kapitonov, whom Brezhnev had appointed head of the party's Organizational Department. Through his introduction of quotas for members of the working class and his failure to incorporate scholars, scientists, and intellectuals into the party's ranks, he was responsible for the party's increasing rigidity.

Kapitonov was replaced by Ligachev, and then Razumovski, both of whom were old friends of Gorbachev, who generally shared his views. Ligachev was an assertive and capable person who applied equal energy to the implementaton of both correct and incorrect ideas, and upheld the principles he believed in. He lacked flexibility, however, and sometimes exposed his authority to criticism. In later years Razumovski, who was milder and more inclined to doubt, realized that he could no longer make any sense of the party's condition and resigned his post and quit party work altogether. Gorbachev was quite happy to see him go.

The appointment of a new head of the Organizational Department, however, merely set up the right conditions for a rectification of the party's cadre policy. Concrete changes would take some time. There was, moreover, a widespread feeling among members that a number of senior party officials had become degraded, losing much of their authority in the eyes of the public. In later years they had also begun to distrust Gorbachev.

Gorbachev tried hard to overhaul the membership of the party's higher echelons, as he should have done. But he did not stop there. At the Twenty-eighth Party Congress in July 1990 he replaced practically the entire Politburo, though his criteria for doing so were not sound in all instances. Many of his former acquaintances from the Komsomol, and others who had been accustomed to working with him, now made their way into the Politburo and Secretariat. Ivashko was elected deputy general secretary. He was a good, likable man, who was tragically stricken with a serious illness and thus denied a chance to show his talents as a political leader. He also suffered from an occupational hazard, in that his work as a teacher had left him with a condescending, moralizing tone. Oleg Shenin was in charge of personnel matters in the Central Committee. He was young, a good organizer, hard-working, and honest: a man of complete integrity. The trouble was that he was not well known, either in the party or the Central Committee, and still less among the general public. The same was true of Boris Pugo, an old friend of Gorbachev's from Komsomol days. A. Dzasokhov, who had been offered the post of ideological chief, should have been able to go far. He too had known Gorbachev since his youth. Although he was a congenial person, flexible in politics, and well versed in international relations, he knew nothing about ideological work. To his credit, he acknowledged that fact and declined the post.

P. Luchinski was ill equipped for a leadership role in the press department; much to his distress, he did not know how to talk to representatives of the press and had only a scant knowledge of journalism. At the same time, an outstanding editor, Galina Semyonova, was dealing with the women's movement in the party and in professional organizations. She became a member of the Politburo in a matter of minutes. During an intermission at a plenum, Gorbachev called her over and told her he intended to make her a member of the Politburo. She was astonished and thereafter made no secret of her ignorance of what membership involved and what her duties would be. There were a number of more extreme instances, in which a particular individual's advancement through the party hierarchy came as a total surprise to the Central Committee membership, as there had been no time to talk to people beforehand.

At the Twenty-eighth Party Congress the first secretaries of the party in each of the union republics joined the Politburo. In some cases the turnover among them was so rapid that Politburo members often asked each other: "Who's that?" Far from strengthening the Politburo, the introduction of the secretaries, including two from Estonia, weakened it

and made its work superficial. Consequently its decisions became meaningless, and its meetings less frequent, until it stopped meeting altogether. Many new Politburo members from the republics did not know
the staff of the Central Committee and did not attend its meetings. Such
was the liaison between the central government and the regions.

All of this resulted from the general secretary's chosen course. Instead
of the obstinate members he had removed, Gorbachev now got a large
number of passive types who said nothing. The organizational capabilities of the Central Committee's ruling body declined. The arrival of people who were ill prepared for such important work lowered the qualifications of those in charge of party organizations, while the extensive
reshuffling of appointments placed many incompetent people in charge
of various sectors of the party's activities. This was a grave miscalculation
on the part of the general secretary—unless it was done deliberately.

Other failings of the Central Committee included the appointment to
high positions of people who were hardly known in the party or in society as a whole. Lenin was wise enough to choose brilliant, clever associates, even from among those whose behavior before October 1917 had
been questionable. Grigory Zimoviev, Lev Kamenev, Leon Trotsky,
Nikolai Bukharin, and other top party figures had different personalities
and abilities, but they were certainly talented people, well known in the
party and the country. Gorbachev should have elevated his new political
appointees gradually, and helped them settle in, thereby enhancing their
authority. Yakovlev certainly favored this approach, but Gorbachev was
too jealous to help any associate of his boost his authority.

When passing judgment on the performance of one of the greatest
political parties in the world, it is important to take these facts into
account. It is equally true that the selection of cadres, particularly at the
highest levels, should not be based on personal friendship, loyalty, or a
common place of origin. That has been, and still is, a serious error. People who are somehow beholden to their master can hardly preserve their
integrity. In the end, neither his former Komsomol friends nor those
appointed for their unquestioning obedience could save Gorbachev. Of
course, in order to prevent such a thing from happening, one should
have integrity oneself. But that is another subject.

Finally, one other conclusion can be drawn from the experience of the
party's ruling organs in recent years: the severe dangers posed by frequent changes of high-ranking politicians. They should not be allowed
to flash briefly across the political firmament, like falling stars, as this

erodes respect for the party. Every effort should be made to ensure that the authority of the departing figure is not splattered with mud and dirt. The more the general secretary and others sought to belittle their predecessors, and often their own associates, the more tainted they themselves became. Moderation is needed in all things. My conclusions are, of course, tentative, as I have only a limited experience of the work of the Politburo and the Secretariat, not to mention other organizations. My observations have generally been proved correct, though I take no particular pleasure in them.

As the party and its highest organs drifted helplessly toward disgrace and disaster, Gorbachev was unable to focus the party's energies on remedying its long-standing ailments. Indeed, he accelerated its downfall. The general secretary, who bore responsibility for the fate of millions of honest Communists who had trusted in him and elected him as their leader, was the first to disown the party. He publicly abandoned and betrayed it, like a coward. History will be his judge. Whatever the country's future—and I hope it is a democratic one—people will never forgive leaders who desert those under their command when danger threatens. They are like the captain who abandons his sinking ship, leaving the crew on board, or the general who flees the battlefield ahead of the cowards among his troops.

This instinctive effort of self-preservation came as no surprise. The general secretary failed to unite the increasingly fractious Central Committee behind a constructive course of action. Having quarreled with practically all those who had minds of their own, he drifted into isolation. He then realized that his days as general secretary were numbered. Both the composition of the Central Committee and the mood of the party were distasteful to him. As he himself told me, he spoke to Yakovlev toward the end of July 1991 about the possibility of detaching the left democratic wing from the party and incorporating it in the Movement for Democratic Reform, which would eventually be turned into a new, independent party. Such a shift really amounted to a schism in the party.

This came as no surprise. Having failed to cope with the party in which he had risen to prominence, Gorbachev was now willing to be content with one part of it. His failure to make his intentions known publicly did nothing to enhance his popularity. No good could possibly come of his devious backstage maneuvering. Four months after losing the party's support, Gorbachev was stripped of his presidential powers and forced out of politics altogether. He was able to travel, like most retired persons in the West, and also to talk about the former glories of the general secretary, the party, and the Soviet Union.

The decline in his authority was matched by the destruction of the state and its economy. There had been a disastrous breakdown in relations between industrial enterprises, while a coal miners' strike had paralyzed production of iron, steel, and other sectors, including large parts of the machine-building sector. In 1991 the gross national product had already fallen more than 10 percent; national income and productivity had both shrunk. All of this was taking place against a background of mounting financial trouble, rising costs, and an increase in the number of unemployed or partially employed workers. Threatened by a tidal wave of economic and financial difficulties, many republics resorted to autarchic methods, sealing themselves off from their neighbors by means of customs and other barriers.

Gorbachev certainly knew disaster was imminent, and even talked about it, though he never proposed viable solutions and, above all, took practically no effective action. He made some revealing remarks at a meeting with the *obkom* and *kraikom* secretaries of the Russian Communist party, in April 1991, in the marble hall on the fifth floor of the Central Committee building. In addition to taking stock of the party's performance at the Congress of People's Deputies of the RSFSR, the meeting also heard Gorbachev refer to the situation in the country as a whole.

"Let me begin with agriculture," he said. "The farm economy is on the brink of collapse. The main reason for this is the disruption of economic links and a massive shift to barter operations. The structure that took decades, and even centuries, to build is now falling apart in a matter of weeks. Industrial and agricultural output is falling. Agreements and obligations are not being honored. Many enterprises have simply stopped entering into contracts for the supply of goods on a cooperative basis; and that is damaging the export trade and reducing hard-currency earnings."

The plight of agriculture was particularly disturbing to the assembled secretaries, who knew only too well that food shortages could spell real trouble. What the general secretary had to say was not reassuring. The harvest was going to be smaller than in 1990, and there would be no industrial workers, military units, or students to help bring it in. For that reason, every effort had to be made to save the crops that had been grown. Even so, the country stood to lose one-third of the harvest: any losses above that limit would be extremely dangerous. The general secretary also emphasized the need for industry to continue functioning.

"The chaos has been compounded by strikes. The fall in the output of coal has had serious effects, cutting into the production of coke, metal, and other vital supplies. The commission headed by V. Doguzhiev has been working on a program designed to bring the economic situation under control. If obstacles arise, we shall not hesitate to introduce tough emergency measures. I hope you will support them.

"This situation has not been brought about by economic difficulties alone. The opposition has been stirring people's emotions and trying to destabilize society; things could get quite out of hand. Of course, the price rise that took effect in April made life difficult for broad segments of the population, but we've got to get through these difficult times.

"The financial situation is particularly troubling. The behavior of the union republics has been destructive: Russia has stopped making payments to the union bank. If this goes on, we shall seize their accounts and dismiss the finance minister of the RSFSR."

Sensing that the president would still not take any effective measures to remedy the grim state of affairs he had described, the secretaries demanded action. They told him bluntly that they had heard more than enough talk, particularly from him, and now wanted concrete effective measures to rectify the situation. They urged him to do his duty as president.

Gorbachev put up a weak defense, essentially trying to lob the ball back into the regional leaders' court. "You're the ones who should be acting," he said. Why leave everything up to the central government? Go ahead and do your job; no one will get in your way." These were remarks that Gorbachev traditionally addressed to regional officials.

Real economic power had slipped away from the central government to the republics, which were busy asserting their sovereignty and electing their presidents. The decisions they made reflected only their own interests, while ignoring the decisions of the Cabinet of Ministers and the decrees of the president of the USSR. Republican leaders, anxious to make their mark and defend their sovereignty as they battled the center, tended less and less to reach mutual understandings. The Soviet finance minister reported a budgetary shortfall of fifty billion rubles and the printing of twenty-eight billion in new paper money in the first six months of 1991. The Russian Federation had not presented a budget at all. Everything was being propped up by the state's reserves of gold and other precious metals and stones. Without resolute measures there could be no way out of this dead end. Economists had drawn up proposals for the shift to a market economy in three hundred to five hundred days, but the president could still not make up his mind. In essence he tended to float with the waves, sinking ever more deeply into the morass and dragging an enormous state down with him. When Lenin was told that there was no force or party in Russia that could lead the way to change, he answered decisively: "There is such a party."

The Communist party was then a serious and authoritative force. It took on the burden of responsibility for change and helped the Soviet Union become a great power. As early as September 1991 one could safely say that, on one-sixth of the earth's surface, that party and that great single state had both ceased to exist.

Epilogue

TAKING STOCK: "WHAT HAVE YOU DONE TO OUR COUNTRY?"

On 11 March 1985, at the age of fifty-four years and nine days, Mikhail Sergeyevich Gorbachev had been elected general secretary of the Communist party of the Soviet Union. On that chilly, overcast day, his meteoric rise to power reached its culmination on the Mount Olympus of political and state power in one of the mightiest and most influential states in the world. Endless opportunities for action stretched before him, like a blank canvas awaiting the artist's brush. He was free to apply whatever solutions his imagination could devise—provided that the people benefited from the results of his creative efforts. He seemed uniquely charming, frank, and persuasive. Not for several decades had the Soviet people welcomed their new leader with such high expectations.

By the time he retired from his position as president and general secretary, six years later, his authority and power were gone, and he had lost the respect of the majority of the Soviet people. It would be truer to say that he was forced into retirement as a failure, after he had lost the state and abandoned the party that had carried him into office. Those six years are described by some as a triumphant dawn, bringing new light to a great country, while others see them as a tragedy leading to the collapse of the Soviet Union and bringing economic ruin, poverty, and hunger to its people. In the United States Gorbachev's rise to power and the results of his rule are viewed as victory for the West over the "evil empire," while in my country it is felt that they were a national disaster, accompanied by the disintegration of the republics and their economies, irreparable damage to science, culture, and the moral values of society, and the beginning of fratricidal bloodshed, poverty, and hunger.

How, then, is one to assess perestroika and the Gorbachev years? As a success or a failure? As a breakthrough into world civilization or as a demonstration of the impotence and surrender of a policy, economic bankruptcy, and the loss of moral values established over many decades? Time will provide exhaustive answers to these questions. At present, however, certain obvious conclusions can be drawn.

It is worth noting, first of all, that perestroika brought a number of positive results, particularly in Gorbachev's early years in office, as well as some grave negative consequences. One early initiative that yielded positive results was a thorough analysis of the state of our society and of the reasons for its economic, financial, and social problems. This analysis served as the basis for a policy of radical reform. Other commendable achievements include decisions in the sphere of democratization, reform of the political system, and glasnost. Certain aspects of Gorbachev's foreign policy, including ways of reducing international tensions and curbing the arms race, may also be considered positive.

The results of perestroika would have been more tangible if the reforms had been elaborated more thoroughly, carried out more consistently, and been properly meshed with other political and economic decisions. The fact that perestroika succeeded best in spheres not requiring much creative effort from society as a whole is most revealing. The economy was another matter altogether: virtually none of the measures adopted to boost productivity or raise living standards had any positive effect. To a large extent that failure invalidated achievements in the democratization of society.

Having been drawn up impulsively and inconsistently, the policy of perestroika was put into effect with depressing incompetence, thus making matters worse and heightening discord in society.

Gorbachev's commendable analysis of Soviet society and the Soviet economy certainly led to a more profound understanding of the country's situation. It also produced some factual conclusions and suggested ways out of the dead end the country found itself in in later years. A study of the state of the economy, finance, science, culture, and education was necessary because official statistics had often told the previous leadership what it wanted to hear, painting an unduly rosy picture.

The analysis was done by a group of experts and academics from a number of major research institutes, the Soviet Academy of Sciences, and statistical organs. The raw data were processed by Academicians Abel Aganbegyan, S. A. Anchishkin, Stanislav Shatalin, V. P. Mozhin, and S. A. Sitaryan, with senior officials from Gosplan and a number of government agencies. The conclusions in the analytical memorandum submitted to the general secretary showed that an industrial and agricultural crisis and grave social tensions were imminent. This had happened because the previous leadership had neglected socioeconomic problems and had failed to take timely measures to rectify the situation. As the situation deteriorated, the accumulated ailments of past decades came to the surface.

One might have expected such an analysis to produce plentiful material on which to base radical reforms in all spheres of society. Yet the conclusions drawn from it were short-term, ideologically biased, and not entirely correct. The document served mainly as a political weapon with which to castigate the past leadership. The analytical memorandum was converted into evidence of incompetence on the part of Brezhnev, the former membership of the Politburo, and the Council of Ministers. Their failings were certainly a fair subject for commentary, but it was wrong to turn a serious analytical document into a slingshot or a means of settling scores and denigrating one's predecessors. It had a great deal more to offer. Its detailed descriptions of Soviet society made it possible to devise a system of corrective measures, make economic forecasts, and formulate a theoretical basis for perestroika and particularly for radical economic reforms. Gorbachev's failure to do this was the major and most tragic reason for his political and economic vacillation and the sad demise of all his planned reforms. Moreover, he did not explain the analysis to the political leadership, preferring instead to disclose it in his speeches.

Gorbachev did not offer any justification for the broad trends of his proposed move to a new system and did not indicate the initial and subsequent phases of radical reform. He then found himself unable to resolve even day-to-day issues or surmount quite minor hurdles. Yet he sought to blame his failures not on his own mistakes but on the inability of others to take effective action. The result was an endless turnover of heads of government, high officials in industry and agriculture, the soviets, and the organs of the party. In six years the entire membership of the Politburo was replaced, along with three prime ministers and almost all the members of the presidium of the Council of Ministers. The Supreme Soviet went through three chairmen in that time: Gromyko, Gorbachev, and Lukyanov. All of this high-level leapfrogging was a grievous blunder on the part of Gorbachev—one that had tragic consequences for the people and the state.

The development of democratization and glasnost enabled the people to say what they really thought of the situation in the country and the policies of the party, and to denounce its monopoly over ideas for the development of society. In the resulting commotion, many energetic and enterprising people came to the fore. The ending of the party's monopoly on power allowed many political factions to compete on an equal footing for the minds and hearts of the people. These processes would have been most laudable if our culture and democratic traditions had been more deeply rooted, and if they had been shorn of the extremist urges of certain leaders and segments of the population. This opening for the democratic process should have been used creatively, as a means of uniting society and improving our legal culture, as well as our culture in general. That would have been the most rational course for the country's development under perestroika. As I see it, however, democratization was used to foster divisiveness, confrontation between opposing political factions, and the settling of personal scores.

The Communist party was the most highly organized force in society, with significant representation of the intelligentsia, workers, peasants, and the military and technological elite. It had set in motion the restructuring of all spheres of society known as perestroika, and was the only organized force capable of carrying it to its logical conclusion with the least pain. Many of its senior officials are still in the forefront of the reform movement. Yet the party was discredited because of the mistakes of its past leaders and essentially shut out of all the creative processes under way in society. Gorbachev's own efforts were a contributing factor. His failure to unite the party behind his leadership, coupled with the erosion of his authority among rank-and-file Communists, led to the destruction of that organization.

The same happened with the army. The psychological attack that began at the first session of the Congress of People's Deputies lasted for four years. As a result, people in military uniform were physically and morally abused and mocked; beatings of military personnel, including officers, became frequent. The president of the Soviet Union and commander-in-chief of its armed forces failed in his duty to protect the army. In fact, he feared and distrusted the army and devoted considerable efforts to weakening it and undermining its authority. He treated the organs of the KGB the same way, refusing even to meet with them.

It was not long before Gorbachev lost his influence among writers, journalists, and academics. The limited scope of his ideas, his passion for speech making, television appearances, and publishing articles and books at home and abroad, and above all his inability to act, caused the intelligentsia to desert the ranks of his supporters. Some simply lost all interest in him, while others became his fierce adversaries.

When workers, peasants, and pensioners started to suffer from declining living standards, Gorbachev lost his support among the population as a whole. The Soviet public quickly rejected him, although his first steps, which led to the subsequent changes in the Soviet Union, had enjoyed broad support. Had it not been for the support of Western leaders and part of Western public opinion, who remembered Gorbachev's selfless political and economic concessions to the United States and Europe, he would long ago have been fully isolated, living in fear of his own people's anger.

The peoples who once made up the USSR, and the world community as a whole, are not likely to forget Gorbachev's years in power; however, regardless of the future course of their development, the descendants of those who lived under him cannot be expected to honor his memory.

For the past few decades the Soviet people have viewed peace as their most pressing necessity—one for which they have been ready to make many sacrifices. The peace to which they aspired had to be achieved by means of balanced disarmament. At its Twenty-seventh Congress the Soviet Communist party called for disarmament in its program of New Thinking in relations between states, primarily the nuclear powers, based on the notion of an interdependent and substantially integrated world. This was a most attractive doctrine, but one that was hard to implement fully until what the military called "major concessions" were made by the Soviet side.

In the early 1990s the process of arms reduction in the Soviet Union ceased to have any real meaning, as the collapse of the state was followed by the disintegration of the army, the air defense system, the strategic air command, and the navy. The withdrawal of military units from the Warsaw Pact countries left some sectors of its territory exposed to attack by weapons of mass destruction. Other factors involved were the collapse of discipline in Soviet army units, the disruption of the chain of command, and the resulting loss of control. Soldiers deserted in large numbers, while the newly formed states of the Commonwealth of Independent States summoned military personnel of their particular nationality back home to form their own national armies. In this way the New Thinking in international affairs, combined with other perestroika measures, however well intentioned, effectively wrecked the country's military defensive complex. This enabled President Bush to talk about the United States' victory in the cold war.

The term "victory in the cold war" is hardly strong enough to convey the truth about what really happened. It was not just a victory: it was a total rout of the disorganized units of the USSR and the moral devastation of a once powerful adversary. But this rout was not the work of American military and technological might, nor of its strategic genius. It resulted from the internal capitulation of those forces opposed to the structure in place in our country.

Beyond a doubt, Gorbachev's coming to power, the notion of perestroika, and the desire for socioeconomic reforms were progressive undertakings. The trouble was that they failed to allow for the real state of society; nor did they have a sound theoretical or organizational basis. The idea of shifting to market relations, for example, was not raised until 1989–90, when it was proposed that the transition be completed in a fantastically short time. This program, though doubtless well intentioned, had the same air of unreality about it as the famous Great Leap Forward.

Gorbachev did not understand that, in a vast territory stretching from Bug to the Kuriles, from Taimyr to Kushka, it was impossible to transform the psychology of the people overnight in one huge market-oriented melting pot, while ignoring their own peculiar ways and traditions. The general secretary had obviously learned little from his efforts to leapfrog over the system formed over the previous few decades: as a result, the country began to burst at the seams from an overload of ideas and schemes, before falling apart in tiny pieces. The latest in a series of experiments performed on our country had failed to produce the miraculous results everyone had expected of it. Miracles do not happen free of charge, however. The issue in this case was just how high the price would be: suffering, hunger, and poverty for the people; interethnic conflicts and bloodshed; a legacy of servitude and debt for future generations?

The pace of economic collapse quickened in the midst of theoretical confusion, inertia, and organizational paralysis. In 1990 began a decline in industrial and agricultural output and in living conditions generally. A number of large metalworks and machine-building plants closed down.

Strikes erupted in the coal, oil, and other industries. In agriculture the situation was grim. Shortages of animal feed, increased prices for manufactured goods, and uncertainty about the future in both state and collective farms caused a sharp drop in the total number and productivity of livestock.

The catastrophic disruption of the supply chain between related industrial enterprises, some of which were located inside former union or autonomous republics, contributed to the overall economic decline.

The worsening state of the economy, coupled with the inability of the central government to keep things under control, served as an additional spur to separatist movements, the formation of independent states, and the unleashing of ethnic strife. The flames of ethnic hatred, and now of violence, had flared in the Caucasus, central Asia, and Moldavia. Relations were tense in many other republics and over large sections of Russia. What had once been a monolithic state, capable of withstanding the hardship of the Second World War, when much of its territory was under occupation, and then the heinous conditions of the postwar period, was now nothing but a pile of fragments.

The consequences were dramatic. Huge masses of Russian-speaking people were forced out of parts of central Asia, the Caucasus, Moldavia, and the Baltic republics. Azeris whose ancestors had lived in Armenia for centuries now found themselves obliged to flee, while tens of thousands of Armenians left Azerbaijan in search of a better life. It is difficult to imagine the anguish this brought to hundreds of thousands of people. Today the blood of innocent citizens of a once huge country is being shed, without eliciting the expressions of outrage such acts would formerly have triggered. Stricken with grief, and numbed by the horrendous prospect of a civil war, people have become so accustomed to the deaths of children and old people that they have begun to shut themselves off from events around them.

Notwithstanding Gorbachev's good intentions—which are increasingly open to question—his actions led to the fall of a once united state, industrial paralysis, rising crime, a lower birthrate, and a lower standard of living.

These are the modest results so highly esteemed in the West but so painful for my fellow citizens residing in the one-sixth of the earth's surface that used to be known as the Soviet Union. The restructuring of all facets of Soviet society, which Gorbachev carried out so incompetently and indecisively, before betraying it, turned into a tragedy for millions of people. People no longer think about the contribution they can make to world culture and human progress. They are too busy struggling to achieve elementary survival.

How was it possible for the noble intentions of perestroika, and its plans for abundance, to lead instead to devastation and ruin in industry and society as a whole, to the degradation of science, culture, and education, and to bloody internecine strife?

The prime reason, as I see it, lies in the character of Mikhail Sergeyevich Gorbachev—in his indecisiveness and his adherence to the underlying assumptions instilled into him from his early youth. The general secretary was, and remained, essentially a product of his age and of the structures that enabled him to grow and propelled him to the top. On the one hand, he could see the absurdity of the existing order and strove to transform society. On the other, he was wedded to the old ways of doing business. Despite all his talk about democratization and glasnost, his alter ego continued to be a crafty, cruel, and perfidious prototype not of Stalin, and not even of Brezhnev, but merely of their pitiful shadow, Suslov—and was only a poor imitation even of him.

His actions bear out this conclusion. Gorbachev advocated democracy and accused his associates of Stalinism; yet he ruled the party and the country practically single-handedly; he decided people's fate as he alone determined the membership of the Central Committee and the Politburo, choosing first secretaries of republican parties, *obkoms*, and *kraikoms* according to his personal likes and dislikes. He talked about collective decision making and the need to uphold the principles of consensus, yet he acted alone when adopting or issuing decisions on the highest matters of state, silencing dissenters and clearing rivals from his path. The general secretary and president fought to expand glasnost, yet he withheld from the people, the party, and even his own associates vital information about the past actions of the Politburo and the domestic and international situation. He threatened to dismiss newspaper editors who published material not to his liking, making good on his threats in several cases. The general secretary and president conducted negotiations with foreign leaders, while not informing the members of the Security Council or the Supreme Soviet of their results. He fought to protect the independence of the judiciary, but instructed the procurator general on how to pursue certain investigations. Gorbachev fought against administrative command methods of management, while keeping a tight grip on ministries and committees and setting policy on all economic issues from the center.

He talked a lot about the need to transfer power to the regions, but actually concentrated unlimited power in his own hands, as general secretary and the head of a party with millions of members. As president of the USSR and head of state, he conducted the meetings of the Council of Ministers, virtually riding roughshod over the prime minister. He was also the commander-in-chief of the armed forces and chairman of the Defense Council, and he exercised sole and direct control over the KGB, the commission on the military industry, and the interior, foreign, and defense ministries.

Gorbachev talked about the need to reduce the size of the government apparatus, yet he expanded the number of bureaucrats in his service and made effective use of them as a weapon against his political opponents. He thought of himself as the incarnation of decency and legality, but he shrank from nothing in his determination to know everything there was to know about those opponents and about his associates and the members of his entourage, and to control their actions. He called for a modest lifestyle and was widely regarded as opposing privileges, yet he stripped his subordinates of all such benefits, while keeping for himself the full range of benefits, either free of charge or on concessionary terms, such as had existed during the heyday of easygoing corruption under Brezhnev.

There was no limit to his double standards. From the foregoing, one can understand why the progress of perestroika followed such a laborious, tortuous path, and why it was doomed to fail. Societies cannot change direction so abruptly and on such a massive scale when guided by weak-willed, vacillating, and timorous leaders. They need leaders who know what they want and can carry their plans through to completion. Life is not a stage, though, even if it were, a clown should not be cast in the role of a great commander.

I do not think that I shall ever forget a letter sent to Gorbachev by a middle-aged woman who had been forced to flee with her daughter and granddaughter from central Asia, where their ancestors had lived for decades, leaving behind the graves of close friends:

"Misha, my darling, what have you done to our country? Was it because you have something against us? Or did you simply want to go down in history as a reformer? We're desperate people, driven this way and that all over the country, like tumbleweed, with no place we can cling to, and violence and spitefulness all around. Tell us how we're going to live now that we've lost everything—friends, property, home. Where are we going to end up? Are we going to make it? We're now reduced to begging for my three-year-old granddaughter and ourselves. If you have any conscience left, why did you have to make people shed so much blood and tears and see their hopes for the future smashed to bits? What's going to become of us? We and our children and grandchildren will always remember you and your children and grandchildren for the kindness you have shown us and the whole nation."

Dozens of letters like this were sent to the president of the USSR. It was frightening and painful to read them, as they told a story of destitute people forced to leave the republics where they had lived; of a collapsing country, economy, and army; of nations that had lived in peace for centuries, but were now at each other's throats. All of this made it essential to stop this disaster, to say out loud that the tragedy could not go on, and to prevent even worse from happening.

In August 1991, some people in positions of authority, seeking nothing but prosperity and peace for their country, with no desire for power yet fearing further bloodshed, tried to avert the impending disaster. Yet they were too scrupulous and decent to use harsh methods, less still to oppose the will of the people.

More than seventy years ago, at the dawn of Soviet rule, the English writer Herbert Wells said he saw Russia in the shadows. History has a way of repeating itself. Once again shadows have spread over the vast expanses of a great country, with renewed bloodshed and suffering. Will Russia rise again as a great power? Will we catch up to the civilized countries within the life span of this generation? Today it is hard to say. Over time everything will fall into place, and a verdict will be reached on the events of the twentieth century. It has been a century of great wars, tragedies, triumphs, and defeats; of magnificent accomplishments and crumbling myths; of spectacular scientific discoveries, brilliant cultural achievements, and mass destruction of human beings.

The twentieth century is ending in turmoil and bloody tragedy over vast stretches of the Eurasian landmass. Will calm return, or is this but the prelude to new upheavals? Time will tell.

NAME INDEX

SUBJECT INDEX